BEER HIKING
NEW ENGLAND

THE TASTIEST WAY TO DISCOVER MAINE, NEW HAMPSHIRE, VERMONT, MASSACHUSETTS, CONNECTICUT AND RHODE ISLAND

Beer Hiking New England
The Tastiest Way to Discover Maine, New Hampshire, Vermont,
Massachusetts, Connecticut and Rhode Island
By: Carey Kish

ISBN: 978-3-907293-74-4
Published by Helvetiq, Lausanne/Basel, Switzerland
Graphic Design and illustration: Daniel Malak
Printed in China
First Edition March 2023

www.helvetiq.com
www.facebook.com/helvetiq
instagram: @helvetiq

BEER HIKING
NEW ENGLAND

THE TASTIEST WAY TO DISCOVER MAINE, NEW HAMPSHIRE, VERMONT, MASSACHUSETTS, CONNECTICUT AND RHODE ISLAND

TABLE OF CONTENTS

1

INTRODUCTION

ABOUT THE AUTHOR

Carey Kish is a seasoned hiker, outdoor and travel writer, beer enthusiast and longtime New England denizen. He forged an enduring love for the outdoors as a youngster in western Massachusetts, where he and his free-range friends explored every patch of woods their sore feet and spider bikes could take them to. When his family relocated to Maine a couple years later, his teenage wanderings continued, ranging from the rocky coastline to the deep forests and mountain peaks.

Carey developed a taste for beer early on when, slightly before reaching the legal age, he absconded with a bottle of Schaefer from his father's stash in the back of the fridge. Carey's passion for beer—and hiking, of course—has continued unabated ever since, and over the course of his adventurous adult life he's logged more than his share of trail miles and beer smiles. Ask him about his favorite beer and the answer will invariably be, "The one in my hand." Much the same goes for hikes, as he always strives to enjoy the moment on whatever trail he's walking.

Among some two-dozen long distance treks in the US, Canada and Europe, Carey has hiked the 2,189-mile Appalachian Trail from Georgia to Maine (twice), the 1,100-mile Florida Trail and the 2,654-mile Pacific Crest Trail from Mexico to Canada. Carey is the author of AMC's *Best Day Hikes Along the Maine Coast* and the editor of the *AMC Maine Mountain Guide*; his hiking and camping column has appeared in the *Portland Press Herald/Maine Sunday Telegram* for two decades. His columns, stories, essays and photographs have also appeared in a wide variety of other print and online publications, including a regular Hikes & Brews piece in *Maine Brew & Bev.*

Carey's basecamp is on the coast of his beloved state of Maine, right next to Acadia National Park on Mount Desert Island, where he lives with his wife and favorite trail companion, Fran Leyman, and a mountain of well-used outdoor gear. You can also find him on Facebook, on Instagram @careykish, and at mainegeographic.com.

ABOUT BEER HIKING IN NEW ENGLAND

With thousands of miles of hiking trails and walking paths rich in scenery, history and wildlife, New England is a hiker's dream destination. And for trampers who appreciate beer, the region has the added appeal of being home to a burgeoning craft brewing industry that has grown to include more than 700 breweries, microbreweries, brewpubs and tasting rooms.

With its high mountain peaks and leafy green hills, sparkling lakes and ponds, clear rushing rivers and streams, sandy dunes, beaches, and rocky coastal headlands, New England has hiking opportunities aplenty to suit every interest and ability. And somewhere in the vicinity of trail's end, you'll always find an inviting spot to enjoy a refreshing craft brew with your trail companions—a fun place to relax and reflect, pint in hand, on the day's outdoor activities amid jovial pub banter, while conjuring up plans for the next hike-and-brew endeavor.

New England comprises six states—Maine, New Hampshire, Vermont, Massachusetts, Connecticut and Rhode Island—in a geographically diverse land area of 72,000 square miles in the northeastern corner of the US. The region is bounded to the west by New York, to the north and northeast by the Canadian provinces of Quebec and New Brunswick, to the southwest by Long Island Sound, and to the east and southeast by the Atlantic Ocean.

Heavily forested Maine is nearly as large as the other five New England states combined, while tiny Rhode Island is the smallest state in the country. The Appalachian Mountains extend across the region's western and northern reaches, notably as the Green Mountains in Vermont and the White Mountains in New Hampshire. Massachusetts is known for its great coastal bays, while the Connecticut River, the region's longest, slices through its namesake state. New England's spectacular fall foliage is world-renowned.

The breweries and beer styles you'll encounter on your travels are as diverse as the region's incredible geography. New Englanders love their beer, and you will too. Several states consistently rank among the highest in the nation in terms of per capita breweries and beer consumption. "We brew the beer we love to drink" is a common refrain among brewers and brewery owners, who exude a palpable enthusiasm for their craft and an amazing passion for their patrons, staff and communities.

From barns and old mill complexes to former machine shops, from main street storefronts to restored train depots, from small rural operations to large urban producers, and from budding new businesses to long-established institutions, every New England brewery has its own unique character and flavor. The hazy, juicy, hop-forward New England IPA may be the dominant beer, but you'll discover a wide range of drinkable brews on tap wherever you go—from traditional favorites to experimental batches and seasonal offerings.

New England. Hiking. Beer. Beer Hiking New England. Great outdoor and indoor adventures await you in the pages of this book. Hike safely, have fun and please drink responsibly.

CHOOSE THE BEER OR THE HIKE

HIKE LOCATION ⟶

REGION ⟶

NAME OF THE BEER ⟶

MAP ⟶

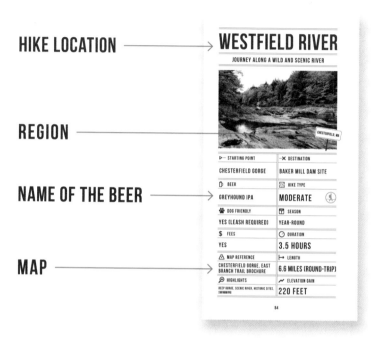

WESTFIELD RIVER
JOURNEY ALONG A WILD AND SCENIC RIVER

CHESTERFIELD, MA

▷— STARTING POINT	—✗ DESTINATION
CHESTERFIELD GORGE	BAKER MILL DAM SITE
🍺 BEER	🏔 HIKE TYPE
GREYHOUND IPA	MODERATE
🐾 DOG FRIENDLY	📅 SEASON
YES (LEASH REQUIRED)	YEAR-ROUND
$ FEES	⏱ DURATION
YES	3.5 HOURS
🗺 MAP REFERENCE	⊢ LENGTH
CHESTERFIELD GORGE, EAST BRANCH TRAIL BROCHURE	6.6 MILES (ROUND-TRIP)
⚡ HIGHLIGHTS	∿ ELEVATION GAIN
DEEP GORGE, SCENIC RIVER, HISTORIC SITES, SWIMMING	220 FEET

94

6.5 % ALCOHOL CONTENT	INDIA PALE ALE
👁	PALE ORANGE
👃	CITRUS GRAPEFRUIT FORWARD
👄	GRAPEFRUITY CITRUS FORWARD

BITTERNESS   SWEETNESS

⟵ INFORMATION
ABOUT THE BEER

⟵ INFORMATION
ABOUT THE HIKE

85

ON THE HIKES AND HIKE RATINGS

The hikes selected for this guide range far and wide across the extraordinary natural landscape of New England. Among them you'll find everything from easy pondside strolls to moderate hill walks and forest forays to strenuous mountain climbs. Hike ratings are subjective and based upon the author's personal experience, considering such factors as terrain, overall mileage and elevation gain. Your experience may be somewhat different; a hike rated moderate, for example, may seem easier or harder than described.

EASY
Easy hikes are generally 2 to 4 miles in length, have a minimal elevation gain and require about 1 to 2 hours to complete.

MODERATE
Moderate hikes are anywhere from 3 to 7 miles long with an elevation gain ranging from around 500 feet to a little over 1,000 feet; they take about 2 to 4 hours. A handful of hikes straddle the moderate line and have hybrid ratings, i.e., easy-moderate or moderate-strenuous.

STRENUOUS
All but one of the strenuous hikes described in this book are mountain climbs. These hikes involve 6 to 10 miles of hiking, have elevation gains ranging from 1,500 feet to as much as 2,700 feet and take from 4 to 6 hours.

Hike length in miles and elevation gain in feet were measured using a GPS app. Duration was calculated using a common formula known in the New England hiking community as "book time," which figures 30 minutes for each mile of distance and 30 minutes for every 1,000 feet of elevation gain. Snack breaks, rest breaks, scenery stops, weather conditions and the like may add more time.

The majority of the hikes in this book are loops, beginning and ending at the same trailhead, while a handful are round-trip (in-and-out via the same trail). Several hikes are one-way or point-to-point hikes, beginning at one trailhead and ending at another, and thus require either a vehicle spot or the use of a taxi or rideshare service (or perhaps a bicycle) to get back to the original trailhead.

On many hikes (but not all), there are opportunities to shorten your journey or alter your route, if so desired. Check your trail map as you go for such options.

A number of hikes involve a fee of some sort, e.g., entrance, parking, toll road. A handful of hikes do not allow dogs, while most require them to be on a leash; please note this in advance to avoid disappointment.

ON THE BREWERIES AND BEER RATINGS

With just a few exceptions, the selected breweries are located a half hour or less from the trailheads. Their days and hours of operation vary; many breweries are open daily or nearly so, while others, especially in the rural areas, are open later in the week and through the weekends (four days is the minimum for this guide). At least two of the breweries are seasonal operations. Some breweries allow dogs and children, while others don't. Given these variables, it's a good idea to consider your intended brewery visit when planning your hike. Check the brewery's website—or even better, in many cases, its social media sites—for the most up-to-date information.

The beer featured with each hike might be that brewery's flagship brew, its most popular offering, a recommendation by bar staff or a patron on the next bar stool, something fun or funky that caught the author's eye, or a brew that simply fit the location or the weather on the day of his visit. Beer ratings are subjective. The color, aroma, taste, bitterness and sweetness of the highlighted beers are based on conversations with the brewers and brewery owners, as well as the author's tasting notes. As with the rated difficulty of the hikes, however, your individual experience with the beers may be a little or a lot different.

The fact is that there's a wealth of really good beer to be enjoyed all over New England, from the ever-popular hazy, juicy, hoppy, smooth-drinking New England IPAs to the more traditional beers—the lagers, IPAs, wheat beers, Belgians, porters and stouts—plus fruit sours and other specialty brews, experimental batches and one-offs. Most breweries feature a tap list of regularly available beers, while some have constantly rotating offerings. What you can always count on is variety and that you'll find one or more beers that will delight your olfactory senses and satisfy your taste buds. Talk with the brewery staff and ask for a taster or two, and consider a flight or sample tray, which is a good way to try a few different brews before selecting a full pour.

To be sure, access to most of the trails and breweries in this book requires a vehicle. Please enjoy your brews responsibly and never drink and drive. Allow at least 45 minutes per beer consumed for your system to process the alcohol before driving. Better yet is to have a designated driver. Another option is to grab a growler, crowler or four-pack to go and enjoy your beer safely, responsibly and comfortably back at home, at your campsite, or in your cabin, hotel room or RV.

PREPARING FOR YOUR HIKE

THE TEN ESSENTIALS (AND THEN SOME)

The day hikes described in this book range from easy pondside strolls of about an hour to rugged mountain climbs requiring the better part of a day. Regardless of the duration or destination, you should always be well prepared. Start with a quality daypack to hold your gear, plus comfortable footwear with good socks (and a spare pair). Here's a list of the other important items you should consider taking with you on the trail to ensure you have a safe, comfortable and enjoyable hike.

- **Navigation.** The maps in this book are for reference only. The most reliable navigation tools are a paper map (preferably topographic) and a compass, and you should know how to use both. Batteries die, so please don't rely solely on your phone (except for photos, of course).

- **Hydration.** Water is essential when you're hiking. Make sure you bring plenty along (2 liters is generally adequate, but you may need more on longer hikes) to keep yourself hydrated and ward off the potential for heat-related illnesses.
- **Nutrition.** Carry and consume high-energy snacks (and lunch foods when you're going to be out for a while). Bring extra food along just in case you're on the trail for longer than planned. Foods high in protein with a good shelf life can be kept in your pack for contingencies.
- **Rain Gear and Insulation.** New England weather can change quickly, especially in the mountains, making rain and wind gear essential for your comfort and safety. Bring a hat and gloves, plus an extra layer or two of clothing (synthetic is best) as added insulation and something dry to change into if needed.
- **Fire Starter.** In case of emergency, a water-tight container of waterproof matches, backed up with a small lighter, is invaluable to a lost hiker for warmth and cheer.
- **First Aid.** From blisters and minor cuts and scrapes to more significant injuries, anything can happen when you're hiking, and you need to be ready. A small first-aid kit, either commercially packaged or put together yourself, along with basic first-aid knowledge will give you peace of mind in the woods. Don't forget any prescription medications.
- **Tools.** Small items, such as pocketknives and multi-tools, can take on big jobs on the trail. A whistle will aid in signaling to companions if you become separated and can also be used to alert rescue personnel in an emergency. And never underestimate the usefulness of duct tape!
- **Illumination.** Delays happen, and getting caught out in the dark is a real possibility, especially in the shorter daylight hours of spring and autumn. Bring a flashlight or headlamp (and spare batteries) so you'll be able to comfortably find your way out.
- **Sun Protection.** Sunscreen, a brimmed hat and sunglasses will help prevent sunburn and protect your eyes from bright glare.
- **Insect Protection.** For bug season, which is generally from late May through mid-July (though it varies by location and latitude), insect repellent for black flies, mosquitoes and the like is a must. Ticks are a growing problem; repellents work, and so do long pants tucked into socks and a long-sleeved shirt. A post-hike tick check is a good idea, too.
- **Sanitation.** When the urge to "go" hits on the trail, you'll be glad you're carrying toilet paper, wet wipes and hand sanitizer. Dig a 6- to 8-inch deep cathole in which to deposit your #2 waste and cover it up when done. Carry out your used TP and wet wipes in a plastic bag.
- **Shelter.** Some form of waterproof protection, be it as simple as a space blanket, a small tarp or even a lawn-size trash bag, will help keep you dry in inclement weather or during an unexpected overnight on the trail.

Finally, pack along a healthy measure of common sense and good judgement and use both liberally on the trail. Have fun, but keep in mind that getting to the summit is optional, while getting back to the trailhead is mandatory.

HIKING SEASON

The hiking season listed for each individual hike is the recommended window, generally from sometime in the spring—after the snows have melted and the trails have had a chance to dry out—until sometime in the fall before the weather turns toward winter again. This optimal period will be longer in southern New England and shorter in the northern regions and at higher elevations. Hikes along the coast and at lower elevations can usually be enjoyed throughout the year. Of course, experienced hikers well equipped with cold-weather gear can tackle the mountain trails right through the shoulder seasons and wintertime. It's a good idea to check with the land/trail manager (listed for each hike) about current trail conditions and any use restrictions in effect.

HUNTING SEASONS

Hunting seasons and rules vary from state to state across New England. In Maine and Massachusetts, for example, hunting isn't allowed on Sundays, while Rhode Island requires anyone out in the woods during hunting season to wear safety orange. To be sure, during the autumn hunting season, plan to carry a couple items of safety orange clothing and be prepared to wear them while hiking. Check these sites for state hunting laws and regulations:

- Maine Dept. of Inland Fisheries and Wildlife, www.maine.gov/ifw/hunting-trapping/
- New Hampshire Fish and Game, wildlife.state.nh.us/hunting/
- Vermont Fish & Wildlife Dept., vtfishandwildlife.com/hunt
- Massachusetts Division of Fisheries and Wildlife, www.mass.gov/hunting-regulations
- Connecticut State Dept. of Energy and Environmental Protection, portal.ct.gov/DEEP/Hunting/CT-Hunting-and-Trapping
- Rhode Island Division of Fish and Wildlife, www.dem.ri.gov/programs/fish-wildlife/

WEATHER

New England weather is notoriously fickle, and conditions can change quickly, especially in the mountains and along the coast. It's best to always be prepared for whatever Mother Nature may bring your way, from sun and wind to rain and cold, and, above tree line, snow even in high summer. For accurate forecasts, check with the National Weather Service at www.weather.gov.

ADDITIONAL RESOURCES

For lots more information on additional hiking opportunities and breweries, plus dining, lodging and camping options and other things to see and do during your beer hiking adventures, check out these helpful sites:

Maine
Hiking: Maine Trail Finder, www.mainetrailfinder.com
Breweries: Maine Brewers Guild, mainebrewersguild.org
Visitor Amenities: Maine Tourism Association, www.mainetourism.com

New Hampshire
Hiking: Trail Finder, www.trailfinder.info
Breweries: New Hampshire Brewers Association, nhbrewers.org
Visitor Amenities: Visit New Hampshire, www.visitnh.gov

Vermont
Hiking: Trail Finder, www.trailfinder.info
Breweries: Vermont Brewers Association, www.vermontbrewers.com
Visitor Amenities: Vermont Dept. of Tourism & Marketing, vermontvacation.com

Massachusetts
Hiking: Massachusetts Dept. of Conservation & Recreation, www.mass.gov/orgs/department-of-conservation-recreation; The Trustees of Reservations, thetrustees.org
Breweries: Massachusetts Brewers Guild, massbrewersguild.org
Visitor Amenities: Visit Massachusetts, www.visitma.com

Connecticut
Hiking: Connecticut Trail Finder, www.cttrailfinder.com
Breweries: Connecticut Brewers Guild, www.connecticut.beer
Visitor Amenities: Connecticut Office of Tourism, www.ctvisit.com

Rhode Island
Hiking: ExploreRI, exploreri.org
Breweries: Rhode Island Brewers Guild, www.ribrewersguild.org
Visitor Amenities: Visit Rhode Island, www.visitrhodeisland.com

The Appalachian Mountain Club (www.outdoors.org), with eight chapters across New England, and the Green Mountain Club (www.greenmountainclub.org) in Vermont, two of the oldest outdoor and conservation organizations in the US, are excellent sources with a wealth of hiking and outdoors-related information, maps and publications.

TRAIL ETIQUETTE

Hiking today is more popular than ever, with an unprecedented number of outdoor enthusiasts—from experienced trampers to those new to the sport—taking to the trails for recreational pleasure. Some of the trails in this book are very popular big-name hikes, others are locally loved favorites, while a few are off-the-beaten-path gems. Regardless of where you go, you're very likely to have some company, especially if it's a weekend or holiday.

Increased hiker use is stressing the carrying capacity of trails, facilities and parking, and challenging the ability of land and trail managers to deal with its many adverse effects. Therefore, it's incumbent upon all of us—that's you and me—to be good stewards and neighbors by following this handful of simple guidelines (in the spirit of Leave No Trace, www.lnt.org) for a safe, enjoyable and environmentally friendly hiking experience.

- **Stay on the trail.** Walk through the mud, not around it, to avoid widening the treadway. Don't cut switchbacks; doing so encourages erosion and creates extra work for trail maintainers. Trampling off trail encourages the start of herd paths and damages fragile flora.
- **Limit your group size.** Many public and private lands cap the size of hiking parties to ten or twelve people. More than that is unwieldly, hard on the environment and a nuisance to other hikers.
- **Hike quietly.** Enjoy the sounds of nature and stay aware of your surroundings by keeping your voice at a respectful volume, turning your cell phone down or off, and leaving your Bluetooth speakers and noise-cancelling headphones at home.
- **Respect wildlife.** Keep wildlife wild by keeping your distance and never, ever feeding the animals.
- **Pack out your trash.** Carry a plastic bag to pack out your garbage (and that of others less thoughtful).
- **Practice good bathroom hygiene.** Know how to pee and poop in the woods. Go at least 200 feet from any trail or water source, dig a proper cathole, and cover up your waste when done.
- **Leave nature as you found it.** Yes, just like the old TV ad said: "Take only pictures and leave only footprints." Don't take souvenirs, build rock art or leave painted rocks behind.
- **Yield to other hikers climbing uphill.** Uphill hikers have the right of way. If you're overtaking others, let them know you're there to avoid any surprise. When taking a break, move entirely off the trail to allow others to pass comfortably.
- **Park responsibly at the trailhead.** And if the trailhead is full, consider returning a little later on.
- **Greet other hikers.** Smile, be friendly and offer help where needed.
- **Hiking with a dog?** Most (but not all) hikes in this book are dog-friendly. A leash is required, usually by state law, to help keep your pet under firm control and avoid being a nuisance to other hikers or a threat to wildlife. Clean up your dog's waste immediately and pack it out.

2

MAP & INDEX

MAP

HIKES

NAME OF THE ROUTE	TOWN, STATE	LENGTH	PAGE
Acadia National Park	Bar Harbor, ME	6.4 Miles (Loop)	280
Adams Reservoir	Bennington, VT	2.4 Miles (Loop)	168
Bangor City Forest & Orono Bog	Bangor and Orono, ME	5.0 Miles (Loop)	286
Barn Island	Stonington, CT	3.8 Miles (Loop)	112
Bear Mountain	Kent, CT	6.3 Miles (Loop)	118
Bluff Head	Guilford, CT	4.3 Miles (Loop)	124
Breakneck Pond	Union, CT	6.3 Miles (Loop)	130
Camel's Hump	Duxbury, VT	7.1 Miles (Loop)	174
Devil's Hopyard	East Haddam, CT	2.8 Miles (Loop)	136
Elmore Mountain	Lake Elmore, VT	4.2 Miles (Loop)	180
Forest City Trail	Portland, ME	10.7 Miles (One Way)	292
Great Island	Wellfleet, MA	7.1 Miles (Loop)	30
Lake Zoar	Sandy Hook, CT	6.5 Miles (Loop)	142
Macedonia Ridge	Kent, CT	6.5 Miles (Loop)	148
Monhegan Island	Monhegan Island, ME	3.1 Miles (Loop)	298
Monument Mountain	Great Barrington, MA	2.6 Miles (Loop)	36
Mount Cardigan	Orange, NH	3.3 Miles (Loop)	230
Mount Greylock	Williamstown, MA	9.4 Miles (Loop)	42
Mount Kearsarge	Wilmot, NH	3.6 Miles (Loop)	236
Mount Mansfield	Underhill Center, VT	7.8 Miles (Loop)	186
Mount Moosilauke	Benton, NH	8.2 Miles (Loop)	242
Mount Pisgah	Westmore, VT	4.2 Miles (One Way)	192
Mount Race	Sheffield, MA	6.4 Miles (Round-Trip)	48
Mount Roberts	Moultonborough, NH	5.3 Miles (Round-Trip)	248
Mount Tom and The Pogue	Woodstock, VT	4.7 Miles (One-Way)	210
Mount Tom	Holyoke, MA	5.4 Miles (Loop)	54
Mount Washington	Sargent's Purchase, NH	6.1 Miles (Loop)	254
Mount Watatic	Ashburnham, MA	3.8 Miles (Loop)	60
Moxie Bald Mountain	Bald Mountain Township, ME	9.4 Miles (Round-Trip)	304
Myles Standish Forest	South Carver, MA	7.2 Miles (Loop)	66
North and Middle Sugarloaf	Bethlehem, NH	3.5 Miles (Round-Trip)	260
Northwood Meadows	Northwood, NH	2.9 Miles (Loop)	224
Old Speck Mountain	Grafton Township, ME	7.0 Miles (Round-Trip)	310
Pisgah Ridge	Winchester, NH	8.6 Miles (Loop)	266
Plum Island	Newburyport, MA	1.5 Miles (Loop)	72
Quoddy Head	Lubec, ME	4.2 Miles (Loop)	316
Ragged Mountain	Berlin, CT	5.7 Miles (Loop)	154
Sachuest Point	Middletown, RI	2.7 Miles (Loop)	92
Shelburne Bay	Shelburne, VT	2.6 Miles (Loop)	198
Snake Mountain	Addison, VT	4.1 Miles (Loop)	204
Talcott Mountain	Simsbury, CT	4.1 Miles (Loop	160
The Sweet Trail	Durham, NH	5.3 Miles (One-Way)	272
Tillinghast Pond	West Greenwich, RI	4.3 Miles (Loop)	98
Tumbledown Mountain	Twp 6 North of Weld, ME	6.4 Miles (Loop)	322
Vaughan Woods	Hallowell, ME	2.1 Miles (Loop)	328
Walden Pond	Concord, MA	2.7 Miles (Loop)	78
Walkabout Trail	Chepachet, RI	7.6 Miles (Loop)	104
Wells Reserve	Wells, ME	3.9 Miles (Loop)	334
Westfield River	Chesterfield, MA	6.6 Miles (Round-Trip)	84
Windmill Ridge	Westminster, VT	4.0 Miles (Loop)	216

BREWERIES & BEERS

BREWERY	BEER	PAGE
Ambition Brewing	Stop. Hammock Time Cream Ale	322
Atlantic Brewing Company, Midtown	Flat Hat American Pale Ale	280
Bangor Beer Co.	Catchphrase NEIPA	286
Barrington Brewery & Restaurant	Barrington Brown Ale	36
Batson River Brewing and Distilling	Cleaves Cove IPA	334
Beer'd Brewing Co.	Dogs & Boats DIPA	112
Big Elm Brewing	413 Farmhouse Ale	48
Black Flannel Brewing Company	Disco Montage NEIPA	186
Bravo Brewing Company	Parliament ESB	104
Bright Ideas Brewing	N.E. Thing IPA	42
Coddington Brewing Company	Blueberry Blonde Ale	92
Drop-In Brewing Company	Heart of Lothian Scottish Ale	204
Elm City Brewing Company	Keene Kolsch	266
Flying Goose Brew Pub & Grille	Long Brothers American IPA	236
Great Falls Brewing Co.	Lazy Hazy Housy NEIPA	118
Hobbs Brewing Company	Black Sheep Pils	248
Hog Island Beer Co.	Outermost IPA	30
Hop Culture Farms & Brew Company	Juicy in the 860 NEIPA	136
Hopmeadow Brewing Co.	Citra Nitra NEIPA	160
Housatonic River Brewing	Gentle On My Mind NEIPA	148
Kennebec River Brewery	Big Mama Blueberry Ale	304
Ledge Brewing Company	As You Wish NEIPA	254
Linesider Brewing Co.	StrIPAh NEIPA	98
Long Trail Brewing Company	Long Trail Ale	210
Lubec Brewing Company	Quoddy Head Red	316
Madison Brewing Company Pub & Restaurant	Old 76 Strong Ale	168
Mayflower Brewing Company	Porter	66
Monhegan Brewing Company	Island Farm Double IPA	298
New City Brewery	Original Ginger Beer	54
Newburyport Brewing Co.	Newburyport Pale Ale	72
Next Trick Brewing	NEKIPA	192
Northampton Brewery	Greyhound IPA	84
Northwoods Brewing Co.	Glass DDH IPA	224
Prohibition Pig Restaurant & Brewery	Bantam Double American IPA	174
Rek'-Lis Brewing Company	Pretentious Hopper Neipa	260
Reverie Brewing Co.	Blimp NEIPA	142
Rising Tide Brewing Company	Ishmael Copper Ale	292
River Styx Brewing	Nectar of Aristaeus: Peach Cobbler IPA Milkshake	60
Rock Art Brewery	Ridge Runner Vermont Ale	180
Shackett's Brewing Company	Newfound Nutbrown Ale	230
Steam Mill Brewing	C-Surplus IPA	310
Stoneface Brewing Co.	Full Clip NEIPA	272
Taylor Brooke Brewery	No Room to Swing a Cat IPA	130
The Liberal Cup Public House & Brewery	Alewife Pale Ale	328
Thimble Island Brewing Company	American Ale	124
True West Brewery	Ruckus! IPA	78
Whetstone Station Restaurant And Brewery	Whetstoner Session IPA	216
Witchdoctor Brewing Company	Pauper's Porridge Oatmeal Amber Ale	154
Woodstock Inn Brewery	Pig's Ear Brown Ale	242
Zero Gravity Craft Brewery	Green State Lager	198

3

THE BEER HIKES

MASSACHUSETTS

GREAT ISLAND

HIKE CAPE COD NATIONAL SEASHORE'S LONGEST TRAIL

WELLFLEET, MA

▷⋯ STARTING POINT	⋯✕ DESTINATION
CHEQUESSETT NECK ROAD TRAILHEAD	**GREAT ISLAND LOOP**
🍺 BEER	🔀 HIKE TYPE
OUTERMOST IPA	**MODERATE** 🥾
🐾 DOG FRIENDLY	📅 SEASON
YES (LEASH REQUIRED)	**YEAR-ROUND**
$ FEES	🕐 DURATION
NO	**3 HOURS 40 MIN.**
⛰ MAP REFERENCE	↦ LENGTH
POSTED AT TRAILHEAD	**7.1 MILES (LOOP)**
🔍 HIGHLIGHTS	〰 ELEVATION GAIN
SAND DUNES, OCEAN SURF, SALT MARSHES, PINE WOODS	**150 FEET**

 AMERICAN IPA

 COPPER

 CITRUS

 CITRUS
HOP BITE

BITTERNESS

SWEETNESS

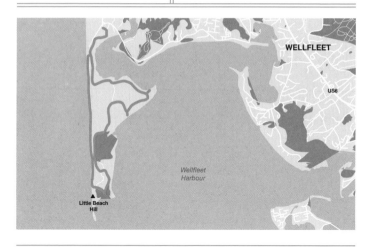

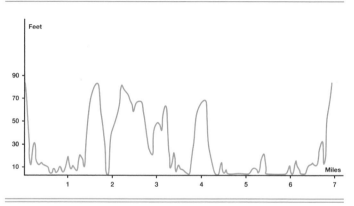

HIKE DESCRIPTION

Ramble around Great Island on Cape Cod's longest trail to enjoy salt marshes, sand dunes, piney woods and a long stretch of sandy oceanfront beach. After your hike, go hog wild with an Outermost IPA at Hog Island Brewery.

Cape Cod is an enormous peninsula extending 60 miles out into the Atlantic Ocean on the southeastern coast of Massachusetts. Its easternmost reaches, known as the Outer Cape, are home to the Cape Cod National Seashore, a 44,600-acre expanse of sand dunes and sandy beaches, salt marshes and estuaries, lakes and ponds, heaths and grasslands and forests of pine and oak.

Great Island Trail is the longest hike at Cape Cod National Seashore. Start by snapping a photo of the trail map, then head out to The Gut, a large semicircular bend in the mouth of the Herring River. A narrow

strip of salt marsh and sand dunes separates The Gut from Cape Cod Bay. Any of several parallel sandy lanes will lead you through the beach rose, beach peas, dune grass and heather, with views across the water to Chequesset Neck and Mayo Beach. As you round the south side of The Gut on the way to the Great Island Tavern Site, keep a sharp eye out so you don't miss the unsigned trail leading right, into the woods. If you can find it, take it. (If not, no worries—just continue walking around the eastern edge of the island. Both routes converge in about a half mile at the old tavern site.)

Twisted woods of pitch pine and black oak lead to the site of the former Great Island Whaler's Tavern, which served local fishermen from 1690 to 1740 in the glory days of Cape Cod whaling when the great mammals were hunted close to shore. An interpretive display shows some old photos of the tavern, but nothing more remains. Beyond the tavern site, the high bluffs on the west shore of the island, reached by a side trail, offer a good view over Wellfleet Harbor. Then it's on to the memorial to William Bradford, who was among the Pilgrims who sailed to the New World on the Mayflower in 1620 and later served as governor of the Plymouth Plantation colony he helped establish.

After rounding the salt marshes of Middle Meadow and then padding through the woods on Great Beach Hill, you'll emerge at a majestic south-facing view of the sandy tip of the island at Jeremy Point. It may look tempting, but realize that it's several long miles away. Work up a thirst by heading for the dunes, then turn north along the beach for the last leg of the walk, an almost 2-mile-long stroll accented by colorful dune bluffs, the rhythmic surf of Cape Cod Bay and plenty of seashells at your feet.

TURN-BY-TURN DIRECTIONS

1. From the trailhead kiosk, follow the gravel trail to the shore of the Herring River, then turn right along the sandy path.
2. At 0.5 miles, bear left at the junction to walk through the dunes along The Gut (to the right is the first beach access and your return route).
3. At 1.2 miles, after passing through an old gate (two concrete and two metal posts), arrive at a signed junction; bear left to walk along the salt marsh shore toward the Great Island Tavern Site.
4. At 1.5 miles, shortly before turning a corner on the point, look for an unmarked trail on the right leading into the woods; take this path.
5. At 2 miles, reach the tavern site marked by an interpretive display. Explore the spur to the beach, then return to continue.
6. At 2.6 miles, a spur on the left leads to a bluff overlooking Wellfleet Harbor.
7. At 3.0 miles, reach a T junction with the main trail; turn left (right leads back to the trailhead).
8. At 3.2 miles, pass the Bradford Memorial.
9. At 4 miles, bear left at a concrete post and climb Great Beach Hill.
10. At 4.5 miles, a spur on the left leads to a view south to Jeremy Point.
11. At 4.8 miles, reach the second beach access; turn right to walk northbound along Cape Cod Bay.
12. At 6.5 miles, turn right off the beach at the first beach access, and ahead, turn left on the main trail to return to the trailhead.

FIND THE TRAILHEAD

In Orleans, from the large traffic circle known as the Orleans Rotary, follow US Route 6 northbound toward Eastham and Provincetown. In 3 miles, pass the Cape Cod National Seashore Salt Pond Visitor Center on the right. In another 8.2 miles, turn left on Main Street toward Wellfleet Center and Wellfleet Harbor. In 0.7 miles, take a left on Holbrook Avenue, and just 0.1 miles beyond, turn right on Chequesset Neck Road. Follow Chequesset Neck Road 2.4 miles to its intersection with Griffin Island Road, where you'll find the Great Island Trail parking area on the left.

HOG ISLAND BEER CO.

Hog Island Beer takes its name from the deserted island in Little Pleasant Bay, a few miles to the east, where Captain Kidd is rumored to have buried his booty of gold. The brewery owners, however, believe they've found treasure of their own: liquid treasure. "Built by locals, brewed by locals, drunk by locals," the "Outermost Brewery on Cape Cod" features a courtyard beer garden where you can enjoy a brew and a bite and maybe a game of corn hole in the warm Cape Cod sun. Outermost IPA, a traditional American IPA sure to quench your thirst, is the signature beer among the seven on draft. Hungry? From New England clam chowder to tavern pretzels, fish and chips to burgers, the talented kitchen staff will feed you well. At Hog Island, you'll feel like a salty local in no time.

LAND MANAGER

Cape Cod National Seashore
Salt Pond Visitor Center
50 Nauset Road
Eastham, MA 02642
(508) 255-3421
www.nps.gov/caco/planyourvisit/greatislandtrail.htm

BREWERY/RESTAURANT

Hog Island Beer Co.
28 West Road
Orleans, MA 02653
(508) 255-2337
www.hogislandbeerco.com
Distance from trailhead: 17 miles

MONUMENT MOUNTAIN

HISTORY AND BEAUTY ABOUND ON THIS NARROW RIDGE HIKE

GREAT BARRINGTON, MA

▷⋯ STARTING POINT	⋯✕ DESTINATION
US ROUTE 7	**PEESKAWSO PEAK**
🍺 BEER	HIKE TYPE
BARRINGTON BROWN ALE	**MODERATE**
🐾 DOG FRIENDLY	SEASON
YES (LEASH REQUIRED)	**MARCH TO NOVEMBER**
💲 FEES	🕐 DURATION
YES	**1 HOUR 40 MIN.**
🗺 MAP REFERENCE	↦ LENGTH
MONUMENT MOUNTAIN	**2.6 MILES (LOOP)**
🔍 HIGHLIGHTS	〰 ELEVATION GAIN
NARROW RIDGE, MOUNTAIN VIEWS, LITERARY HISTORY	**675 FEET**

ENGLISH BROWN ALE

MAHOGANY BROWN

NUTTY
COFFEE
CHOCOLATE

CARAMEL
COFFEE
CHOCOLATE

BITTERNESS   SWEETNESS

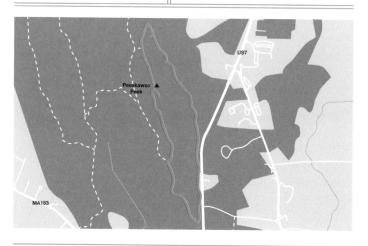

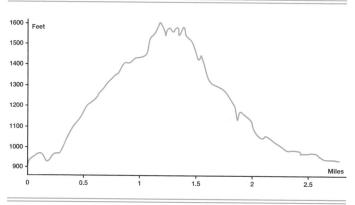

HIKE DESCRIPTION

Enjoy outstanding views of the Berkshire Hills from this craggy ridgeline rising high above the Housatonic River valley. Then head for Barrington Brewery in lively Great Barrington for a fine pint of English ale.

Monument Mountain is a 2.5-mile knife-edge ridge of gray quartzite rising high above the bucolic Housatonic River Valley in southern Berkshire County. Monument Mountain Reservation encompasses the mountain and its spectacular cliffs: 555 acres altogether. The property belongs to the Trustees of Reservations, which has been protecting places of ecological, scenic and historic importance throughout Massachusetts since 1891.

History and beauty abound on this loop hike, which follows three trails: Hickey, Peeskawso and Mohican Monument. At the start of the Hickey Trail is an interpretive sign, "The Melville Trail." Literary giants Nathaniel Hawthorne and Herman Melville were among a group of friends who met here for a picnic hike on August 5, 1850. Caught in a thunderstorm partway up the mountain, the pair sought refuge in a cave and a lengthy, spirited discussion ensued. This conversation provided the inspiration for Melville's most famous work, *Moby-Dick*. The Hickey trail (marked with yellow dots) leads up the eastern side of the peak. In a ravine along the way, a short side trail will take you to the cave Melville and Hawthorne took cover in.

At the junction of the Mohican Monument Trail and the Peeskawso Trail is Inscription Rock. Dedicated in 1899, it reads: "In fulfillment of a wish of Rosalie Butler that such portions of this mountain might be preserved to (sic) the people of Berkshire as a place of free enjoyment for all time." The Peeskawso Trail (marked with red dots) follows the narrow ridge, which affords fine views to the east. The wooded, craggy knife-edge leads on to several rocky outlooks at about 640 feet on the summit ridge of Peeskawso Peak. The vista from the east side of the peak ranges north to Mount Greylock, the highest mountain in

Massachusetts, and south to Mount Everett, Mount Race and the slopes of the Ski Butternut resort. From the west-facing rocks, you can look out over the broad Housatonic River valley and on to the Taconic Range, which straddles the Massachusetts-New York state line, and thence to the lofty Catskill Mountains of New York.

Drop down off the narrow ridge to skirt the main summit of Peeskawso Peak and arrive at a side trail to Devil's Pulpit; take this short detour to enjoy a look at the striking free-standing rock pillar. After passing a series of cliffs and ledges, you'll reach the Mohican Monument Trail. Blue dots mark the old carriage road, which swings east around the base of the mountain. The great cliffs and talus slopes of the mountain's east face loom above as you make your way around a large finger of rock on the last leg of the hike.

TURN-BY-TURN DIRECTIONS

1. From the trailhead info kiosk, look right for the Hickey Trail and follow its yellow dots up the east side of the mountain.
2. At 1.0 miles, reach Inscription Rock. Turn here onto the Peeskawso Trail.
3. At 1.2 miles, reach the rock outcrops and lookouts on the summit ridge of Peeskawso Peak.
4. At 1.3 miles, take the side trail on the left to a viewpoint overlooking Devil's Pulpit.
5. At 1.8 miles, turn left on the Mohican Monument Trail to return to the base of the mountain.

FIND THE TRAILHEAD

From the junction of MA Route 41 and US Route 7/MA Route 23 in Great Barrington, drive north on US Route 7 for 3.6 miles to the Monument Mountain trailhead parking area on the left.

BARRINGTON BREWERY & RESTAURANT

Barrington Brewery, housed in two former dairy barns that were once part of the old Christie Farms established in the 1850s, has been serving "barn-brewed" beers and food made from scratch since 1995. In 2007, the brewery became the first on the East Coast to install a solar-energy hot-water system, and 10 years later it added a 480-panel photovoltaic system that generates 85 percent of the brewery's electrical needs. Pretty cool. Warm colors and dark wood give the comfortable taproom

an English pub feel—and why not, since the town and the brewery were named after the village of Great Barrington in Gloucestershire, England? Choose from six signature ales or select a brew from the seasonal tap list and pair it with something delicious from the pub's extensive menu, like the awesome BBQ beef brisket with mac and cheese. Yum!

LAND MANAGER

The Trustees of Reservations
Boston, MA
(617) 542-7696
Info and trail map: thetrustees.org/place/monument-mountain/

BREWERY/RESTAURANT

Barrington Brewery & Restaurant
420 Stockbridge Road
Great Barrington, MA 01230
(413) 528-8282
www.barringtonbrewery.net
Distance from trailhead: 2.2 miles

MOUNT GREYLOCK

TACKLE THE HIGHEST MOUNTAIN IN MASSACHUSETTS

WILLIAMSTOWN, MA

▷··· STARTING POINT	···✕ DESTINATION
HOPPER ROAD	MOUNT GREYLOCK SUMMIT AND WAR MEMORIAL
🍺 BEER	HIKE TYPE
N.E. THING IPA	STRENUOUS
🐾 DOG FRIENDLY	SEASON
YES (LEASH REQUIRED)	MAY TO OCTOBER
$ FEES	🕐 DURATION
NO	6 HOURS
⛰ MAP REFERENCE	↦ LENGTH
MT. GREYLOCK STATE RESERVATION & GREYLOCK GLEN	9.4 MILES (LOOP)
🔎 HIGHLIGHTS	〰 ELEVATION GAIN
HISTORIC SUMMIT TOWER, 4-STATE PANORAMA	2,650 FEET

7.6 %
ALCOHOL CONTENT

NEW ENGLAND IPA

HAZY GOLD

FRUITY
CITRUS

GRAIN
FRUIT

BITTERNESS

SWEETNESS

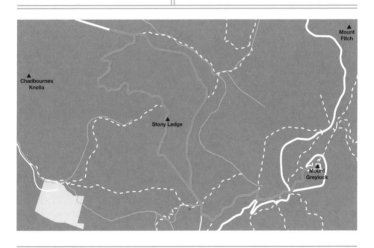

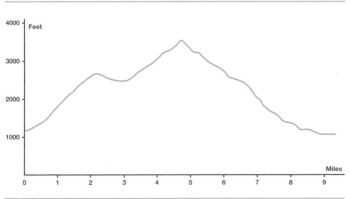

HIKE DESCRIPTION

Hike over Stony Ledge to the historic tower on the summit of Mount Greylock, the highest peak in Massachusetts, for a four-state panorama. Bright Ideas Brewing is a bright idea for a post-hike brew.

Mount Greylock rises to 3,491 feet in the northwest corner of Massachusetts. It is the highest peak in the Bay State and the crown jewel of the 12,500-acre Mount Greylock State Reservation. Designated in 1968, Mount Greylock became the first reservation in the state's forests and parks system. A graceful 92-foot granite tower adorns the summit of Mount Greylock amid the only subalpine terrain in the state.

Just minutes into the hike, the Haley Farm Trail crosses a lovely grassy meadow with an excellent view into the Hopper, an enormous cirque walled in by Mount Prospect, Mount Greylock and Stony Ledge. The Haley Farm Trail and then the Stony Ledge Trail lead to the top of Stony Ledge, where there's an expansive vista eastward over the Hopper to the rounded dome of Mount Greylock. Sperry Road leads along the ridge through the primitive campsites of Sperry Road Campground. The Hopper Trail joins the road, eventually leaving it to begin the ascent of Mount Greylock proper. Amid the woods of yellow birch, balsam fir and mountain ash, you'll climb higher until you meet the Appalachian Trail, which coincides with the Hopper Trail from here to the summit.

When you arrive at a small pond with an old pumphouse in view, you'll know you don't have far to go. With auto roads from North Adams to the north and Lanesborough to the south converging near the top, Greylock can be a busy place on a nice day, and rightly so. You'll break out of the woods for good at a stone patio; just beyond, there's a

bronze profile of Mount Greylock to enjoy before heading for the tower to claim your summit. Topped with a powerful beacon, the Massachusetts Veterans War Memorial was erected in 1932. Circle around the tower to enjoy the architecture, then duck inside the chamber and climb the 89-step spiral staircase to the viewing platform for an incredible four-state panoramic view that takes in Massachusetts, New York, Vermont and Connecticut. Back on the ground, check out the schist outcroppings beyond the tower, which offer another view northward, complete with a profile map of what you're looking at.

After carousing on top, head over to Bascom Lodge, a rustic arts-and-crafts-style structure built by the Civilian Conservation Corps in 1938. The lodge has a small gift shop and offers meals and accommodation to visitors. When you're ready to move on, follow the Hopper Trail down to Sperry Road Campground, then veer right into the woods for a fairly steady descent back to the valley.

TURN-BY-TURN DIRECTIONS

1. From the trailhead kiosk, follow the old farm road east.
2. At 0.3 miles, turn right on the Haley Farm Trail.
3. At 2.1 miles, turn left on the Stony Ledge Trail.
4. At 2.2 miles, reach a clearing atop Stony Ledge (2,560 feet); beyond, follow Sperry Road.
5. At 3.1 miles, the Hopper Trail enters from the left; continue ahead on Sperry Road.
6. At 3.4 miles, just beyond the Sperry Road Campground fee station, turn left on the Hopper Trail to enter the woods.
7. At 4.1 miles, the Overlook Trail leaves to the left; turn sharply right to stay on the Hopper Trail.
8. At 4.3 miles, where the Cheshire Harbor Trail heads right, bear left to stay on the Hopper Trail; just ahead, the Appalachian Trail joins up with the Hopper Trail.
9. At 4.4 miles, just after passing around a small pond, cross Notch Road.
10. At 4.8 miles, follow a paved drive between a communications tower and a maintenance building (toilets), crossing Summit Road just ahead.
11. At 4.9 miles, cross Summit Road again, then take the paved path to the tower on the summit of Mount Greylock.
12. At 5.2 miles, reach Bascom Lodge. From the lodge, cross Summit Road to the Hopper Trail (AT), then turn left to descend.
13. At 7.1 miles, at Campsite 1, the Hopper Trail leaves Sperry Road to the right; turn here to complete the descent via the Hopper Trail.

FIND THE TRAILHEAD

From the junction of US Route 7 and MA Route 43 in South Williamstown, turn north on MA Route 43 (Green River Road) and drive 2.3 miles to Mount Hope Park. Alternatively, from the junction of US Route 2 and MA Route 43 in Williamstown, drive south on MA Route 43 for 2.4 miles to Mount Hope Park. Either way, from the entrance of Mount Hope Park, follow Hopper Road, cross the bridge over Green River and continue onward. In another 1.3 miles, where Potter Road diverges right, stay left on Hopper Road, now gravel-surfaced. Hopper Road Trailhead is 0.8 miles ahead, on the right at the end of the road.

BRIGHT IDEAS BREWING

Bright Ideas Brewing checks all the boxes for beer types—from light beer and red ale to NEIPAs and fruited sours—thanks to its talented head brewer, Danny Sump. Owner Orion Howard, an oncologist by day and beer guru by night, opened the brewery in 2016 on the campus of the Massachusetts Museum of Contemporary Art in the former Sprague

Electric complex in historic downtown North Adams. Ever since, they've been going gangbusters, pouring "accessible, affable, quaffable brews that inspire conversation, creativity, and community" among the thirsty, happy throngs of locals and visitors from near and far. Order up a brew, grab a tasty bite from AOK BBQ or the Chingon Taco food truck and join the eclectic mix in the taproom or outside in the courtyard. "Get Right. Drink Bright."

LAND MANAGER

Mount Greylock State Reservation
Visitors Center/Park Headquarters
30 Rockwell Road
Lanesborough, MA 01237
(413) 499-4262
Info and trail map: www.mass.gov/locations/mount-greylock-state-reservation

BREWERY

Bright Ideas Brewing
111 MASS MoCA Way
North Adams, MA 01247
(413) 346-4460
www.brightideasbrewing.com
Distance from trailhead: 9.6 miles

MOUNT RACE

HIKE TO MOUNTAINSIDE WATERFALLS AND MOUNTAINTOP VISTAS

SHEFFIELD, MA

▷⋯ STARTING POINT

MA ROUTE 41

⋯✕ DESTINATION

**MOUNT RACE
SUMMIT LEDGES**

🍺 BEER

413 FARMHOUSE ALE

🎫 HIKE TYPE

STRENUOUS

🐾 DOG FRIENDLY

YES (LEASH REQUIRED)

📅 SEASON

MAY TO OCTOBER

$ FEES

NO

🕐 DURATION

4 HOURS 10 MIN.

⛰ MAP REFERENCE

**MT. WASHINGTON
STATE FOREST**

↦ LENGTH

6.4 MILES (ROUND-TRIP)

🔎 HIGHLIGHTS

WATERFALLS, MOUNTAIN VIEWS,
APPALACHIAN TRAIL

〰 ELEVATION GAIN

1,850 FEET

FARMHOUSE ALE

STRAW

BANANA
ORANGE PEEL

CHAMOMILE
ORANGE

BITTERNESS   SWEETNESS

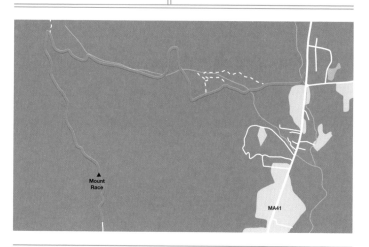

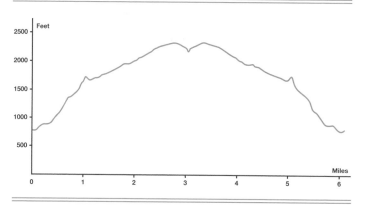

HIKE DESCRIPTION

Follow the falling waters of Race Brook and hike the Appalachian Trail to great summit and ledge vistas on Mount Race. Then go big with a farmhouse brew at Big Elm Brewing.

Mount Race is located on the border of the towns of Mount Washington and Sheffield in the southwest corner of Berkshire County. Part of the Taconic Range and rising to 2,365 feet in the Mt. Washington State Forest, the mountain's long, mostly open ridgeline rewards hikers with a sweeping 360-degree panorama across four states.

Follow the Race Brook Trail to the side trail leading to Lower Falls, then head for Upper Falls, ascending through laurel, hemlocks and mixed hardwoods. You'll cross Race Brook and pass by the Lower Falls Loop Trail on the way to rock-hopping across the base of Upper Race Brook Falls. Altogether, Race Brook Falls drops 300 feet down the mountainside over five distinct falls. Climb along the course of Race Brook to a shady grove of mature hemlocks. Cross the brook again to reach Race Brook Falls Campsite, where there's a privy, tent sites and tent platforms. The north ridge of Mount Race and the Appalachian Trail (AT) aren't far beyond the campsite.

Extending 2,192 miles from Springer Mountain in Georgia to the summit of Katahdin in Maine's Baxter State Park, the AT is perhaps the most beloved long-distance trail in the US. In high summer, you may encounter northbound AT "thru-hikers," the moniker given to those hearty souls who make the entire end-to-end trek in a single push. Follow the white blazes of the AT over the rocky north ridge of Mount Race at a moderate

grade at first, then more gradually. It's a lovely walk to the top of the mountain over bedrock outcrops and through woods of scrub oak, laurel, mountain ash, pitch pine and huckleberry. If you're visiting between mid-June and early July, the laurel thickets will be in full bloom.

Three miles into the hike, the summit of Mount Race rewards hikers with views northward to the fire tower atop the rounded dome of Mount Everett and beyond to Mount Greylock, the highest peak in Massachusetts; west to more peaks of the Taconic Range along the MA–NY border and further to the high peaks of the Catskill Mountains (some over 4,000 feet) in New York; south to Mt. Frissell, Connecticut's highest point; and east over the broad Housatonic River valley, a sublime scene of farms, woods and hills.

Continue south on the AT for less than a quarter-mile, ambling through the shrubby woods to an enormous open ledge on the eastern edge of the south ridge. This is a wonderful spot to enjoy your trail lunch and the fantastic wide-open 180-degree view to the east, north and south. The wavy bedrock you're relaxing on is called gneiss, a type of metamorphic rock. Retrace your steps over the summit to return to the trailhead.

TURN-BY-TURN DIRECTIONS

1. From the trailhead information kiosk, follow the blue-blazed Race Brook Trail into the woods.
2. At a fork at 0.25 miles, a side trail to Lower Falls heads right; bear left to stay on the Race Brook Trail.
3. At 1.0 miles, cross Race Brook below Upper Race Brook Falls.
4. At 1.8 miles, reach Race Brook Falls Campsite.
5. At 2.1 miles, turn left (south) on the white-blazed Appalachian Trail.
6. At 3 miles, arrive at the unsigned summit of Mount Race.
7. At 3.2 miles, reach huge open ledges on the south ridge of Mount Race.
8. From the ledges, retrace your steps up and over the mountain.

FIND THE TRAILHEAD

From the south end of Great Barrington, at the junction of US Route 7 and MA Routes 41/23, drive south on MA Routes 41/23 for 3.9 miles to Egremont. At Mill Pond, MA Route 41 and MA Route 23 split; continue left on MA Route 41 and follow it for 5.2 miles to the trailhead parking area, a paved pullout on the right side of the road.

BIG ELM BREWING

Christine Bump and Bill Heaton each brought 20 years of brewing experience to this rural southwestern corner of Massachusetts in 2012, when they opened Big Elm Brewing "to make beer and smiles." Housed in an old warehouse space and named after a stately 400-year-old elm

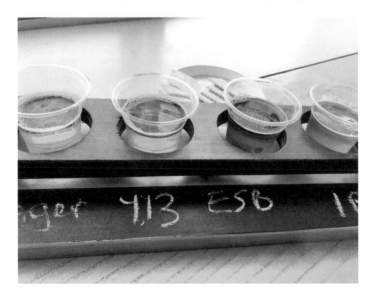

that used to stand at the end of the street, Big Elm produces a year-round lineup of six traditional beers and a handful of newer styles for a pleasing, balanced menu. In 2018, the brewery went solar, with panels on the roof for hot water and three large rotating arrays in the yard for electricity. Nestle into the cozy taproom or spread out outside—either way, it's a real family-fun and dog-friendly place to enjoy great brews and good times.

LAND MANAGER

Mount Washington State Forest
545 East Street
Mount Washington, MA 01258
(413) 528-0330
Info and trail map: www.mass.gov/locations/mount-washington-state-forest

BREWERY

Big Elm Brewing
65 Silver Street
Sheffield, MA 01257
(413) 229-2348
www.bigelmbeer.com
Distance from trailhead: 5.1 miles

MOUNT TOM

ENJOY SPECTACULAR CLIFFTOP VIEWS FROM WHITING PEAK AND GOAT PEAK

HOLYOKE, MA

▷⋯ STARTING POINT	⋯✕ DESTINATION
LAKE BRAY	**GOAT PEAK LOOKOUT**
🍺 BEER	🎫 HIKE TYPE
ORIGINAL GINGER BEER	**MODERATE**
🐾 DOG FRIENDLY	📅 SEASON
YES (LEASH REQUIRED)	**MARCH TO NOVEMBER**
$ FEES	🕐 DURATION
YES	**3 HOURS 10 MIN.**
⛰ MAP REFERENCE	↦ LENGTH
MT. TOM STATE RESERVATION	**5.4 MILES (LOOP)**
🔍 HIGHLIGHTS	〰 ELEVATION GAIN
TRAPROCK CLIFFS, LOOKOUT TOWER, VALLEY VIEWS	**1,000 FEET**

GINGER BEER

BRIGHT GOLD

FRESH GINGER

SPICY GINGER
TROPICAL FRUIT, CITRUS
HINT OF MOLASSES

BITTERNESS

SWEETNESS

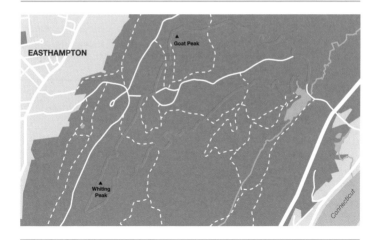

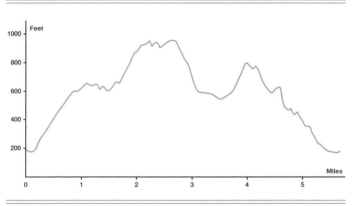

HIKE DESCRIPTION

Hike a section of the New England Trail for spectacular views from the traprock cliffs on Mount Tom's Whiting Peak and Goat Peak. Then quench your thirst with a ginger beer at New City Brewery.

The 1,967-acre Mount Tom Reservation, located in the south-central Pioneer Valley just west of the Connecticut River, encompasses the peaks of the Mount Tom Range from Mount Tom, Whiting Peak and Goat Peak to Dry Knoll and Mount Nonotuck. The range, part of the Metacomet Ridge that extends 100 miles from Long Island Sound into southern New Hampshire, is a steep, narrow ridgeline of volcanic basalt or traprock as well as sedimentary rock that has faulted and tilted over the eons.

This loop hike follows six different color-coded trails and features dramatic vistas from numerous lookouts atop the 1,000-foot cliffs on the west side of Whiting Peak and Goat Peak. From Lake Bray, an artificial lake created by the damming of Bray Brook, follow the Accessible Trail to the Kay Bee Trail, where the ascent begins in earnest. A series of switchbacks will lead you gradually over the western slopes of Whiting Peak, which is cloaked in a mix of hardwoods and softwoods, some quite large in diameter.

On the Keystone Extension, climb around several rocky knobs to meet the D.O.C. Trail, which weaves through low, rocky outcrops, then contours around the west side of Whiting Peak to the ridge crest, where it

joins the New England Trail. The white-blazed New England Trail, established in 2009, is comprised of the historic Mattabesett, Metacomet and Monadnock trail systems. The NET extends 215 miles from Long Island Sound north through Connecticut and Massachusetts and into southern New Hampshire.

Sharp, broken rocks and a series of open ledges mark the NET route along the western edge of Whiting Peak, revealing vistas over the town of Easthampton (in one of those old mill buildings in view is New City Brewery) and north to Northampton along the Connecticut River. You'll scamper down a chimney to reach another ledge with a view before arriving at a wildflower garden area in a meadow. Ahead at a lookout with two benches, a short side trail leads to Goat Peak Tower. Built in 1928, the tower offers a fine view of the Holyoke Range, Mount Tom, the Connecticut River and the University of Massachusetts campus. Continue on to the T. Bagg Trail, which winds back down the mountain to Lake Bray.

TURN-BY-TURN DIRECTIONS

1. From the trailhead kiosk, walk the Accessible Trail along the north end of Lake Bray.
2. At 0.2 miles, turn right on the blue-blazed Kay Bee Trail.
3. At 0.6 miles, at the intersection with the Link Trail, continue straight on the Kay Bee Trail.
4. At 0.9 miles, at an offset junction with the Keystone Trail, bear right and then immediately left on the Keystone Extension (orange blazes).
5. At 1.5 miles, at the intersection with the Quarry Trail (yellow blazes), proceed straight on the D.O.C. Trail (red blazes).
6. At 2.3 miles, reach the ridge crest below Whiting Peak. Turn right to follow the New England Trail (also signed as the Metacomet-Monadnock Trail).
7. At 2.6 miles, reach a round outcrop and lookout below Whiting Peak.
8. At 3 miles, proceed through the intersection with the Quarry Trail, remaining on the white-blazed NET/MMT.
9. At 3.3 miles, turn right along paved Reservation Road, then left into the woods again.
10. At 3.6 miles, where the Dynamite Trail continues straight, turn right to stay on the NET/MMT.
11. At 3.7 miles, reach a lookout and two benches. To climb Goat Peak, walk between the benches to a kiosk in the dip beyond, then climb steeply up the steps to the Goat Peak Tower. Return to the main trail to continue on the NET/MMT.
12. At 4.2 miles, soon after crossing the old tower road, the Beau Bridges Trail departs to the right; stay straight on the NET/MMT. In another 100 feet, where the NET/MMT leaves to the left, turn right to descend via the T. Bagg Trail (red blazes).
13. At 5.1 miles, turn left on Reservation Road.
14. At 5.3 miles, just before Lake Bray, turn right (restrooms just ahead on the left) to finish the hike.

FIND THE TRAILHEAD

From the junction of I-91, Exit 23 (old Exit 18) and US Route 5 in Holyoke, drive south on US Route 5 for 3.4 miles. Turn right (west) on Reservation Road (sign for Mount Tom State Reservation), go under the I-91 overpass, pass the gatehouse and then Lake Bray. Just beyond, turn left, pass restrooms on the left and reach the Mount Tom trailhead parking lot, where there is an information kiosk, picnic tables and a bench.

NEW CITY BREWERY

Opened in 2015, New City Brewery occupies the old boiler room of a long-abandoned and now beautifully redeveloped mill complex in the historic New City neighborhood of Easthampton. Look for the towering 200-foot brick smokestack of the former home of the National Felt Company (circa 1890s) and you'll have discovered this unique brewery. New City features Original Ginger Beer among its creative tap list of ales, alongside IPAs, lagers, a mule and even fresh-squeezed mimosas. This pre-Prohibition, Jamaican-style ginger beer is made according to the recipe of owner and brewmaster Sam Dibble, who loves to put his own spin on traditional brewing styles. Enjoy a refreshing pour, and perhaps a bite of locally sourced deliciousness from New City's kitchen, in the patio beer garden out front where there's a fine view across bucolic Lower Mill Park to the rolling ridgeline of Mount Tom.

LAND MANAGER

Mount Tom State Reservation
125 Reservation Road
Holyoke, MA 01040
(413) 534-1186
Info and trail map: www.mass.gov/locations/mount-tom-state-reservation

BREWERY

New City Brewery
180 Pleasant Street (rear of old mill building)
Easthampton, MA 01027
(413) 529-2000
www.newcitybrewery.com
Distance from trailhead: 4.9 miles

MOUNT WATATIC

REVEL IN A SWEEPING THREE-STATE PANORAMA FROM HUGE OPEN LEDGES

ASHBURNHAM

▷⋯ STARTING POINT	⋯✕ DESTINATION
MA ROUTE 119	**MOUNT WATATIC SUMMIT**
🍺 BEER	HIKE TYPE
NECTAR OF ARISTAEUS: PEACH COBBLER IPA MILKSHAKE	**MODERATE**
🐾 DOG FRIENDLY	SEASON
YES (LEASH REQUIRED)	**MARCH TO NOVEMBER**
$ FEES	⏲ DURATION
NO	**2 HOURS 15 MIN.**
⛰ MAP REFERENCE	↦ LENGTH
MOUNT WATATIC & NUTTING HILL	**3.8 MILES (LOOP)**
🔎 HIGHLIGHTS	〰 ELEVATION GAIN
STATE LINE, WIDE OPEN LEDGES, HUGE 3-STATE VIEW	**700 FEET**

IPA MILKSHAKE

GOLDEN ORANGE

PEACH
FLORAL

PEACH
VANILLA

BITTERNESS

SWEETNESS

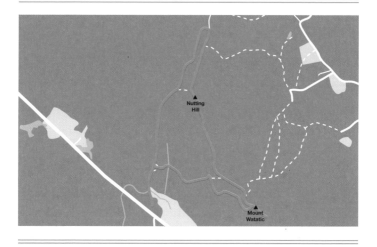

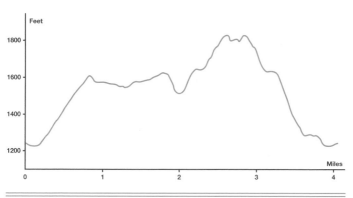

HIKE DESCRIPTION

Hike to the Massachusetts–New Hampshire state line, then climb up to the huge open ledges atop Mount Watatic for a three-state, 360-degree panorama. Post-hike, head for the underworld of beers at River Styx Brewing.

At 1,832 feet, Mount Watatic is the second-highest peak east of the Berkshire Hills in Massachusetts. The mountain's bald summit ledges offer sweeping views stretching from east to west across almost the entire length of Massachusetts––from the Boston skyline to Mount Greylock and north into New Hampshire. In 2002, the Mount Grace Land Conservation Trust purchased 281 acres on Mount Watatic after a proposal to erect a communications tower on the peak met with fierce opposition. Ashburnham State Forest, Watatic Mountain Wildlife Sanctuary and Ashby Wildlife Management Area serve as buffers around the Mount Watatic Reservation.

Mount Watatic marks the southern end of the Wapack Range, a series of peaks and ledges extending north to Pack Monadnock Mountain—a 20-mile distance covered by the Wapack Trail. The Midstate Trail also winds across Watatic near the end of its 92-mile route from the Rhode Island border. Our loop hike follows portions of both trails.

Soon after the start, the coinciding Midstate and Wapack trails give way to the State Line Trail, which ascends in a northeasterly direction through woods of oak, beech and maple to a stone wall and monument marking

the MA–NH state line. Once you pass the 1834 border monument, you're back on the combined Wapack/Midstate trails. A large cairn on the exposed bedrock marks the top of Nutting Hill, and just beyond there's a view of the north slope of Watatic. Ledges, hemlock woods and more old stone walls distinguish the next section of trail, which leads up to the concrete stanchions of the former fire tower (removed in 1984) and then over the final ledges to the summit of Mount Watatic. A large stone monument honors the citizens of Ashburnham and Ashby and the Commonwealth of Massachusetts for their efforts in protecting this special place.

Push on into the obvious dip, then scamper out to the huge open ledges beyond. The vista is magnificent, ranging southeast to the Boston skyline, south to Wachusett Mountain, north to Pack Monadnock, far beyond to the high peaks of the White Mountains, and even to Killington Peak in Vermont's Green Mountains. This is a popular spot for watching hawks soaring on thermals, so keep an eye out for these raptors while you relax and revel in the big view. The descent via the Wapack/Midstate trail is mostly moderate, but there are several steep, rocky sections as you hike through the shady hemlock forest. You'll pass through a cool split boulder before returning to the highway.

TURN-BY-TURN DIRECTIONS

1. Beginning at the brown gate, follow yellow triangle markers on the Wapack/Midstate trails.
2. At 0.3 miles, the Wapack/Midstate trails lead off to the right; continue straight ahead on the State Line Trail (blue triangle markers).
3. At a junction at 0.8 miles, bear left to stay on the State Line Trail.

4. At 1.2 miles, reach the NH–MA state line monument and the northern terminus of the Midstate Trail. Turn sharply right here on the Midstate Trail to quickly reach the "Border 1834" monument and then a T-junction. Turn right and continue on the Wapack/Midstate trails.
5. At 1.7 miles, reach the open ledges atop Nutting Hill.
6. At 2.4 miles, join the Emergency Access Road and follow it for 75 feet, then leave the road and take the path on the right.
7. At 2.5 miles, pass the concrete stanchions of the former fire tower to reach the summit of Mount Watatic. Continue into the dip ahead, then head out to the huge open ledges.
8. Return to the summit and turn left on the Wapack/Midstate trails to descend the mountain.
9. At 3.5 miles, at the base of the descent, reach the junction with the State Line Trail; turn left to continue on the Wapack/Midstate trails to return to the trailhead.

FIND THE TRAILHEAD

From the junction of US Route 2, Exit 90 (old Exit 24) and MA Route 140 in Westminster, drive north on MA Route 140. In 2.8 miles, turn right (north) on MA Route 101 and follow it for 4.3 miles to the village of Ashburnham. Turn right on MA Routes 101/12, and in just 0.1 miles, turn left (north) on MA Route 101. In 4.0 miles, turn left (west) on MA Route 119 and drive 1.4 miles to the trailhead parking area on the right. If the small parking lot is full, there's additional parking across MA Route 119 along Old Pierce Road.

RIVER STYX BREWING

When longtime homebrewers Jackie and Scott Cullen opened River Styx Brewing in 2017 in the old General Electric manufacturing plant in downtown Fitchburg, they brought a host of gods and goddesses from Greek mythology along and named their beers after them. The brewery's logo features Charon, the hooded ferryman of Hades who carried souls across the River Styx from the world of the living to the world of the dead. Inspired by Scott's favorite sweet treats, the Nectar of Aristaeus series of milkshake IPAs is made by adding lactose to peach, blueberry and even rainbow sherbet for a deliciously cool, creamy treat on a warm summer day. Enjoy a pour from the extensive menu of great brews in the dark-walled taproom lined with murals of mythological characters and illuminated by 100 lanterns, or outside on the sunny, sprawling patio.

LAND MANAGER

Mount Grace Land Conservation Trust
1461 Old Keene Road
Athol, MA 01331
(978) 248-2043
Info: www.mountgrace.org/visit/conserved/mount-watatic
Trail map: www.mountgrace.org/about/publications/conservation,
"Twenty Years, Twenty Hikes"

BREWERY

River Styx Brewing
166 Boulder Drive, Suite 112
Fitchburg, MA 01420
(978) 696-5176
riverstyxbrewing.com
Distance from trailhead: 14 miles

MYLES STANDISH FOREST

EXPLORE THE WORLD'S THIRD-LARGEST PINE BARRENS ECOSYSTEM

SOUTH CARVER, MA

▷··· STARTING POINT	···✕ DESTINATION
FOREST HEADQUARTERS, CRANBERRY ROAD	EAST HEAD LOOP AND BENTLEY LOOP
🍺 BEER	🔳 HIKE TYPE
PORTER	MODERATE
🐾 DOG FRIENDLY	📅 SEASON
YES (LEASH REQUIRED)	YEAR-ROUND
$ FEES	🕐 DURATION
NO	3 HOURS 45 MIN.
🗺 MAP REFERENCE	↦ LENGTH
MYLES STANDISH STATE FOREST	7.2 MILES (LOOP)
🔎 HIGHLIGHTS	〰 ELEVATION GAIN
PINE BARRENS, TWO RESERVOIRS, KETTLE HOLES	240 FEET

 PORTER

 DARK BROWN
RUBY

 COFFEE
CHOCOLATE
CARAMEL

 ROASTED COFFEE
BITTERSWEET CHOCOLATE
SMOKY

BITTERNESS SWEETNESS

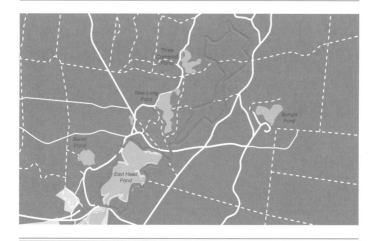

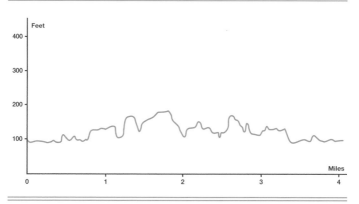

HIKE DESCRIPTION

Explore the world's third-largest pine barrens ecosystem on a circuit hike through one of the most extensive public open spaces in Massachusetts. Then make like a Pilgrim and set sail for Plymouth and a cold beer at Mayflower Brewing.

Shaped by powerful glaciers, changing climate, natural fires and human activity over the eons, the sprawling landscape of Myles Standish State Forest features the third-largest pine barrens ecosystem in the world. Established in 1916, the 12,400-acre state forest is one of the largest properties in the Massachusetts reservation system. The East Head Loop and Bentley Loop provide hikers with a wonderful tour of the terrain and its dry, sandy woods of pitch pine and scrub oak with understories of blueberries, huckleberries and crowberries.

Before you leave Forest Headquarters, grab a copy of the East Head Reservoir Nature Trail Guide for the hike around East Head Reservoir, where 14 trailside posts describe the fascinating natural history of the forest. The first 1.5 miles of the hike take you along the eastern shore of the reservoir, with numerous side paths leading to viewpoints at the water's edge. Trail markers with blue diamonds and black acorns guide the way. Southeastern Massachusetts is home to one of the largest commercial cranberry-growing industries in the world, and in 1868, this 86-acre reservoir was created not for drinking water but to irrigate the nearby cranberry bogs.

On the Bentley Loop, make sure to follow the blue trail markers, as many game trails cross the main path, which also turns on and off quite a few old dirt and grass fireroads. Landmarks en route include the

Bentley Loop trailhead parking area on the east side and Round Pond on the west. Along the loop there are numerous examples of frost pockets: grassy, shrubby depressions that accumulate cooler air. These were created when enormous ice chunks left behind by the retreating glaciers of the last ice age settled in place some 10,000 years ago before finally melting away. Kettle holes (like Round Pond) were also formed in this manner. The white pine plantations you'll see are remnants of Depression-era plantings by the Civilian Conservation Corps, which worked on forest improvement and built recreation infrastructure at Myles Standish and across the U.S. from 1933 through the 1940s.

The woods of pitch pine and scrub oak around you have evolved to thrive in this region dry, sandy, nutrient-poor soils prone to forest fires. The oaks produce an important supply of acorns for forest wildlife and their roots can survive fires and quickly regenerate, while the serotinous cones of the pitch pines will only open and drop seeds after being heated by fire. Round Pond, a classic kettle hole filled with groundwater but with no inlet or outlet, is a lovely spot worth enjoying for a spell before carrying on.

Six miles into the walk, close the Bentley Loop and return to the East Head Loop. Follow it around the west side of East Head Reservoir back to Forest Headquarters. And oh yeah—Myles Standish. Standish was an English military officer who accompanied the Pilgrims on the Mayflower voyage in 1620 and served as commander of Plymouth Colony.

TURN-BY-TURN DIRECTIONS

1. From the information kiosk at the trailhead parking area, walk to the black gate and proceed on Fearing Pond Road; cross the East Head Pond outlet dam and then bear left into the woods on the Reservoir Trail.
2. At 1.4 miles, in a cleared gas-line corridor, turn right on a connector trail to reach the Bentley Loop.
3. At 1.7 miles, after crossing Halfway Pond Road, join the Bentley Loop. Turn right to follow it in a counterclockwise direction.
4. At 3.1 miles, reach the Bentley Loop trailhead parking area.
5. At 4.4 miles, a spur trail on the right leads to Round Pond.
6. At 5.7 miles, complete the Bentley Loop. Turn right on a connector trail to return to the East Head Loop.
7. At 6.0 miles, turn right on the East Head Loop and proceed along the gas-line corridor.
8. At 6.5 miles, cross paved Lower College Pond Road, and at 6.6 miles, re-cross the road.
9. At 7.1 miles, with Forest Headquarters in view to the right, leave the East Head Loop and follow the paved path back to the trailhead parking area.

FIND THE TRAILHEAD

From the junction of I-495, Exit 2 and MA Route 58 in Wareham, drive north on MA Route 58 for 2.5 miles. In South Carver, where MA Route 58 bears left, continue straight ahead on Tremont Street. In 0.8 miles, turn right on Cranberry Road and proceed 2.8 miles to Myles Standish State Forest. Forest Headquarters is on the left, where you will find trailhead parking, an interpretive center and restrooms.

MAYFLOWER BREWING COMPANY

When the Mayflower dropped anchor at Plymouth, Massachusetts on December 20, 1620, the Pilgrims were cold and tired from their long voyage and desperately low on food and beer. There's no shortage of beer in the former colony today, though, thanks to Mayflower Brewing, "America's Hometown Brewery," which opened in 2007. Incredibly, founder Drew Brosseau is a tenth great-grandson of John Alden, the beer barrel cooper on the Mayflower. Pull up a chair in the taproom or beer garden and "taste the history" with a good pour from one of Mayflower's 14 taps (plus two nitros and the occasional cask). The smooth-drinking English-style Porter is a favorite among the core brews available year-round, and with the limited-edition Cooper's Series plus several seasonal specialties, Mayflower's beer lineup offers a plentiful variety to enjoy no matter when you visit.

LAND MANAGER

Myles Standish State Forest
194 Cranberry Road
South Carver, MA 02366
(508) 866-2526
Info and trail map: www.mass.gov/locations/myles-standish-state-forest

BREWERY

Mayflower Brewing Company
12 Resnik Road
Plymouth, MA 02360
(508) 746-2674
www.mayflowerbrewing.com
Distance from trailhead: 14 miles

PLUM ISLAND

GO BOARDWALKING THROUGH A DIVERSE COASTAL ECOSYSTEM

NEWBURYPORT, MA

▷⋯ STARTING POINT	⋯✗ DESTINATION
HELLCAT WILDLIFE OBSERVATION AREA	**MARSH OVERLOOK, DUNES OVERLOOK**
🍺 BEER	🎛 HIKE TYPE
NEWBURYPORT PALE ALE	**EASY**
🐾 DOG FRIENDLY	📅 SEASON
NO	**YEAR-ROUND**
$ FEES	🕐 DURATION
YES	**1 HOUR**
⛰ MAP REFERENCE	↦ LENGTH
HELLCAT BOARDWALK TRAIL (POSTED AT TRAILHEAD)	**1.5 MILES (LOOP)**
🔍 HIGHLIGHTS	〜 ELEVATION GAIN
SALT MARSHES, SAND DUNES, BIRD AND ANIMAL LIFE	**15 FEET**

 PALE ALE

 AMBER

 CITRUSY

 CITRUSY
WELL-BALANCED

BITTERNESS

SWEETNESS

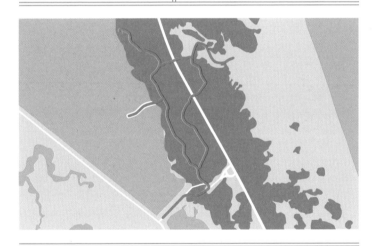

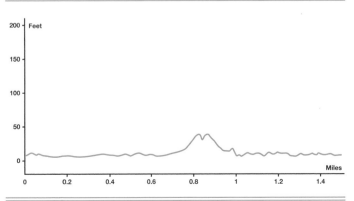

HIKE DESCRIPTION

Hellcat Boardwalk Trail winds through a diverse coastal ecosystem of upland and wetland habitats. Post-hike, head into historic downtown Newburyport for pale ale, pizza and lively music at Newburyport Brewing.

The Parker River National Wildlife Refuge occupies much of the southern three-quarters of Plum Island, an 8-mile barrier island that separates the Atlantic Ocean from Plum Island Sound and serves as a natural buffer against fierce storms headed for the mainland beyond. The 4,662-acre refuge was established in 1942 as an important resting, feeding and nesting ground for migratory birds on the Atlantic Flyway.

The Hellcat Boardwalk Trail weaves through a pretty cross-section of the refuge's upland and wetland habitat—from freshwater marshes and shrubs to dunes, vernal pools and maritime woods. The trail, the most popular feature in the refuge, is used by some 150,000 visitors annually. The original wooden boardwalk, built in the 1970s, was redesigned and replaced with plastic decking in 2020 and is now universally accessible.

Take a photo of the posted trail map, then begin the Boardwalk Trail Loop. At a fork in 250 feet, bear left to walk the loop clockwise. Wander ahead to the Wetland Spur, which leads west to an observation platform overlooking a freshwater marsh of tall grasses and cattails. Next up is the Marsh Spur; follow this out to an observation platform at Marsh Overlook. The marsh was artificially created to provide a habitat for waterfowl and other birds and wildlife. Beyond the marsh is the North Pool Dike and then Plum Island Sound.

Back on the Boardwalk Trail Loop, you'll soon cross Refuge Road to get to the Dunes Spur; take this and head for Ocean Overlook. Note the plaque here dedicated to Ludlow Griscom, an early supporter of the refuge. The boardwalk rises gently through a woodland of black oak and black pine, which help stabilize the shifting sands of the wind-blown dunes. At Ocean Overlook, an expansive view extends east over the dunes to the cold waters of the Atlantic Ocean.

Continuing on the Boardwalk Trail Loop, you'll recross Refuge Road. Saunter slowly along this final leg to soak in the beauty of the woods and swamp around you and consider the importance of this place to a host of wild critters. Back at the trailhead, continue through the lot to the path across the grassy dike, passing Bill Forward Pool on your left and North Pool on the right. At the junction of North Pool Dike and South Pool Dike, climb the observation tower for a 360-degree panorama over the refuge and much of your walk.

TURN-BY-TURN DIRECTIONS

1. From the posted map at the parking area, begin the Boardwalk Trail Loop. In 250 feet, bear left where the boardwalk splits.
2. At 0.2 miles, take the Wetland Spur on the left to visit an observation platform on the edge of a freshwater marsh.
3. At 0.4 miles, where the Boardwalk Loop Trail bears right, continue straight ahead on the Marsh Spur, which leads to Marsh Overlook in 0.1 miles.
4. At 0.7 miles, cross Refuge Road to reach the junction with the Dunes Spur. Turn left to explore the boardwalk to Ocean Overlook, which is reached at 0.8 miles.
5. At 1.0 miles, cross Refuge Road.
6. At 1.3 miles, reach the trailhead parking area. Continue through the lot to the wide gravel path, which crosses a grassy causeway to reach an observation tower.
7. Return to the parking area to complete the hike.

FIND THE TRAILHEAD

From the junction of US Route 1 and Merrimac Street in downtown Newburyport, drive east on Merrimac Street for 0.3 miles, then bear left on Water Street. In another 1.5 miles, enter Parker River National Wildlife Refuge and reach the refuge visitor center and Joppa Flats Education Center on the left. Continue ahead on the same road, which is now Plum Island Turnpike. Pass the Plum Island Airport, cross the bridge over Plum Island River, and at 1.9 miles from the visitor center turn right on Sunset Drive. In 0.6 miles, reach the refuge entrance station (the refuge information center and restrooms are on the left). Continue along Refuge Road for another 3.5 miles to the Hellcat Wildlife Observation Area trailhead parking area on the right.

NEWBURYPORT BREWING CO.

Newburyport Brewing is "a no-frills place where music pours out like beer, and beer pours out one cold, fresh pint at a time." Chris Webb and Bill Fisher, longtime friends and musicians in a seven-piece funk band, left their corporate jobs behind to pursue their passion for beer and music, opening Newburyport's first brewery in 2013. Located on a dead-end street in an industrial park, this self-described "dive bar" is a down-to-earth, unpretentious place. Sit at a community table and enjoy a great pint from the diverse selection of approachable ales and lagers, a hot slice from Anchor Stone Deck Pizza and awesome live music five nights a week. Raise your glass of Newburyport Pale Ale or Green Head Lager—the two most popular brews—and exclaim "Yeat!" (a Newburyport colloquialism) just like a local.

LAND MANAGER

Parker River National Wildlife Refuge
6 Plum Island Turnpike
Newburyport, MA 01950
(978) 465-5753
Info: fws.gov/refuge/parker_river/

BREWERY

Newburyport Brewing Co.
4 New Pasture Road
Newburyport, MA 01950
(978) 463-8700
www.nbptbrewing.com
Distance from trailhead: 8.8 miles

WALDEN POND

WALK IN THE FOOTSTEPS OF HENRY DAVID THOREAU

CONCORD, MA

▷⋯ **STARTING POINT**	⋯✘ **DESTINATION**
WALDEN POND VISITOR CENTER	**WALDEN POND, EMERSON'S CLIFF**
🍺 **BEER**	**HIKE TYPE**
RUCKUS! IPA	**EASY**
🐾 **DOG FRIENDLY**	**SEASON**
NO	**YEAR-ROUND**
$ **FEES**	⏱ **DURATION**
YES	**1 HOUR 30 MIN.**
⌂ **MAP REFERENCE**	↦ **LENGTH**
WALDEN POND STATE RESERVATION	**2.7 MILES (LOOP)**
👁 **HIGHLIGHTS**	～ **ELEVATION GAIN**
KETTLE HOLE POND, LITERARY HISTORY, SWIMMING	**160 FEET**

AMERICAN IPA

OPAQUE GOLD-ORANGE

CITRUS
FLORAL

FLORAL
BITTER
CITRUS

BITTERNESS

SWEETNESS

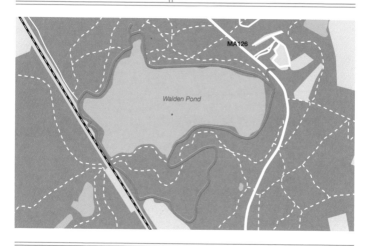

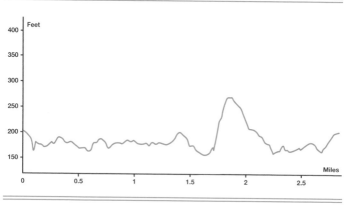

HIKE DESCRIPTION

Take a contemplative walk in the woods around idyllic Walden Pond, following in the footsteps of renowned author, naturalist and philosopher Henry David Thoreau; then head west to True West Brewery to ponder some refreshing brews and good eats.

Walden Pond in Concord is renowned as the former home of Henry David Thoreau, who lived in a small cabin on its north shore in the mid-1800s, taking daily walks and dutifully recording his observations in a journal. Drawing on the inspiration provided by this simple life of independence and self-reflection, Thoreau later wrote *Walden*, an enduring classic in the nature-writing genre that is credited with sparking the modern environmental movement.

In 1922, the Emerson, Forbes and Heywood families deeded 80 acres around Walden Pond to the Commonwealth of Massachusetts for use as a public space. In 1965, the National Park Service designated Walden Pond a National Historic Landmark, and in 1975, Walden Pond became part of the state's reservation system, which placed 462 acres of mostly pitch pine, oak and hickory woods around the famous pond under protection.

Amble over to Main Beach for a look west over the length of Walden Pond. The 62-acre kettle hole pond, formed by the action of retreating glaciers more than 10,000 years ago, is 103 feet deep, making it the deepest natural body of water in Massachusetts. It is popular with

hikers, but you're also likely to see boaters, paddlers, anglers, swimmers and stand-up paddleboarders enjoying the beauty of this special place. Pond Path, which forms the core of our hike, circumnavigates Walden Pond. You'll walk the circuit counterclockwise, passing Red Cross Beach on the way to Wyman Meadow. Access points to the pond are numerous, so take advantage at will.

The Thoreau House Site is located in the woods a short distance from Thoreau's Cove. It was here that 27-year-old Henry David Thoreau lived for two years, two months and two days—from July 1845 to September 1847—on a small plot of land owned by his good friend, the essayist and transcendentalist Ralph Waldo Emerson. Thoreau built a simple, sturdy one-room cabin himself with materials and furnishings that cost 28 dollars and 12½ cents. A replica of Thoreau's cabin sits across from the visitor center and is a must-visit after the hike.

The Bay Circuit Trail joins Pond Path in the course of its 230-mile greenway arc around Greater Boston. Pond Path remains close to the shore, passing Ice Fort Cove on a stretch bordered by the tracks of the Massachusetts Bay Transportation Authority's Fitchburg Line. At Long Cove you'll leave Walden Pond on Fire Road South, which morphs into Heywood's Meadow Path along the wetland of the same name. Partway around the pretty meadow, the Emerson's Cliff Trail climbs through tall white pines. The rocky ridge of Emerson's Cliff may once have offered views, but no more, so carry on over the north side to the Esker Trail. The Esker Trail and a short connector bring you back to Pond Path at Little Cove.

Saunter along, as carefree as Thoreau might have been, enjoying the last half-mile back to Main Beach. Restrooms are available in the bathhouses, and a swim might well be in order if it's a warm and sunny day. Be sure to check out the visitor center and gift shop—and the Thoreau cabin replica, of course.

TURN-BY-TURN DIRECTIONS

1. Begin at the information kiosk adjacent to Walden Pond Visitor Center. Walk across MA Route 126 and down to Main Beach on Walden Pond. Turn right on the Pond Path.
2. At 0.6 miles, opposite Thoreau's Cove on Walden Pond, a path on the right leads to the Thoreau House Site.
3. At 1.3 miles, at Long Cove, leave the Pond Path and continue straight on Fire Road South.
4. At 1.4 miles, the trail takes a sharp left and continues as Heywood's Meadow Path.
5. At 1.6 miles, turn left to ascend the Emerson's Cliff Trail.
6. At 1.9 miles, turn left to follow the Esker Trail, a wide track.
7. At 2.0 miles, at a fork, stay right on the Esker Trail, and 0.1 miles later, turn right on a short connector path leading to Walden Pond. Turn right to follow the Pond Path back to Main Beach and the end of the hike.

FIND THE TRAILHEAD

From I-95, Exit 45 (old Exit 29) in Lexington, take US Route 2 West toward Fitchburg. In 4.4 miles, turn left on MA Route 126 (Walden Street). Drive 0.4 miles, then turn left into the main entrance of Walden Pond State Reservation and proceed to any of the six parking lots.

TRUE WEST BREWERY

Opened in 2016 by brothers Pete and Matt Henry, True West Brewery is an authentic community meeting place in the heart of the West Acton Village Historic District, a vibrant, walkable old New England–style town center of galleries, shops, restaurants and churches. More than just a brewery or a restaurant, True West is a crucible of family-oriented, passionate and skilled craftspeople focused on fresh farm-to-table foods and great craft beer. The taproom features community tables made of large slabs of spalted maple, and the beautiful bell-shaped bar is specially designed to foster friendly banter among patrons. Belly up to the bar for a pour of the best-selling Ruckus!, a big, Citra-based American IPA. Pair your brew with a Beef-on-Weck: mouthwatering prime rib on a special Kimmelweck roll with au jus and horseradish sauce.

LAND MANAGER

Walden Pond State Reservation
915 Walden Street (MA Route 126)
Concord, MA 01742
(978) 369-3254
Info and trail map: www.mass.gov/locations/walden-pond-state-reservation

BREWERY/RESTAURANT

True West Brewery
525 Massachusetts Avenue
Acton, MA 01720
(978) 206-1600
www.brewtruewest.com
Distance from trailhead: 7.6 miles

WESTFIELD RIVER

JOURNEY ALONG A WILD AND SCENIC RIVER

CHESTERFIELD, MA

▷⋯ STARTING POINT	⋯✗ DESTINATION
CHESTERFIELD GORGE	**BAKER MILL DAM SITE**
🍺 BEER	▦ HIKE TYPE
GREYHOUND IPA	**MODERATE** 🚶
🐾 DOG FRIENDLY	📅 SEASON
YES (LEASH REQUIRED)	**YEAR-ROUND**
$ FEES	🕐 DURATION
YES	**3.5 HOURS**
⌂ MAP REFERENCE	↦ LENGTH
CHESTERFIELD GORGE, EAST BRANCH TRAIL BROCHURE	**6.6 MILES (ROUND-TRIP)**
🔍 HIGHLIGHTS	〰 ELEVATION GAIN
DEEP GORGE, SCENIC RIVER, HISTORIC SITES, SWIMMING	**220 FEET**

INDIA PALE ALE

PALE ORANGE

CITRUS
GRAPEFRUIT FORWARD

GRAPEFRUITY
CITRUS FORWARD

BITTERNESS   SWEETNESS

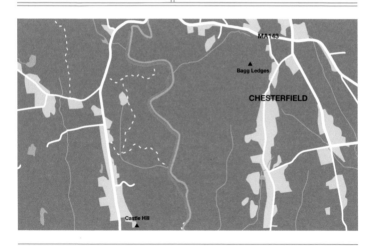

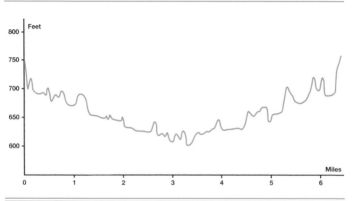

HIKE DESCRIPTION

Enjoy dramatic views of Chesterfield Gorge, then saunter along the East Branch of the Westfield River to an old dam site. Refreshing brews and delish pub grub await at Northampton Brewery afterward.

Chesterfield Gorge is a dramatic canyon on the East Branch of the Westfield River, which slices through the rural hills of Hampshire County. Over 78 miles of the river are designated as a National Wild and Scenic River—the first in Massachusetts and one of just a few in the eastern US—while 166 acres around the gorge are protected by the Massachusetts Trustees of Reservations. Beginning at Chesterfield Gorge, the East Branch Trail, a multi-use recreation route, extends south for more than 9 miles to Knightville Dam, connecting a half dozen historical sites. On this out-and-back hike, you'll explore the upper 3 miles of the East Branch Trail along the winding Westfield River.

At the safety fence above the chasm, look left to see the stone abutments of the old High Bridge, the former Albany Post Road crossing that once connected Boston with Albany, New York. Traversed by both British and American troops during the Revolutionary War, the bridge was destroyed by floodwaters in 1835. The fence line provides an excellent look at Chesterfield Gorge, its walls of gneiss, schist and quartzite towering 70 feet over the river. Ahead on the old River Road, now the route of the East Branch Trail, you'll descend easily to the level

of the river and a catch-and-release fishing area. The area is famous for its native populations of brook and brown trout, so you may see anglers casting about along this stretch of the rushing river.

Padding through a forest of ash, beech, maple, oak, hemlock and laurel, you'll enter a section of the 2,343-acre Gilbert Bliss State Forest where the river makes a wide bend to the east. The trail, marked occasionally with small, diamond-shaped blue and white "East Branch Trail" signs, passes a "Mile 1" post just before an old quarry site. Note the evidence of rock extraction on both sides of the road. Where the river bends south again, there's a brown gate; this marks the end of vehicular access on River Road. Around the "Mile 2" post, there are large boulders in the river worth investigating. Scramble down the bank to get a look upriver from the bedrock slabs.

Field stone walls appear along the trail around the 3-mile mark. Saunter through a grove of huge old oaks and hemlocks to reach the "Mill Site" and "Mile 3" posts and the rock walls at the site of the former Baker Mill and Dam. In 1848, Lemuel Baker built a dam here and then erected a sawmill that used an undershot waterwheel—a vertically mounted wheel with a horizontal axle that turns when water hits its bottom quarter—to generate power. The dam site is a pretty spot to poke around, enjoy a snack and perhaps have a swim before retracing your steps back along the river.

TURN-BY-TURN DIRECTIONS

1. From the information kiosks, walk left past a barn to the safety fence above Chesterfield Gorge, then turn right along the gorge.
2. At 0.2 miles, soon after passing through a gate, the fence ends; turn left to follow the old River Road, now the route of the East Branch Trail along the Westfield River.
3. At 0.9 miles, enter Gilbert Bliss State Forest.
4. At 1.2 miles, pass the site of an old quarry.
5. At 1.6 miles, at a bend in the Westfield River, pass left around a brown gate.
6. At 3.4 miles, reach the site of the former Baker Mill Dam.
7. From the old dam site, retrace your steps to return to the trailhead.

FIND THE TRAILHEAD

From the intersection of MA Route 143, Cummington Road and Ireland Street in West Chesterfield, turn south on Ireland Street. In 0.9 miles, turn left on River Road (gravel) and in another 0.1 miles, turn left into the semicircular Chesterfield Gorge parking lot. Additional parking is available just ahead on River Road at the Chesterfield Four Seasons Club.

NORTHAMPTON BREWERY

Established in 1987, Northampton Brewery is one of the oldest continuously operating brewpubs in the eastern US. "Peace, love and beer"—and excellent food—is what you'll find at this fun, funky spot at 11 Brewster Court (no kidding) in the heart of beautiful downtown Northampton. Originally an 18th-century carriage house, its well-appointed interior features a large bar, lots of wood and a cozy fireplace. Additions and renovations over the years have included a sunroom, a balcony and a three-tiered outdoor beer garden. Greyhound IPA, a juicy, citrus forward and the favorite of head brewer Steve Bilodeau, is the brewery's most popular pour. Try it with an appetizer of catfish bites, a house specialty; then go for a wood-fired pizza served straight from the stone-hearth oven.

LAND MANAGER

The Trustees of Reservations
Boston, MA
(617) 542-7696
Info: thetrustees.org/place/chesterfield-gorge/

TRAIL MANAGER

Wild & Scenic Westfield River Committee
Huntington, MA
Trail map: www.westfieldriverwildscenic.org/documents/East-BranchTrailBrochure.pdf

BREWERY/RESTAURANT

Northampton Brewery Bar + Grille
11 Brewster Court
Northampton, MA 01060
(413) 584-9903
northamptonbrewery.com
Distance from trailhead: 19 miles

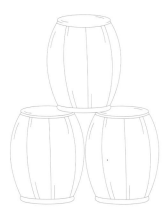

RHODE ISLAND

SACHUEST POINT

TAKE A SALTY WALK AROUND A WINDSWEPT PENINSULA

MIDDLETOWN, RI

▷⋯ STARTING POINT	⋯✗ DESTINATION
REFUGE VISITOR CENTER	**SACHUEST POINT, FLINT POINT**
🍺 BEER	🔀 HIKE TYPE
BLUEBERRY BLONDE ALE	**EASY**
🐾 DOG FRIENDLY	📅 SEASON
NO	**YEAR-ROUND**
$ FEES	🕐 DURATION
NO	**1 HOUR 20 MIN.**
⛰ MAP REFERENCE	↦ LENGTH
SACHUEST POINT NATIONAL WILDLIFE REFUGE	**2.7 MILES (LOOP)**
👁 HIGHLIGHTS	〰 ELEVATION GAIN
BAY VIEWS, BIRD LIFE, SALTY AIR, SCENIC OVERLOOKS	**30 FEET**

BLONDE ALE

GOLDEN

BLUEBERRY

BLUEBERRY

BITTERNESS   **SWEETNESS**

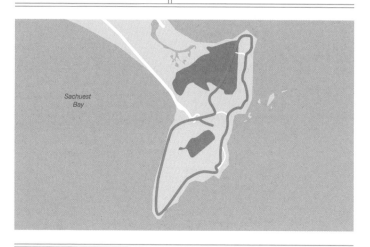

Sachuest
Bay

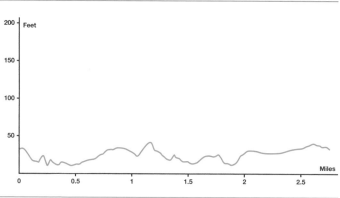

HIKE DESCRIPTION

Wander around the windswept margins of Sachuest Point for big oceanfront vistas and plenty of bird life. Then relax with a fine pint in the English-style pub at Coddington Brewery.

Sachuest Point National Wildlife Refuge protects 242 acres on the spectacular point of the same name at the southeastern tip of Aquidneck Island. One of five national wildlife refuges in Rhode Island, it is an important stopover for migratory birds. From the middle of the 1600s until the early 1900s, Sachuest Point consisted of farmland and pasture for sheep. The point was used as a rifle range and communications center by the US Navy during World War II. The wildlife refuge was established in the 1970s with a 70-acre donation from the Audubon Society of Rhode Island and land transfers from the Navy.

Pick up the Ocean View Loop at the visitor center and follow it to the bluff overlooking Sachuest Bay, where there's a good view to Second Beach and across to the historic town of Newport. Stroll along the wide gravel path to a bench, one of many along the way, and the first of eight shoreline access points where you can get down to the water's edge to poke around. You'll soon reach the first of five interpretive displays on the fascinating natural history of Sachuest Point. Ahead on the rocks at windswept Sachuest Point, your view across the water to the west ranges from Easton Bay to Land's End, taking in the route of Newport's famous Cliff Walk, a fine stroll that combines the bold natural beauty of the town's rugged eastern shore with the historical architecture of its Gilded Age.

As you head up the east side of Sachuest Point you'll get a lovely look out over Sakonnet Bay to Breakwater Point and Sakonnet Light on Sakonnet Point. The 66-foot cylindrical cast-iron tower on Little Cormorant Rock has stood watch through countless storms since its beacon was first lit in 1884. After a display describing resident and migratory raptors, turn left onto the Price Neck Overlook Trail and walk across ancient rock ledges.

A mile and a half into the hike, you'll continue on the Flint Point Loop to reach Island Rocks Scenic Overlook, where you might spy some of the birds that rest, feed and nest on the rocky islands just offshore. At Flint Point, climb the observation tower for a last look over the Sakonnet River to the arc of Third Beach. After the point, the trail passes through an area of habitat restoration where crews are working to eliminate harmful invasive plants. Before you make the turn for the visitor center, sidle out to the third observation tower for a 360-degree view of your walk.

TURN-BY-TURN DIRECTIONS

1. From the kiosk next to the visitor center, take the Ocean View Loop around the front of the building, then continue right, following the dirt path to the water's edge.
2. At a fork at 0.6 miles, bear right on a spur out to Sachuest Point. Return to the fork and turn right to continue.
3. At 1.0 miles, leave the main path for the narrower Price Neck Overlook Trail, which rejoins the Ocean View Loop in about 500 feet.
4. At 1.4 miles, where the path on the left leads back to the visitor center, continue straight ahead on the Flint Point Loop.
5. At 1.5 miles, reach the observation platform at Island Rocks Scenic Overlook.
6. At 1.9 miles, reach the observation tower at Flint Point.
7. At 2.4 miles, arrive at a T-junction and turn right; after another 150 feet, turn left at the kiosk and take the spur to the observation tower. Retrace your steps to the Flint Point Loop and turn left to return to the visitor center.

FIND THE TRAILHEAD

From the Newport Gateway Transportation and Visitor Center on RI Route 138A in downtown Newport (1.2 miles south of Claiborne Pell Bridge and RI Route 138), drive south and then east through town on RI Route 138A. In 2.2 miles, after crossing the neck of Easton Beach, turn right on Purgatory Road. At 3.1 miles, bear right on Hanging Rock Road, and shortly after, bear right on Sachuest Point Road. Pass Second Beach, enter Sachuest Point National Wildlife Refuge, and arrive at the visitor center and trailhead parking on the left at 4.6 miles.

CODDINGTON BREWING COMPANY

Coddington Brewing was founded in 1995, the first brewpub in Newport County. The warm, well-appointed interior with its beautiful mahogany bar is reminiscent of many a fine English pub—and why not, considering that the place is named after the Englishman William Coddington, governor of the Colony of Rhode Island and Providence Plantations in the 1600s. Order a sample tray of the brewery's six original beers plus a seasonal brew, or settle into a pint, like a refreshing Blueberry Blonde, for some relaxing downtime with locals and visitors alike. Try the mango habanero wings if you dare, or one of the "brewery favorites" on the great menu—like the William Coddington turkey platter, a traditional favorite.

LAND MANAGER

Sachuest Point National Wildlife Refuge Visitor Center
769 Sachuest Point Road
Middletown, RI 02842
(401) 619-2680
Info and trail map: fws.gov/refuge/Sachuest_Point/

BREWERY/RESTAURANT

Coddington Brewing Company
210 Coddington Highway
Middletown, RI 02842
(401) 847-6690
coddbrew.com
Distance from trailhead: 5.3 miles

TILLINGHAST POND

WANDER THROUGH THE NATURE CONSERVANCY'S LARGEST RHODE ISLAND PRESERVE

WEST GREENWICH, RI

▷··· STARTING POINT	···✕ DESTINATION
PLAIN ROAD	**TILLINGHAST POND, HEMLOCK RIDGE**
🍺 BEER	HIKE TYPE
STRIPAH NEIPA	**EASY-MODERATE**
🐾 DOG FRIENDLY	SEASON
NO	**YEAR-ROUND**
$ FEES	⏲ DURATION
NO	**2 HOURS 10 MIN.**
⛰ MAP REFERENCE	↦ LENGTH
TILLINGHAST POND TRAIL SYSTEM	**4.3 MILES (LOOP)**
🔎 HIGHLIGHTS	〜 ELEVATION GAIN
PONDSIDE VIEWS, PLEASANT WOODS, FIELDS, CASCADES	**120 FEET**

NEW ENGLAND DOUBLE IPA

STRAW/ORANGE

TROPICAL FRUIT
STONE FRUIT
PINE

GRAPEFRUIT
STONE FRUIT
MANGO, PINE

BITTERNESS

SWEETNESS

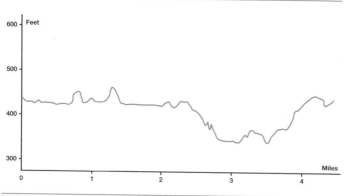

HIKE DESCRIPTION

Take a relaxing hike around scenic Tillinghast Pond and through stands of mature pine, oak and hemlock. Then head east for a cold StrIPAh at Linesider Brewing.

Located in a remote area of west-central Rhode Island, Tillinghast Pond Management Area is part of the largest block of undeveloped coastal forestland between Boston and Washington, D.C. Established in 2006, the 2,200-acre preserve protects the headwaters of the Wood River, one of the state's most prized trout fisheries. Tillinghast Pond is owned by The Nature Conservancy and is the largest of the dozen wildlife preserves in the state under the organization's care.

This pleasant circuit hike combines the Tillinghast Pond Loop and the Coney Brook Loop to explore the environs around Tillinghast Pond, cascading Coney Brook and the impressive stands of white pine, red oak and hemlock on Hemlock Ridge. Halfway along the east side of Tillinghast Pond is Phebe's Grove. Phebe McAlpine Shepard's generous gift of 500 acres in 2006 sparked the conservation effort to save Tillinghast Pond from a large housing development. A bench and picnic table accompany the dedication marker at this lovely spot.

At the north end of the pond, old stone walls are reminders of the farming and pastoral lives of the past, and another bench beckons you to sit for a while to enjoy the view. At a meadow on the pond's west shore there's an observation deck worthy of a short pause for a good look around. Leaving the meadow, the path enters the woods, crosses a creek, and then edges along a field from which you'll see a farmstead several hundred yards away. You'll return to the pond at Howard's Rest, which honors the naturalist and humanitarian Howard White Murre.

On the west side of Plain Road, the Coney Brook Loop leads through meadows to two small ponds, then to a sluice and cascades and the remains of an old dam on Coney Brook. Beyond, there's a narrow valley of pines and oaks and then Hemlock Ridge. Wetlands are interspersed with low ridges along this stretch of trail, and young hemlocks are prevalent. On the return leg, the Coney Brook Loop passes the remains of the old Parker Homestead before returning to Plain Road.

TURN-BY-TURN DIRECTIONS

1. The Tillinghast Pond Loop (white blazes) begins left of the information kiosk.
2. At 0.2 miles, the Flintlock Loop merges from the east. Turn left here, following the white and yellow blazes of the Tillinghast Pond Loop and the Flintlock Loop, which coincide for the next 0.6 miles.
3. At 0.4 miles, a short side trail on the left leads to Phebe's Grove on the east shore of Tillinghast Pond.
4. At 0.8 miles, the Flintlock Loop diverges right; bear left to stay on the Tillinghast Pond Loop.

5.   At 1.4 miles, a spur on the left leads to an observation deck looking over the pond.
6.   At 1.7 miles, a spur on the left leads to the site of Howard's Rest on the pond.
7.   At 2.1 miles, cross Plain Road to pick up the Coney Brook Loop (orange blazes).
8.   At 2.3 miles, the Logger's Trail turns off to the left; continue straight on the Coney Brook Loop.
9.   At 3.4 miles, the Shepard Trail leaves right for Hazard Road; continue ahead on the Coney Brook Loop.
10.   At 4.1 miles, the Logger's Trail joins from the left; continue straight, cross Plain Road and turn right to return to the trailhead.

FIND THE TRAILHEAD

From the junction of I-95 (Exit 5A [southbound] or Exit 5B [northbound]) and RI Route 102 in West Greenwich, head west on RI Route 102. In about 3 miles, turn left on Plain Meeting House Road. In another 3.9 miles, turn right on Plain Road and drive 0.5 miles to the Pond Loop Trailhead of the Tillinghast Pond Management Area on the right.

LINESIDER BREWING CO.

Linesider Brewing is a welcoming, family-friendly place with a little something for everybody on the menu, which is exactly what Jeremy Ruff, a former aerospace engineer, and Dan Koppen, a retired NFL player, had in mind when they opened the place in 2018 in a renovated industrial space. Linesider is another name for striped bass, and the brewery's deliciously popular NEIPAs—StrIPAh and VII Stripes—are both nods to Rhode Island's state fish, which just so happens to have seven stripes. As many as 14 different beers are on tap at any time, so grab a pint, pull up a chair in the casual, comfy taproom or in the outdoor courtyard and enjoy some live music, the jukebox or a trivia contest along with some good eats from one of the rotating food trucks. You may also BYOF (Bring Your Own Food).

LAND MANAGER

The Nature Conservancy
Providence, RI 02906
(401) 331-7110
Info and trail map: www.nature.org/en-us/get-involved/how-to-help/
places-we-protect/tillinghast-pond-management-area/

BREWERY

LineSider Brewing
1485 South County Trail, Suite 201
East Greenwich, RI 02818
(401) 398-7700
www.linesiderbrewing.com
Distance from trailhead: 19 miles

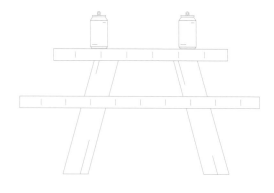

WALKABOUT TRAIL

TAKE A HIKE WITH AN AUSTRALIAN CONNECTION

CHEPACHET, RI

▷⋯ STARTING POINT	⋯✕ DESTINATION
EAST END OF BOWDISH RESERVOIR	**8-MILE ORANGE LOOP**
🍺 BEER	🀫 HIKE TYPE
PARLIAMENT ESB	**MODERATE** 🚶
🐾 DOG FRIENDLY	📅 SEASON
YES (LEASH REQUIRED)	**YEAR-ROUND**
💲 FEES	🕐 DURATION
YES	**4 HOURS**
⛰ MAP REFERENCE	↦ LENGTH
WALKABOUT TRAIL	**7.6 MILES (LOOP)**
🔎 HIGHLIGHTS	〰 ELEVATION GAIN
LARGE RESERVOIR, PRETTY PONDS, BIG WOODS, HISTORY	**275 FEET**

EXTRA SPECIAL BITTER

DARK AMBER/LIGHT RED

TOFFEE
BISCUIT

BALANCED SWEET
AND BITTER

BITTERNESS

SWEETNESS

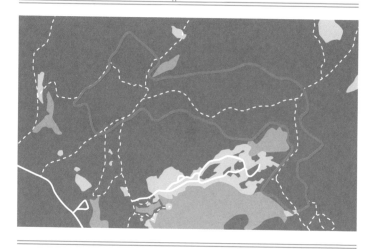

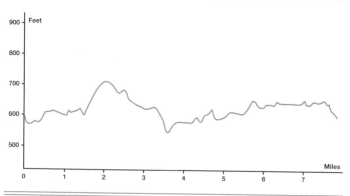

HIKE DESCRIPTION

Go for an Aboriginal Australian–inspired "walkabout" on the Walkabout Trail, a meandering 8-mile circuit that'll surely earn you a "bravo!" later at Bravo Brewing in tiny Pascoag.

The Walkabout Trail meanders through the remote woods of the 4,000-acre George Washington Management Area (GWMA) in the rural northwest corner of Rhode Island. The trail traces a scenic wildlife-rich route that visits a large reservoir, two ponds, hemlock groves and marshy wetlands over nearly 8 miles, which allows plenty of time to consider its interesting historical connection to faraway Australia.

In the summer of 1965, a crew of Australian sailors found themselves in Rhode Island with a month's time on their hands while they waited for their ship, the *HMAS Perth*, to be commissioned. The state forestry department was developing trails in the GWMA and needed help. When officials asked the Aussies if building miles of trails would fill the bill, the sailors readily agreed and got to work. The result of the men's efforts was a network of trails they collectively named the Walkabout Trail after the indigenous Aboriginal tradition of their Down Under homeland. A "walkabout" is a rite of passage during which individuals, typically young males, make a spiritual journey into the wilderness, sometimes for months at a time. Many young Australians still go on such adventures, better known today as "holidays." A bronze plaque on a large boulder at the start of the hike honors the Aussies and their trail work.

Walkabout Trail follows orange markers throughout its length, which partly coincides with a blue-blazed loop (2 miles long) and a red-blazed

loop (6 miles long), both of which can serve as good bailout points, if needed. Rhode Island's North-South Trail, a 78-mile trail extending from Charlestown on the Atlantic coast to the Massachusetts border, also coincides with portions of the Walkabout Trail.

The Walkabout Trail skirts the park campground as it threads its way beside the 226-acre Bowdish Reservoir, where there are several access points to the water. After the Blue Trail connector, you'll walk along the north shore of Wilbur Pond. Bowdish Lake Camping Area is in view across the water. Beyond the Red Trail connector, you'll cross a number of gravel and grassy roads and pass by at least one gate. The Walkabout Trail follows several other park trails and tracks, all designated by triangles of different colors. To avoid confusion, always stick to the orange markers of the Walkabout Trail.

After a sign for Pulaski Park, the Walkabout Trail meanders onward to Richardson Pond. The grassy earthen dam at the pond's west end is a real pretty spot that's great for a break. From the pond, it's about 3 miles back to the start, and soon enough you'll again be following the combination of orange and red and then orange, red and blue markers on this last leg of the walk.

TURN-BY-TURN DIRECTIONS

1. Begin at the large boulder with a bronze plaque ("The Walkabout Trail") and brown trail sign above the beach at Bowdish Reservoir; walk to the obvious trail marker post with colored bands on it, then bear left into the woods on the orange-blazed Walkabout Trail.
2. At 0.8 miles, the Blue Trail leaves to the right (the 2-mile loop hike); bear left to stay on the Walkabout Trail, which soon reaches a spur on the left to Wilbur Pond.
3. At 2.0 miles, where the Red Trail continues straight ahead, turn left to stay on the orange Walkabout Trail.
4. At 3.0 miles, cross the Center Trail, a wide dirt road.
5. At 3.4 miles, at the sign "Pulaski Park," leave the old forest road for the foot trail on the right.
6. At 4.0 miles, cross a dirt road signed the Inner Border Trail.
7. At 4.8 miles, bear left to cross a grassy earthen dam at the west end of Richardson Pond.
8. At 5.4 miles, the Red Trail departs to the right; stay straight on the orange-blazed Walkabout Trail.
9. At 6.2 miles, cross the Center Trail, a wide gravel road.
10. At 7.0 miles, the Blue Trail enters from right; continue straight ahead on the Walkabout Trail to return to the trailhead.

FIND THE TRAILHEAD

From I-395, Exit 47 in Putnam, CT, drive east on US Route 44 toward Providence, RI. In 5 miles, cross the state line into Glocester, RI. In another 2.3 miles, turn left into George Washington State Campground. Pass through the campground entrance station and proceed to the trailhead parking lot on the left.

BRAVO BREWING COMPANY

Chris Mishoe, an Air Force veteran and longtime home brewer, opened Bravo Brewing in 2019 on Main Street in the village of Pascoag (pop. 4,500) in rural northwest Rhode Island. As a "Salute to Craft Beer," the small-batch brewery specializes in English ales and lagers and is well-known for its flagship, the Parliament ESB. Its eclectic blend of other styles, including New England IPAs and fruited sours, ensures there's something for everyone's beer palate among the other eleven taps. A big hit with locals, family and dog-friendly Bravo Brewing draws beer travelers from afar, which is great news for this small community working hard to revitalize its downtown. The brewery donates one percent of its annual sales to Homes For Our Troops, a disabled veterans adaptive home-building assistance program. Brew beer, drink beer, have fun, do good. Bravo!

LAND MANAGER

George Washington Management Area Headquarters
2185 Putnam Pike
Chepachet, RI 02814
(401) 568-6700
Info and trail map: www.riparks.com/Locations/LocationGeorgeWashington.html

BREWERY

Bravo Brewing Company
75 Pascoag Main Street
Pascoag, RI 02859
(401) 710-4242
bravobrewingcompany.com
Distance from trailhead: 6.3 miles

CONNECTICUT

BARN ISLAND

EXPLORE THE FINEST WILD COASTAL AREA IN CONNECTICUT

STONINGTON, CT

▷⋯ STARTING POINT	⋯✗ DESTINATION
PALMER NECK ROAD	**IMPOUNDMENTS 1-5**
🍺 BEER	HIKE TYPE
DOGS & BOATS DIPA	**EASY**
🐾 DOG FRIENDLY	📅 SEASON
YES (LEASH REQUIRED)	**YEAR-ROUND**
$ FEES	🕐 DURATION
NO	**2 HOURS**
⛰ MAP REFERENCE	↦ LENGTH
BARN ISLAND WILDLIFE MANAGEMENT AREA	**3.8 MILES (LOOP)**
🔎 HIGHLIGHTS	〰 ELEVATION GAIN
BAY VIEWS, SALT MARSHES, BIRD AND ANIMAL LIFE	**65 FEET**

DOUBLE IPA

PALE STRAW

CITRUS RIND
TROPICAL FRUIT

CITRUS
BISCUIT
TROPICAL FRUIT

BITTERNESS

SWEETNESS

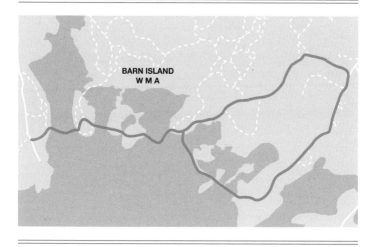

BARN ISLAND
W M A

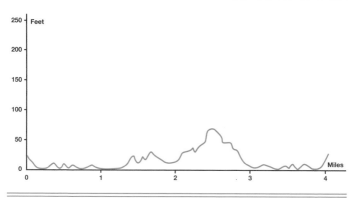

HIKE DESCRIPTION

Take a meandering walk through the wonderfully wild wetlands and woods of Connecticut's finest coastal preserve. Then relax with a heady brew at nearby Beer'd Brewing.

Barn Island Wildlife Management Area in the far southeastern corner of Connecticut is the largest, most diverse and most ecologically significant in the state's inventory of wildlife management properties. Established in 1944, Barn Island protects 1,103 acres of prime habitat: from saltwater and freshwater wetlands and hardwood forests to old fields and grasslands.

Just 100 feet into the hike, you'll reach Marsh Overlook and Demonstration Garden. Check out the interpretive displays, then follow the wide path down to the open marshlands and over a causeway with a culvert. Impoundment 1 on the left is the first of five impoundments you'll pass on a series of old roads through the marshes on the edge of Little Narragansett Bay. In the 1940s, four dikes were constructed across the estuary. The impounded waters were designed to enhance tidal wetland habitat for migratory and resident birds and muskrat, and to reverse the damage done to open water habitat by the mosquito ditches dug in the early 1930s, which drained the marshes in an effort to eliminate the pest. Look for these long, straight mosquito ditches as you walk. In 1968, a fifth dike was built.

You'll bear right at the next two forks over the next mile or so and be in and out of the impressive deciduous forest of oak, hickory and maple as you pass the next four impoundments. The open stretches are a delight and you're likely to see plenty of birdlife. The shallow pools and depressions along the route provide important habitat for waterfowl, shorebirds and wading birds. The culverts at each impoundment were installed in the late 1970s to increase tidal flow to help restore the natural balance of the tidal marshes.

Look out across the marshlands toward the bay to see a large, forested island; this is Barn Island. Historically it was known as Stanton Island, but during the late 1800s the Burdicks erected a huge barn (long gone) that was visible for miles around, and the name Barn Island has stuck. Before you enter the woods at the far end of Impoundment 5, look for the osprey nesting platform sticking out of the marsh grass.

Stone walls line the old road as you hike through the woods to the Burdick-Culver Cemetery. Gravestones in the cemetery date from 1793 to 1881. Beyond the stone pillars of an old gate, the trail leads onto Stewart Road through a rural neighborhood. Turn left on gravel Brucker Parkway and walk past a farmstead to a large parking area for Barn Island WMA. Take the wide grassy track and meander through the pretty fields, noting the many bluebird nest boxes. Re-enter the woods and make your way back to the marsh to connect the loop and return to Palmer Neck Road.

TURN-BY-TURN DIRECTIONS

1. Begin at the information kiosk across Palmer Neck Road from the trailhead parking; walk ahead to the overlook, then out to the open marshland.
2. At a fork at 0.3 miles, bear right at the interpretive display.
3. At a fork at 0.9 miles, bear right toward the open marsh.
4. At 1.5 miles, reach Burdick-Culver Cemetery on the right.
5. At 1.8 miles, pass around a green metal gate onto Stewart Road.
6. At 2.1 miles, turn left to follow the gravel Brucker Parkway.
7. At 2.4 miles, where the road ends at a gravel parking lot, bear left past the green gate into the meadow.
8. At a junction at 2.7 miles, bear left.
9. Close the lollipop loop at 3 miles and bear right to retrace your steps.
10. At 3.6 miles, bear left at the interpretive display to return to the trailhead.

FIND THE TRAILHEAD

From I-91, Exit 91 in Stonington, head south on CT Route 234. In 0.3 miles, turn left on Main Street and drive 1.6 miles to US Route 1. Turn left on US Route 1 and continue 1.8 miles to Greenhaven Road. Turn right, and in 100 feet, turn right again on Palmer Neck Road. In 1.2 miles, pass a sign on the left for Barn Island Wildlife Management Area. In another 0.3 miles, trailhead parking is on the right. Additional parking can be found just ahead where the road ends at the boat launch.

BEER'D BREWING CO.

Like many old New England mills, the American Velvet Mill (circa 1891) has been repurposed and today houses a thriving mix of artists, crafts-people and entrepreneurs, including Beer'd Brewing, which set up shop here in 2011. Living out their motto, "Don't just stand out in the crowd, stand somewhere else," the passionate crew at Beer'd believes in making beer accessible to everyone, and with their Signature, Limited Release and Experimental Series, you're sure to find a brew or two that suits your palate. One of Beer'd Brewing's popular staples is a juicy Imperial IPA called Dogs & Boats. Whatever beer you choose, enjoy it with a slice of Woodfellas pizza (one of several terrific food vendors inside the mill) in the taproom or out in the Beer'd Garden in the spacious, sunny atrium.

LAND MANAGER

Connecticut Dept. of Energy and Environmental Protection – Bureau of Natural Resources
Hartford, CT
(860) 424-3011
Trail map: portal.ct.gov/-/media/DEEP/stateparks/maps/BarnIslandTrail2012pdf.pdf

BREWERY

Beer'd Brewing Co.
22 Bayview Ave, Unit 15 (Velvet Mill)
Stonington, CT 06378
(860) 213-9307
beerdbrewing.com
Distance from trailhead: 3.7 miles

BEAR MOUNTAIN

HIKE TO CONNECTICUT'S HIGHEST MOUNTAINTOP

KENT, CT

▷⋯ STARTING POINT	⋯✕ DESTINATION
CT ROUTE 41/UNDER MOUNTAIN ROAD	BEAR MOUNTAIN SUMMIT
🍺 BEER	🗺 HIKE TYPE
LAZY HAZY HOUSY NEIPA	**STRENUOUS**
🐾 DOG FRIENDLY	📅 SEASON
YES (UNDER CONTROL)	APRIL TO NOVEMBER
$ FEES	🕐 DURATION
NO	**4 HOURS**
⛰ MAP REFERENCE	↦ LENGTH
POSTED AT UNDER MOUNTAIN TRAIL TRAILHEAD	**6.3 MILES (LOOP)**
🔍 HIGHLIGHTS	〰 ELEVATION GAIN
STONE MONUMENT, MOUNTAIN VIEWS, APPALACHIAN TRAIL	**1,550 FEET**

NEW ENGLAND IPA

 TANGERINE

 TROPICAL FRUIT
CITRUS

TROPICAL FRUIT
CITRUS

BITTERNESS   SWEETNESS

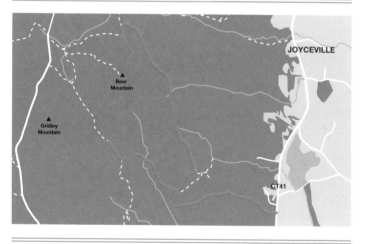

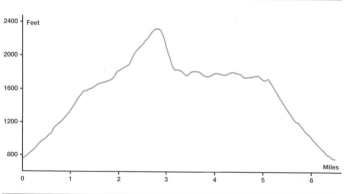

HIKE DESCRIPTION

Follow a segment of the famous Appalachian Trail to the summit of Bear Mountain for stunning 360-degree views. Then head for a frosty brew in a refurbished railroad depot.

The 2,316-foot summit of Bear Mountain was long considered to be Connecticut's highest point. But when the United States Geological Survey resurveyed the area in the 1940s, a point on the southern slope of Mount Frissell (it's summit is just across the Massachusetts state line) a couple miles northwest was discovered to be 2,380 feet high, 64 feet higher than Bear Mountain. The matter of highest point versus highest peak need not concern everyday hikers, however, as Bear Mountain rewards visitors with outstanding views in every direction.

This hike combines the Under Mountain Trail, the Appalachian Trail (AT) and the Paradise Lane Trail for a lollipop loop on Bear Mountain. The Under Mountain Trail climbs westerly up the valley of Brassie Brook to meet the AT at Riga Junction. From this point, you'll follow the famously well-trodden long-distance footpath over Bear Mountain. It's delightful walking through the laurel along the mountain's south ridge, where several rocky outcrops offer excellent views west to Round Mountain, Mount Frissell and Mount Brace, and south to Lions Head.

The AT threads through woods of pitch pine, scrub oak and dwarf birch before breaking out on top of Bear Mountain at the 20-foot stone monument. Scramble up the rock pile for a fabulous 360-degree panorama that includes Mount Race and Mount Everett in Massachusetts to the north. The Twin Lakes and Housatonic River Valley are off to the east, while New York's Taconic Range and Catskill Mountains can be seen to the west. According to the inscription at its base, the monument was erected in 1885 by Owen Travis, a mason. The original pyramid-shaped monument was much higher, perhaps three times its current height. After it had collapsed multiple times over the years, state officials finally decided in 1978 to stabilize the rock pile instead of rebuilding the monument.

The AT descends the steep ledges on the north side of Bear Mountain to reach a junction. Here, the AT continues north into Sages Ravine, but you'll turn right to follow the Paradise Lane Trail through a beautiful grove of mature hemlocks. On its contouring route around the eastern base of Bear Mountain, the trail passes a shallow pond, crosses a small brook and skirts a wetland before angling down to join the Under Mountain Trail for the final leg back to the trailhead.

TURN-BY-TURN DIRECTIONS

1. Start to the left of the information kiosk and follow the Under Mountain Trail (blue blazes).
2. At 1.2 miles, where the Paradise Lane Trail continues straight ahead, bear left to stay on the Under Mountain Trail.
3. At 1.9 miles, turn right (north) on the Appalachian Trail (white blazes).
4. At 2.1 miles, where Bear Mountain Road goes left, bear right to stay on the AT.
5. At 2.8 miles, reach the stone monument on the summit of Bear Mountain.
6. At 3.3 miles, where the AT continues straight toward Sages Ravine, turn right on the Paradise Lane Trail (blue blazes).
7. At 5.1 miles, turn left on the Under Mountain Trail to return to the trailhead.

FIND THE TRAILHEAD

From the junction of US Route 44 and CT Route 41 in Salisbury, drive north on CT Route 41 (Under Mountain Road) for 3.2 miles to trailhead parking for the Under Mountain Trail on the left.

GREAT FALLS BREWING CO.

Named for the huge waterfall on the Housatonic River 6 miles to the south, Great Falls Brewing opened in 2018 in a refurbished section of the historic Canaan Union Depot Railroad Station. Living up to its motto "community, beer, life," the brewery is committed to the town of Canaan and regularly holds fundraising events for local causes. The taproom is festooned with historic artifacts, many from the old train depot, and often hosts dart leagues and trivia contests. Beers on Great Falls Brewing's diverse menu are named for significant features in this rural northwest corner of Connecticut, like the flagship Lazy Hazy Housy, a juicy, tangerine-colored New England IPA that's a nod to the meandering Housatonic River nearby. Bar snacks plus local food trucks on weekends help keep the munchies in check.

TRAIL MANAGER

Appalachian Mountain Club – Connecticut Chapter
Info and trail map: ct-amc.org/trails/trails-hiking-on-the-at/

BREWERY

Great Falls Brewing Co.
1 Railroad Plaza
Canaan, CT 06018
(860) 453-4076
www.greatfallsbrews.com
Distance from trailhead: 9.2 miles

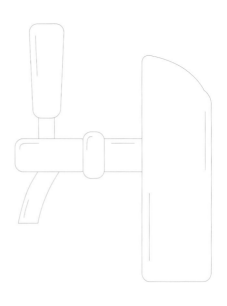

BLUFF HEAD

ENJOY CLIFFTOP VIEWS OVER A VAST MOSAIC OF RURAL CONSERVATION LANDS

GUILFORD, CT

▷⋯ STARTING POINT	⋯✗ DESTINATION
CT ROUTE 77	**BLUFF HEAD**
🍺 BEER	🗺 HIKE TYPE
AMERICAN ALE	**MODERATE**
🐾 DOG FRIENDLY	📅 SEASON
YES (LEASH REQUIRED)	**MARCH TO NOVEMBER**
$ FEES	🕐 DURATION
NO	**2 HOURS 25 MIN.**
⛰ MAP REFERENCE	↦ LENGTH
NORTHWOODS: JAMES VALLEY & BLUFF HEAD	**4.3 MILES (LOOP)**
🔍 HIGHLIGHTS	〰 ELEVATION GAIN
CLIFFTOP VIEWS, PRETTY POND, RURAL COUNTRYSIDE	**475 FEET**

AMBER ALE

DEEP RED

FLORAL
SWEET

CARAMEL
PINE AND CITRUS NOTES

BITTERNESS   SWEETNESS

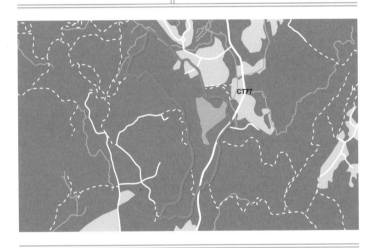

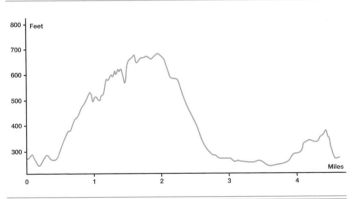

HIKE DESCRIPTION

Scamper up to the airy clifftop on Bluff Head for outstanding views over the rolling rural countryside of coastal Connecticut. Then head down to Thimble Island Brewing for classic beers and good eats in a chill atmosphere.

Since 1965, the Guilford Land Conservation Trust (GLCT) has been hard at work protecting open spaces and preserving recreational access to lands within the Town of Guilford in south-central Connecticut. Today, the organization has conserved close to 3,200 acres, some 3,000 through acquisition and the rest as conservation easements. The trust's work in the area called Northwoods, north of Lake Quonnipaug in North Guilford on both sides of CT Route 77, is particularly impressive and includes the beloved landmark of Bluff Head.

Bluff Head, a 500-foot cliff composed of basalt or "traprock," is considered the crown jewel among the many and varied land holdings of the GLCT. The airy open ledges atop the precipitous east face yield far-reaching views across the rural wooded hills east of the Connecticut River, north 25 miles to the skyline of the capital city of Hartford and south a dozen miles to the state's coastline along Long Island Sound. At the bluff's base is Meyerhuber Pond, a shallow, heart-shaped gem and one of the sources of the Coginchaug River.

Bluff Head is the focus of this hike, which winds through Bluff Head Preserve by way of four trails. A segment of the New England National Scenic Trail (NET), a 215-mile long-distance hiking route from Long

Island Sound in Guilford through Connecticut and Massachusetts to the New Hampshire border, leads hikers up and over Bluff Head, passing several lookouts over Meyerhuber Pond along the way. The North Slope Trail winds down to the valley below to meet the Lone Pine Trail, which runs along clear-running Hemlock Brook. Ahead, the George Etzel/Meyerhuber Trail meanders past the pond and its beaver dams, then across the highway and back to complete the loop.

These trails and many more are all part of an extensive network known as the Northwoods of Guilford, which links more than 1,000 acres of conservation properties owned and managed by either the GLCT or the Town of Guilford. From Bartlett Land Preserve, GCLT's newest acquisition, one could actually walk on protected open spaces across the town from its border with North Branford east to Madison, connecting the James Valley and Meyerhuber Preserves west of CT Route 77 with Broomstick Ledges and Braemore Preserves east of the highway. —a distance of close to 4 miles as the crow flies. The fun spills over the Madison line, with more trails connecting to two additional preserves.

TURN-BY-TURN DIRECTIONS

1. Begin left of the information kiosk. Pass through the wooden fence and follow the light blue blazes of the New England National Scenic Trail (NET), avoiding the Bluff Loop Trail on the right (light blue/orange blazes).
2. At 0.4 miles, avoid the orange-blazed trail ahead and turn sharply right uphill to continue on the NET.
3. At 1.2 miles, reach the first of two ledge viewpoints overlooking Meyerhuber Pond.
4. At 1.3 miles, bear right, away from the blue-blazed NET, on a narrow path across the east face of Bluff Head.
5. At 1.4 miles, reach the huge open ledges at the second viewpoint overlooking Meyerhuber Pond. Just beyond, the path rejoins the blue-blazed NET and continues.
6. At 2.0 miles, where the NET continues straight ahead, turn right to descend on the North Slope Trail (light blue/white blazes).
7. At 2.5 miles, reach a junction. Here, the Lone Pine Trail (light blue/red blazes) splits. To the right is a high-water alternative path; go straight to cross Hemlock Brook on a footbridge.
8. At 2.6 miles, the high-water alternative rejoins from the right.
9. At 2.7 miles, ford or rock-hop across Hemlock Brook (no bridge).
10. Pass through a former horse farm, and at a junction at 3.2 miles, where the Lone Pine Trail departs to the left, continue straight ahead on the George Etzel/Meyerhuber Trail (light blue/yellow blazes) along Meyerhuber Pond.
11. At 3.6 miles, cross CT Route 77 and walk (carefully!) along its east shoulder.
12. At 3.8 miles, leave the road and turn left at an old road with a metal gate. In 50 feet, the trail continues to the right.
13. At 4.1 miles, reach a T-junction. Turn right on the NET to reach CT Route 77 and soon after, the trailhead.

FIND THE TRAILHEAD

From I-95, Exit 58 in Guilford, travel north on CT Route 77 for 8.5 miles to trailhead parking on the left and a kiosk that reads "Welcome to Northwoods."

THIMBLE ISLAND BREWING COMPANY

Growing up in Branford, Justin Gargano spent a lot of time exploring the Thimble Islands just offshore in Long Island Sound, so when he embarked on his brewery adventure in 2011, the name came easily. Thimble Island Brewing has grown into a locals' joint; it is a comfortable, family-friendly place known for its classic beers, good eats and chill atmosphere. American Ale, a refreshingly drinkable amber, is the

original and still popular flagship brew among the 24 taps that pour a little something for everyone. Enjoy a pint with a tasty Thimble Smash Burger, the #1 seller on the eclectic, locally-sourced menu. Hang out on the lawn or stone patio or in the taproom, where a colorful mural, hand-painted by a local artist, depicts squid tentacles grasping a can of ale adorned with Neptune's trident.

LAND MANAGER

Guilford Land Conservation Trust
Guilford, CT 06437
(203) 457-9253
Info and trail map: guilfordlandtrust.org

BREWERY/RESTAURANT

Thimble Island Brewing Company
16 Business Park Drive
Branford, CT 06405
(203) 208-2827
www.thimbleislandbrewery.com
Distance from trailhead: 13 miles

BREAKNECK POND

CIRCUMNAVIGATE REMOTE BREAKNECK POND IN THE QUINEBAUG HIGHLANDS

UNION, CT

▷⋯ STARTING POINT	⋯✗ DESTINATION
BIGELOW POND	**BREAKNECK POND**
🍺 BEER	🏷 HIKE TYPE
NO ROOM TO SWING A CAT IPA	**MODERATE**
🐾 DOG FRIENDLY	📅 SEASON
YES (LEASH REQUIRED)	**APRIL TO OCTOBER**
💲 FEES	🕐 DURATION
YES	**3 HOURS 15 MIN.**
⛰ MAP REFERENCE	↦ LENGTH
NIPMUCK STATE FOREST– BIGELOW HOLLOW STATE PARK	**6.3 MILES (LOOP)**
🔍 HIGHLIGHTS	〰 ELEVATION GAIN
REMOTE POND, DEEP GREEN VALLEY, MOSSY BOULDERS	**190 FEET**

INDIA PALE ALE

HAZY YELLOW

TROPICAL FRUIT
GUAVA

MELON, GRAPEFRUIT
PEACH
PASSION FRUIT

BITTERNESS

SWEETNESS

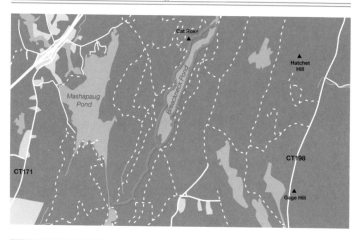

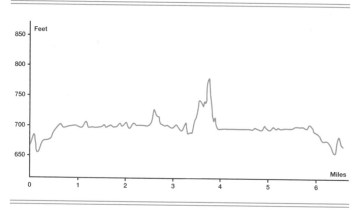

131

HIKE DESCRIPTION

Circumnavigate Breakneck Pond in the remote woods of Nipmuck State Forest. A No Room to Swing a Cat IPA at Taylor Brooke Brewing is your thirst-quenching after-hike reward.

Bigelow State Park and Nipmuck State Forest, located in the Quinebaug Highlands in the rural northeast corner of Connecticut, are part of one of the largest tracts of undeveloped forest in the state. The two properties, a combined 9,526 acres of remote woods and waters, are both managed by the Connecticut Department of Energy and Environmental Protection. The mountainous area around the state park and forest, which spills over into Massachusetts, features more than 40,000 acres of protected lands. One of the last remaining swaths of green in the heavily urbanized Boston-to-Washington, D.C. metro corridor, the region has been designated a "Last Green Valley National Heritage Corridor."

Enjoy the wild character of Nipmuck State Forest on a counterclockwise circuit hike around Breakneck Pond. The East Ridge Trail and then Park Road lead through woods of mountain laurel, hemlock, fir, oak and beech to the south end of Breakneck Pond. Join the Nipmuck Trail here to wend your way along the east shore of the pond, which is hemmed in by ridges as high as 1,000 feet. Several islands come into view as you hug the shoreline on the pleasant path through the stately white pines and laurel thickets. The three-sided East Shelter, one of several official overnight camping sites on the pond (permit required), is a good break spot.

The undulating path alternates between the edge of the pond and the slope above it. Views of the pond are lovely, so take advantage of each

opportunity to see it. More islands come into focus as you stride north to the Massachusetts state line, which is marked by a granite post. The Breakneck Pond View Trail continues on from the state line to the north end of Breakneck Pond, where you'll cross to the west side on a wooded causeway.

Climb to the ridge above the pond and cross back into Connecticut (no marker). Pass through Cat Rocks, an area of lichen and moss-covered boulders, and then climb higher onto the ridge and proceed south through thickets of mountain laurel. The rolling path continues down the west side of Breakneck Pond, eventually reaching a campsite on a point dotted with oaks and pines and with a sweeping view over the water. Several more ups and downs lead to a rocky stretch of treadway on the slope above the pond. Close the loop at the pond's south end and make your way back to Bigelow Pond.

TURN-BY-TURN DIRECTIONS

1. From the Bigelow Pond trailhead, cross the park road to follow the East Ridge Trail (white blazes).
2. At 0.3 miles, turn left on Park Road (a wide trail).
3. At 1.1 miles, just past the concrete stanchions of an old gate and a faded map table, turn right to proceed on the Nipmuck Trail (blue blazes).
4. At 1.9 miles, reach East Shelter on the east shore of Breakneck Pond.
5. At 3.0 miles, reach a granite post marking the Massachusetts state line. Continue ahead on the Breakneck Pond View Trail (blue and red blazes).
6. At 3.2 miles, bear left to cross the north end of Breakneck Pond on a causeway.
7. At 4.5 miles, pass through a campsite.
8. At 5.2 miles, close the loop around Breakneck Pond, turn right at the concrete stanchions and map table, and return to the trailhead via Park Road and the East Ridge Trail.

FIND THE TRAILHEAD

From I-84, Exit 73 in Union, drive north on CT Route 190 for 2.1 miles, then turn right on CT Route 171. Follow CT Route 171 for 1.4 miles, then turn left into Bigelow Hollow State Park–Nipmuck State Forest. Follow Bigelow Hollow Road for 0.7 miles to trailhead parking on the left at Bigelow Pond, passing the park entrance station and an information kiosk en route.

TAYLOR BROOKE BREWERY

With a pint of the popular No Room to Swing a Cat IPA in hand, there's plenty of room to roam on the sprawling 46-acre farmstead that's home to Taylor Brooke Brewery. Located pretty much in the middle of nowhere in rural Woodstock, the big red dairy barn–like brewery is tucked into the grassy slopes of Rocky Hill adjacent to Taylor Brooke Winery and surrounded by tall trees, vineyards and gardens. Pull up an Adirondack chair, sit down at a picnic table or bring your own camp chair and join happy beer lovers from near and far for fun conversation, cornhole, trivia and live music. Order up some good chow from the rotating food trucks (think pit BBQ, sourdough pizza and lobster rolls), settle in for a spell, and the next thing you know you'll be enjoying one of Taylor Brooke's fantastic sunsets.

LAND MANAGER

Bigelow Hollow State Park
c/o Shenipsit State Forest
(860) 684-3430
Info and trail map: portal.ct.gov/DEEP/State-Parks/Parks/Bigelow-Hollow-State-Park-Nipmuck-State-Forest

BREWERY

Taylor Brooke Brewery
818 CT Route 171
Woodstock, CT 06281
(860) 315-7503
www.taylorbrookebrewery.com
Distance from trailhead: 11 miles

DEVIL'S HOPYARD

60 FOOT CHAPMAN FALLS STEALS THE SHOW ON THIS HIKE

EAST HADDAM, CT

▷··· STARTING POINT	···✗ DESTINATION
FOXTOWN ROAD	**CHAPMAN FALLS, TABLET ROCK**
🍺 BEER	🎲 HIKE TYPE
JUICY IN THE 860 NEIPA	**EASY-MODERATE** 🚶 🎒
🐾 DOG FRIENDLY	📅 SEASON
YES (LEASH REQUIRED)	**YEAR-ROUND**
💲 FEES	🕐 DURATION
NO	**1 HOUR 40 MIN.**
⌂ MAP REFERENCE	↦ LENGTH
DEVIL'S HOPYARD STATE PARK	**2.8 MILES (LOOP)**
👁 HIGHLIGHTS	〰 ELEVATION GAIN
THUNDERING WATERFALL, ROCK OUTLOOK, SCENIC RIVER	**470 FEET**

7.0 %
ALCOHOL CONTENT

NEW ENGLAND IPA

HAZY GOLD/ORANGE

CITRUS
TROPICAL

PASSION FRUIT
MANGO

BITTERNESS

SWEETNESS

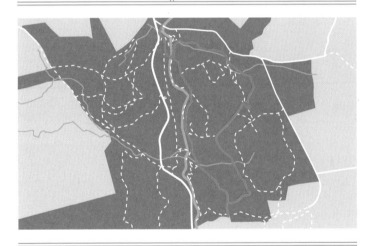

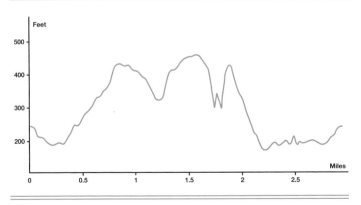

HIKE DESCRIPTION

Devil's Hopyard is highlighted by 60-foot Chapman Falls on the wild and scenic Eight Mile River, while Hop Culture Farms features Juicy in the 860, an unfiltered, pulpy and delicious New England IPA.

Established in 1919, the 900-acre Devil's Hopyard State Park features an extensive network of hiking trails, as well as outstanding birding and excellent trout fishing. This hike combines the White Trail and the Vista Trail for a nice loop through the woods of Devil's Hopyard, beginning with Chapman Falls, the park's signature natural attraction. Head for the base of the falls for a fabulous view of the 60-foot, three-step drop over the rocks of Scotland schist.

The origin of the name Devil's Hopyard is steeped in lore and legend. A farmer named Dibble is said to have grown a garden of hops that he used for brewing beer. Over time, "Dibble's Hopyard" morphed into "Devil's Hopyard." Another tale has to do with the natural potholes near the falls—some as large as several feet in diameter—formed by the action of stone and water over the eons. Supposedly, the Devil passed by the falls, got his tail wet, and became so enraged that he burned these holes in the rock. The supernatural accounts continue with alleged sightings of Satan sitting on a boulder atop the falls, playing his violin while the witches of East Haddam brewed an evil potion in the potholes. Fact or fiction? You decide, but it's certainly fun to consider as you enjoy Chapman Falls.

After Chapman Falls, you'll cross Eight Mile River on a covered pedestrian bridge. Follow the White Trail left along the river to a pool at the base of the falls. For the next 0.5 miles, the trail ascends along a brook through a narrow valley of mountain laurel, pine and hemlock, oak, poplar and beech. There's a brook to hop across before you level out on the ridge above. Passing several trails leading to the park's backcountry camping sites, you'll eventually wander down to the Vista Trail. This wide, rooty, eroded path climbs back to the ridge and soon arrives at a side trail leading to Tablet Rock.

It's a few hundred feet to the open ledges of Tablet Rock, which look south over the bucolic valley of the Eight Mile River. This exceptional river, the most prized in the Lower Connecticut River region, is under consideration for federal designation as a Wild and Scenic River. In fact, the region, also called "the Tidelands," is so ecologically valuable that it was named one of the 40 "last great places in the Western Hemisphere" by The Nature Conservancy. From the Tablet Rock junction, the Vista Trail returns to the Eight Mile River. Not far ahead, a short, steep side trail leads to Devil's Oven, a shallow cave in the cliffside rocks. Continue on to the covered bridge and make your way back to the Foxtown Road trailhead, no doubt with another stop at Chapman Falls.

TURN-BY-TURN DIRECTIONS

1. From the information kiosk, cross Foxtown Road and descend along Chapman Falls to a spur on the left, which leads to the base of the falls.
2. At 0.2 miles, cross Eight Mile River on a covered pedestrian bridge, then turn left on the White Trail (white blazes).
3. At 1.3 miles, turn left on the Vista Trail (orange blazes).
4. At 1.6 miles, a spur trail on the left leads several hundred feet to a lookout at Tablet Rock.
5. At 2.2 miles, a side trail on the right climbs up to Devil's Oven.
6. At 2.6 miles, turn left to recross Eight Mile River via the covered bridge.
7. At 2.8 miles, end the hike at the original Chapman Falls trailhead.

FIND THE TRAILHEAD

If traveling southbound on I-95: From Exit 70 in Old Lyme, follow US Route 1 south for 0.7 miles to the junction with CT Route 156. *If traveling northbound on I-95:* From Exit 70, drive north under the overpass to the junction of US Route 1 and CT Route 156. From this common point at the junction of US Route 1 and CT Route 156, continue north on CT Route 156 for 8.4 miles. Turn right onto CT Route 82, and in 0.2 miles, turn left on Hopyard Road. In 3.1 miles, pass the entrance to Devil's Hopyard State Park on the right. Drive another 0.3 miles and then turn right on Foxtown Road. The parking area for Chapman Falls is immediately on the left.

HOP CULTURE FARMS & BREW COMPANY

"Great Beer Grows Here" at the family-owned and operated Hop Culture Farms in the rural countryside of Colchester. Longtime homebrewers Heather and Sam Wilson, a nurse practitioner and firefighter respectively, purchased the 40-acre plot in 2017. Over the next two years, despite being novice farmers, the pair successfully turned the land into a working hops farm and opened their craft brewery and taproom in a converted cattle barn. Sitting outdoors in the grassy field out back is a bit like attending a fun family reunion, with happy beer drinkers convening around community tables, kids and dogs cavorting about, live music filling the air, and an assortment of delicious munchies being handed out the food truck window. Juicy in the 860, a veritable juice bomb of a New England IPA, is the flagship among Hop Culture's diverse craft offerings.

LAND MANAGER

Devil's Hopyard State Park
366 Hopyard Road
East Haddam, CT 06423
(860) 526-2336
Info and trail map: portal.ct.gov/DEEP/State-Parks/Parks/Devils-Hop-yard-State-Park

BREWERY

Hop Culture Farms & Brew Company
144 Cato Corner Road
Colchester CT, 06415
(860) 305-9556
hopculturefarms.com
Distance from trailhead: 8.7 miles

LAKE ZOAR

HIKE ALONG A LARGE RESERVOIR ON THE HOUSATONIC RIVER

SANDY HOOK, CT

▷··· STARTING POINT	···✕ DESTINATION
GREAT QUARTER ROAD	LAKE ZOAR, PRYDDEN BROOK FALLS
🍺 BEER	🔀 HIKE TYPE
BLIMP NEIPA	**MODERATE** 🚶
🐾 DOG FRIENDLY	📅 SEASON
YES (LEASH REQUIRED)	APRIL TO NOVEMBER
$ FEES	🕐 DURATION
NO	**3 HOURS 40 MIN.**
⛰ MAP REFERENCE	↦ LENGTH
PAUGUSSETT STATE FOREST– LOWER BLOCK	**6.5 MILES (LOOP)**
🔎 HIGHLIGHTS	〰 ELEVATION GAIN
SCENIC RESERVOIR, WATERFALL, OUTCROPS, LEDGES	**850 FEET**

NEW ENGLAND IPA

STRAW YELLOW/ORANGE

PEACH
NECTARINE
STONE FRUIT

TROPICAL
CITRUS

BITTERNESS   SWEETNESS

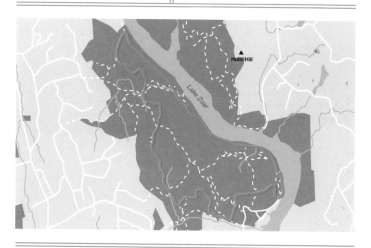

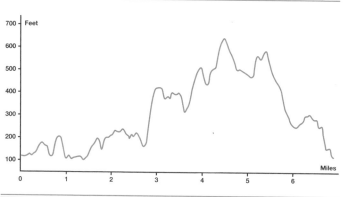

HIKE DESCRIPTION

Amble along Lake Zoar on this scenic loop through Paugussett State Forest. Then get pleasantly lost in your thoughts with a fine pint of Blimp NEIPA at Reverie Brewing.

The Zoar Trail winds for more than six pleasant miles through the southern portion or "lower block" of Paugussett State Forest, a 1,200-acre expanse of woodlands owned by the Connecticut Department of Energy and Environmental Protection along a dammed stretch of the Housatonic River. The trail is maintained by the Connecticut Forest & Park Association as part of its Blue-Blazed Hiking Trails System, an impressive 825 miles of marked hiking trails across the state.

Lake Zoar is a 975-acre reservoir that backs up a 10-mile stretch of the Housatonic River, which flows 149 miles southward from its source in northern Berkshire County in western Massachusetts through western Connecticut before emptying into Long Island Sound. The lake (and the hiking trail) is named for the community of Zoar that was flooded after the Stevenson Dam, a couple miles downriver from the Zoar Trail trail-head, was completed in 1919.

Follow the Zoar Trail's blue blazes to the west shore of Lake Zoar, then turn north to hike the route counterclockwise. Depending upon the water level, you may be able to access several small beach areas as you hike along the lake, which features some 27 miles of scenic shoreline. You're also likely to share the view with anglers fishing for trout and other game fish. The route along Lake Zoar undulates through a forest of oak and hemlock, from the water's edge to the hillside above and back, with filtered views of the hills on the opposite side. It's not long before the Oxford town beach at Jackson Cove Park comes into view where the lake bends to the west. Beyond that point, you're looking across at the lands of Kettletown State Park.

Not quite two miles into the hike, at a spot high on a bluff above the lake, an unmarked spur trail on the right leads to Prydden Brook Falls, a 35-foot plunge and cascade drop. The pretty falls are seasonal, so if it's a dry spell, the falls may be too. The Zoar Trail angles down to Lake Zoar one last time around the 2.5-mile mark. Take a good look, because soon after you'll bear sharply left and away from the lake to begin a steady climb up the west slope via switchbacks and rock stairs.

Several old forest roads coincide with and cross the main trail over the next 3 miles or so as you meander southeast on a rolling course of wooded outcrops and ledges through the quiet backcountry of Paugussett State Forest west of the lake. You can avoid any confusion en route by sticking with the blue blazes of the Zoar Trail. You'll cross back over Prydden Brook on your way to a cold glass of post-hike craft beer.

TURN-BY-TURN DIRECTIONS

1. From the trailhead information kiosk, bear right into the woods, following the blue blazes of the Zoar Trail along the west shore of Lake Zoar.
2. At 1.6 miles, an unmarked spur on the right leads to Prydden Brook Falls.
3. At 1.8 miles, a marked spur on the right leads back to the falls.
4. At 1.9 miles, where the Blue/White Trail goes left, bear right to stay on the Zoar Trail.
5. At 2.6 miles, the Zoar Trail turns sharply left away from Lake Zoar to climb the slope beyond.
6. At 3.4 miles, the Blue/White Trail enters from the right; continue ahead on the Zoar Trail on an old forest road and soon cross Prydden Brook on a footbridge.
7. At 4.7 miles, the Blue/Red Trail merges from the right and both trails cross the brook ahead; follow the Zoar Trail as it turns sharply right while the Red/White Trail goes sharply left.
8. At 4.9 miles, where the Blue/Yellow Trail leaves to the right, bear left to continue.
9. At 5.7 miles, follow the Zoar Trail on the path to the left where the Blue/Yellow Trail goes straight on an old forest road.
10. At 6.2 miles, continue straight where the Blue/White Trail crosses the Zoar Trail just 0.3 miles from the end of the loop.

FIND THE TRAILHEAD

From I-81, Exit 11 in Newtown, turn right on CT Route 34. In 4.9 miles, turn left on Great Quarter Road. Trailhead parking is at the end of the road 1.3 miles ahead.

REVERIE BREWING CO.

The renovated industrial space at Reverie Brewing, once a mechanic shop for working on coach buses, is now a large tasting room resplendent with a beautiful bar and wooden tables. Walls painted a warm and welcoming gentle blue feature a splashy mural that defines the place: "Don't Quit Your Daydream" is the modus operandi for the brewery's founders, who all daydreamed of owning their own operation before turning their reverie into reality in 2018. Variety is what pours from Reverie's twelve rotating tap lines, and Blimp, a juicy NEIPA that bears the Reverie blimp logo, will have you pleasantly relaxed and lost in your own thoughts in no time. Outdoor patio seating and tent space complete the family-friendly community feel. BYOF or sample something delish from the regular food truck lineup.

LAND MANAGER

Connecticut Dept. of Energy and Environmental Protection
(860) 424-3000
Trail map: portal.ct.gov/-/media/DEEP/stateparks/maps/Paugus-settSouthpdf.

TRAIL MANAGER

Connecticut Forest & Park Association
(860) 346-8733
Info: www.ctwoodlands.org/blue-blazed-hiking-trails/zoar-trail

BREWERY

Reverie Brewing Co.
57B Church Hill Road
Newtown, CT 06470
(203) 872-2124
reveriebrewing.com
Distance from trailhead: 8 miles

MACEDONIA RIDGE

HIKE A ROLLING RIDGELINE CIRCUIT HIGH ABOVE MACEDONIA BROOK

KENT, CT

▷··· STARTING POINT	···✗ DESTINATION
MACEDONIA BROOK ROAD	**COBBLE MOUNTAIN**
🍺 BEER	📅 HIKE TYPE
GENTLE ON MY MIND NEIPA	**STRENUOUS**
🐾 DOG FRIENDLY	📅 SEASON
YES (LEASH REQUIRED)	**MAY TO OCTOBER**
$ FEES	🕐 DURATION
NO	**4 HOURS**
⛰ MAP REFERENCE	↦ LENGTH
MACEDONIA BROOK STATE PARK	**6.5 MILES (LOOP)**
🔎 HIGHLIGHTS	〰 ELEVATION GAIN
WOODED RIDGES, RUSHING BROOK, POND, LEDGE OUTLOOKS	**1,550 FEET**

NEW ENGLAND IPA

HAZY APRICOT

CITRUS
TROPICAL

TANGERINE
GRAPEFRUIT

BITTERNESS

SWEETNESS

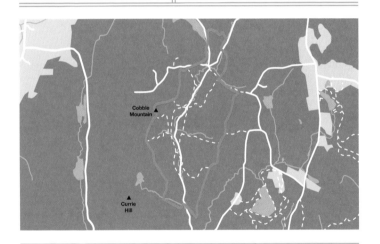

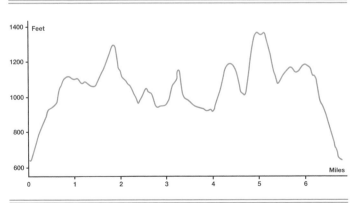

HIKE DESCRIPTION

Follow the wooded ridges encircling the valley of Macedonia Brook to Cobble Mountain for expansive views west into New York. Then enjoy a delicious pint and a game of cornhole in the riverside beer garden at Housatonic River Brewing.

The Macedonia Ridge Trail makes a circuit over the wooded peaks and ridges on the east and west sides of rushing Macedonia Brook, which slices through the heart of Macedonia Brook State Park. Established in 1918, the park encompasses 2,300 acres in the Litchfield Hills of far western Connecticut along its boundary with New York. The Macedonia Ridge Trail is the longest of the color-coded hiking trails that depart from Macedonia Brook Road in the central valley that extends the length of the park. This blue-blazed hike is described in a counterclockwise direction. It crosses rolling terrain, so be prepared for a healthy dose of ups and downs.

From the start, it's a fairly steady climb to gain the eastern ridgeline. You'll get occasional views of Cobble Mountain as you amble north along the ridge through the oak and hickory woods with their understory of huckleberry and blueberry. An old stone fireplace and beautiful stone walls punctuate the route. Reach a saddle, then descend to an old forest road. Within sight of one of the park's camping areas, leave the road and take the trail out to Keeler Road, where you'll cross Macedonia Brook to the west side of the valley.

Crest the ridge beyond, then descend through hemlocks on tight switchbacks to reach Hilltop Pond, where the grassy promenade atop the earthen dam provides a sweet spot for a break. In the next half-mile

or so, you'll pass by three gates, cross a couple roads and follow a wide old stone-lined road built by the Civilian Conservation Corps in the early 1930s. Beyond Chippewalla Road and a fourth gate, the climbing begins again. Atop the first hill, you'll enjoy nice views to the west and south from an open ledge. Next, the trail makes its way down sloping ledges and a steep rocky pitch. Continue into a ravine, then ascend steeply over rocks. Scramble up an interesting crevice, then up the rock face above.

Once atop the 1,350-foot summit ridge of Cobble Mountain, numerous open ledges facing west provide excellent views to New York's Taconic Range, and some 35 miles farther, to the high peaks of the Catskills, the home of some 30 peaks over 3,500 feet in elevation. All too soon, you'll drop down off the peak to follow a mildly undulating route along the mountain's south ridge. Six miles into the hike, enjoy the last of the views from ledges, this time of the opposite ridge to the east and along Macedonia Brook valley to the south.

TURN-BY-TURN DIRECTIONS

1. From the trailhead, follow Macedonia Brook Road south across the bridge; then turn left onto the blue-blazed Macedonia Ridge Trail.
2. At 2.8 miles, after passing junctions with the Yellow Trail, the Green Trail and the Orange Trail, arrive at Keeler Road. Turn left along the road, cross the bridge, and then turn right to stay on the Macedonia Ridge Trail.
3. At 3.4 miles, reach a spur on the right to Hilltop Pond, and not far ahead, emerge on Weber Road. Turn left here along the road toward a trailhead parking area; then walk around a green gate onto an old CCC road.
4. At 3.9 miles, pass around a gate, cross paved Chippewalla Road, pass around the next gate, and just ahead, take the trail on the right into the woods.
5. At 4.5 miles, the Green Trail joins from the left; keep on straight ahead.
6. At 4.8 miles, reach the summit ridge of Cobble Mountain, which offers several outstanding open ledges facing west over the next quarter mile. The White Trail joins the route and then departs during this stretch.
7. At 6.0 miles, enjoy the last of the views before commencing the descent to the valley.

FIND THE TRAILHEAD

From US Route 7 and CT Route 341 in Kent, drive north on CT Route 341. In 1.8 miles, turn right on Macedonia Brook Road and follow this for 1.5 miles. The road turns to dirt just 0.1 miles before the unsigned trailhead, on the left just after a bridge over Macedonia Brook.

HOUSATONIC RIVER BREWING

The rustic taproom interior at Housatonic River Brewing looks a lot like a log cabin, and with its large fieldstone fireplace, barrel tables and long wood bar, it's just the right place for cozying up with a pint. It has exactly the comfortable, woodsy atmosphere that Dave Littlefield, the founder, brewer and chief bottle washer, was aiming for when he opened the place in 2018. The 7-acre riverside property also features a lively beer garden complete with picnic tables, big wire spools for sitting around, and firepits. Along with live music or a friendly game of cornhole, there are eleven diverse taps of the good stuff to enjoy. Apricot-colored and oh so juicy, Gentle on My Mind is the ever-popular New England IPA. Bar snacks and rotating local food trucks help stave off the munchies.

LAND MANAGER

Macedonia Brook State Park
159 Macedonia Brook Road
Kent, CT 06757
(860) 927-3238 Info and trail map: portal.ct.gov/DEEP/State-Parks/
Parks/Macedonia-Brook-State-Park

BREWERY

Housatonic River Brewing
30 Kent Road
New Milford, CT 06776
(860) 946-0266
www.housatonicriverbrewing.com
Distance from trailhead: 17 miles

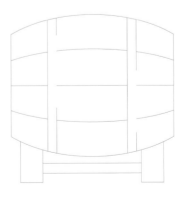

RAGGED MOUNTAIN

REVEL IN EXTENSIVE VIEWS FROM ATOP RUGGED TRAPROCK CLIFFS

BERLIN, CT

▷⋯ STARTING POINT	⋯✗ DESTINATION
WEST LANE	**RAGGED MOUNTAIN SUMMIT**
🍺 BEER	🗺 HIKE TYPE
PAUPER'S PORRIDGE OATMEAL AMBER ALE	**MODERATE**
🐾 DOG FRIENDLY	📅 SEASON
YES (LEASH REQUIRED)	**MARCH TO NOVEMBER**
$ FEES	🕐 DURATION
NO	**3 HOURS**
🗻 MAP REFERENCE	↦ LENGTH
RAGGED MOUNTAIN PRESERVE TRAIL SYSTEM	**5.7 MILES (LOOP)**
🔍 HIGHLIGHTS	〰 ELEVATION GAIN
TRAPROCK CLIFFS, PONDS, RESERVOIRS, ROCK CLIMBERS	**650 FEET**

6.0% ALCOHOL CONTENT

OATMEAL AMBER ALE

DEEP TAN/AMBER

OATMEAL

BISCUIT
CARAMEL
TOASTED OATS

BITTERNESS

SWEETNESS

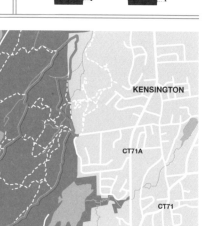

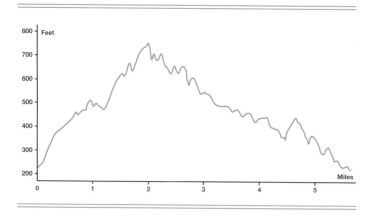

HIKE DESCRIPTION

Take a circuit hike on Ragged Mountain for extensive views from atop its rugged traprock cliffs. Then ease into a Pauper's Porridge oatmeal amber, "the cure for what ales you," at Witchdoctor Brewing.

Reaching to 761 feet above the Quinnipiac River Valley, Ragged Mountain is one of the most popular hiking destinations in Connecticut, rewarding hikers with outstanding vistas from its high bluffs and ledges. The mountain and its 563 acres are protected and managed cooperatively by several conservation and recreation advocates. This hike combines the Ragged Mountain Preserve Trail and the New England Trail (NET) for a scenic loop over the mountain.

Climb gently on the Preserve Trail to attain Ragged's ridge, then hike along its steep eastern face. Upper Hart Pond comes into view as you weave between rock outcrops. There are numerous viewpoints over the course of the next mile as the ascent continues, interrupted occasionally by small ravines that require some scrambling. Lovely Lower Hart Pond soon appears below as the trail climbs a narrow ridge to a detached slab.

Feel free to explore any and every lookout on the way to meeting the New England Trail, which enters from the left though a rock crevice. The NET, federally designated in 2009, extends 215 miles from Long Island Sound through Connecticut and Massachusetts to the Vermont border, following portions of the historic Mattabesett, Metacomet and Monadnock trail systems. After a few more minor ups and downs, the NET reaches the main summit cliffs and an extraordinary vista that

takes in West Peak (look for the multiple antennas on its top) in the Hanging Hills to the south, as well as Wassel Reservoir and Shuttle Meadow Reservoir to the north.

On this southwestern edge of Ragged Mountain, you may find brightly colored ropes anchored to the rock and climbers with clanking gear tackling the impossibly vertical traprock or volcanic basalt cliffs amid shouts of climbing lingo like "Belay on!" and "Climbing!" Ragged is the state's most popular traditional climbing venue, with routes for all abilities. The cliffs were once owned by Stanley Hart, who wanted the property to be forever protected. Shortly before he passed away in 1989, Hart donated the land to The Nature Conservancy, and 10 years later, ownership was transferred to the Ragged Mountain Foundation to support its continuing efforts to protect access to high and wild places across Connecticut.

From the clifftop, the NET follows the northwestern margin of Ragged Mountain for the next 2 miles on a mildly undulating but gradually descending route to the northern edge of the peak. From here you'll scamper around the mountain's northeastern base, then climb a ravine past a seasonal cascade to rejoin the ridge before making the final descent to close the loop and return to the trailhead at West Lane.

TURN-BY-TURN DIRECTIONS

1. Go past the brown gate to the information kiosk, then proceed to a junction; bear left, and soon after, bear left again, following the blue and red blazes of the Preserve Trail.

2. At 0.8 miles, the Blue/Yellow Trail enters from the right; continue ahead on the Preserve Trail.

3. At 1.6 miles, turn right to join the blue-blazed New England Trail.

4. At 2.0 miles, reach the summit cliffs atop Ragged Mountain.

5. At 2.7 miles, the Blue/Yellow Trail leaves to the right; continue straight on the NET.

6. At 3.4 miles, the Blue/Orange Trail leaves to the right; bear left to continue on the NET.

7. At 4.1 miles, at a three-way junction where the NET continues to the left and the Blue/White Trail goes to the right, continue straight ahead on the Preserve Trail (blue and red blazes).

8. At 5.0 miles, after climbing a ravine past a small cascade (seasonal), the Blue/White Trail enters from the right; continue left on the Preserve Trail.

9. At 5.6 miles, close the loop and bear left to reach the trailhead in 0.1 miles.

FIND THE TRAILHEAD

In Berlin, at the junction of CT Route 71A and West Lane, drive west on West Lane for 0.5 miles; roadside parking for Ragged Mountain Memorial Preserve is on the right.

WITCHDOCTOR BREWING COMPANY

Witchdoctor Brewing is the anchor tenant in the renovated Factory Square Building, which dates back to 1883, when it first opened as Southington Tool Manufacturing. The taproom is a warm, rich space that features lots of exposed wood and brick, Edison lighting and a long bar. Operations Manager and Brewer Josh Norris says Witchdoctor has the "cure for what ales you," and no doubt among the 16 taps there's a little something for everyone. Pauper's Porridge, a smooth oatmeal amber ale with biscuit and caramel notes, is one of the original brews and a staple on the menu. Darts, pool, board games, cornhole and live music make Witchdoctor a go-to spot for good times.

LAND MANAGER

Town of Berlin Parks and Recreation
230 Kensington Road
Berlin, CT 06037
(860) 828-7009

TRAIL MANAGER

Connecticut Forest & Park Association
(860) 346-8733
Trail map: www.ctwoodlands.org/sites/default/files/Ragged New Trail Map.pdf

BREWERY

Witchdoctor Brewing Company
168 Center Street
Southington, CT 06489
(860) 426-1924
witchdoctorbrewing.com
Distance from trailhead: 7.8 miles

TALCOTT MOUNTAIN

CLIMB THE HEUBLEIN TOWER FOR SPECTACULAR MOUNTAINTOP VIEWS

SIMSBURY, CT

▷⋯ STARTING POINT	⋯✕ DESTINATION
SUMMIT RIDGE DRIVE	**HEUBLEIN TOWER**
🍺 BEER	🁢 HIKE TYPE
CITRA NITRA NEIPA	**MODERATE** 🚶
🐾 DOG FRIENDLY	📅 SEASON
YES (LEASH REQUIRED)	**MARCH TO NOVEMBER**
$ FEES	⏲ DURATION
NO	**2 HOURS 20 MIN.**
⛰ MAP REFERENCE	↦ LENGTH
TALCOTT MOUNTAIN STATE PARK	**4.1 MILES (LOOP)**
🔍 HIGHLIGHTS	〰 ELEVATION GAIN
HISTORIC SUMMIT TOWER, CLIFFTOP LOOKOUTS, SCENIC VALLEY	**640 FEET**

NEW ENGLAND IPA

HAZY GOLD

CITRUS
TROPICAL FRUIT

CITRUS
TROPICAL FRUIT

BITTERNESS   SWEETNESS

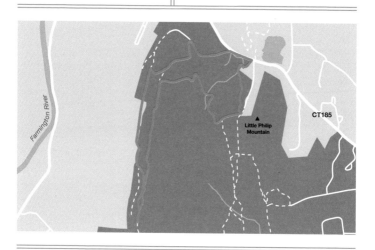

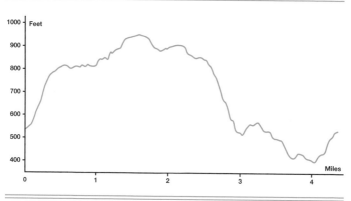

HIKE DESCRIPTION

Wander along the precipitous western escarpment of Talcott Mountain to the marvelous 165-foot Heublein Tower for spectacular views. Then head for Hopmeadow Brewing and a Citra Nitra, a juicy New England IPA that's been "hopped to hell."

Rising to 950 feet above the Farmington River Valley, Talcott Mountain is crowned by the 165-foot Heublein Tower, one of Connecticut's most popular hiking destinations. The tower is the former summer home and retreat of Gilbert Heublein, the food and beverage magnate (think A1 Steak Sauce and Smirnoff Vodka), and 565 acres around it are preserved as Talcott Mountain State Park.

This hike combines the Yellow Trail with a portion of the New England Trail (NET) for a great loop hike. Starting on the Yellow Trail, you'll climb up a ravine to the ridgeline. Here, rather than following the Yellow Trail through the woods, walk along the unmarked paths on the lip of the precipitous west face of Talcott Mountain for the next half-mile or so. Many lookouts make this gently rolling stretch a lot of fun, with great views over the scenic valley.

When you rejoin the Yellow Trail, it's just a short climb to meet the NET, which leads easily to the base of the spectacular stone Heublein Tower. The museum inside welcomes visitors; hikers are invited to climb to the observation lounge on the top floor, where it's possible to see the Hartford skyline to the east, the Berkshires in Massachusetts to the northwest, Mount Monadnock in southern New Hampshire to the northeast and a sliver of Long Island Sound to the south. Should the tower be closed when you arrive, the view from the piazza is also quite lovely.

Hiking Talcott Mountain with his fiancée, Louise Gundlach, Gilbert Heublein promised to build her a castle on the peak. True to his word, Heublein Tower was completed in 1914, an architectural marvel that resembled structures in Heublein's native Bavaria in Germany. In 1943, the tower was purchased by the *Hartford Times* newspaper, and finally, threatened by development, it was conserved as public property in 1965.

From the tower steps, wander ahead through the park-like summit area. A signpost on the way to the picnic pavilion marks the tri-corner boundary of the towns of Avon, Simsbury and Bloomfield. From the pavilion, retrace your steps to the tower, then follow the NET north over the narrow ridge. A half-mile along, the NET leaves the ridge and descends the mountain's east slope to return to CT Route 185, not far from the trailhead.

TURN-BY-TURN DIRECTIONS

1. From the information kiosk, pass the brown gate and follow the Yellow Trail, an old carriage road, toward Heublein Tower.
2. At 0.4 miles, where the Yellow Trail goes left, veer right on another old road leading up and then left to the ridge crest.
3. At 0.6 miles, the unmarked old road rejoins the Yellow Trail. In 200 feet, step right to a viewpoint, then continue on an unmarked foot trail along the edge of the precipice.
4. At 1.0 miles, turn right onto the wide Yellow Trail.
5. At 1.2 miles, the blue-blazed New England Trail enters from the left; turn right to follow the trail, now marked with blue and yellow blazes.
6. At 1.3 miles, bear right to stay on the NET and reach the base of Heublein Tower.
7. At 1.4 miles, pass a signpost marking the intersection of the Avon, Simsbury and Bloomfield town lines.
8. At 1.5 miles, reach a pavilion, your turnaround point. Return to the tower, then follow the Yellow Trail around the tower's right side to join the NET.
9. At 1.8 miles, bear right on the NET and follow it across the ridge and then down the mountain's east side.
10. At 3.1 miles, the red- and blue-blazed Metacomet Bypass goes right; stay left to continue on the NET.
11. At 3.7 miles, turn left to walk along CT Route 185 to the park entrance road; bear left on it and return to the trailhead at 4.1 miles.

FIND THE TRAILHEAD

From either I-91 or I-84 in Hartford, travel west on US Route 44 for about 4 miles. At the junction of US Route 44 and CT Route 218 in West Hartford, turn right on CT Route 218. In 1.4 miles, turn left on CT Route 185 and drive 3.1 miles to the entrance of Talcott Mountain State Park on the left. Follow Summit Ridge Drive for 0.7 miles to trailhead parking on either side of the road.

HOPMEADOW BREWING CO.

Hopmeadow Brewing is nestled in the Farmington River Valley a mile south of historic US Route 44 in Avon. Longtime homebrewer Bryan Hickey opened the small-batch brewery in an old industrial space in the summer of 2020 and turned it into a hopping good spot to "hop into craft beer." Hop vines appear on the town seal of neighboring Simsbury, and Hickey grew up in Granby, the next town over, and traveled Hopmeadow Street every day for years—so giving the brewery a name was a bit of a no-brainer. Hopmeadow specializes in IPAs (try the

"hopped to hell" Citra Nitra NEIPA), stouts, fruited sours and lagers. With 18 taps plus two side-pours from the Czech Republic, there's plenty to enjoy amid the fun, relaxed vibe of this craft brewery gem. Rotating food trucks serve up tasty grub every day.

LAND MANAGER

Talcott Mountain State Park
c/o Penwood State Park
57 Gun Mill Road
Bloomfield, CT 06002
(860) 242-1158
Info and trail map: portal.ct.gov/DEEP/State-Parks/Parks/Talcott-Mountain-State-Park

BREWERY

Hopmeadow Brewing Company
205 Old Farms Road
Avon, Connecticut 06001
(860) 470-5787
www.hopmeadowbrewingcompany.com
Distance from trailhead: 5.7 miles

VERMONT

ADAMS RESERVOIR

ENJOY A STROLL AROUND A BEAUTIFUL RESERVOIR

BENNINGTON, VT

▷⋯ STARTING POINT	⋯✕ DESTINATION
RESERVOIR TRAIL TRAILHEAD	**ADAMS RESERVOIR LOOP**
🍺 BEER	▦ HIKE TYPE
OLD 76 STRONG ALE	**EASY** 🚶
🐾 DOG FRIENDLY	📅 SEASON
YES (LEASH REQUIRED)	**MAY TO OCTOBER**
$ FEES	🕐 DURATION
YES	**1 HOUR 20 MIN.**
⌂ MAP REFERENCE	↦ LENGTH
WOODFORD STATE PARK HIKING TRAILS	**2.4 MILES (LOOP)**
🔍 HIGHLIGHTS	〜 ELEVATION GAIN
SCENIC RESERVOIR, WILDERNESS AREA, SWIMMING AREA	**160 FEET**

YORKSHIRE ALE

DARK AMBER BROWN

MALTY

HINT OF WHISKY
MALTY SWEET

BITTERNESS

SWEETNESS

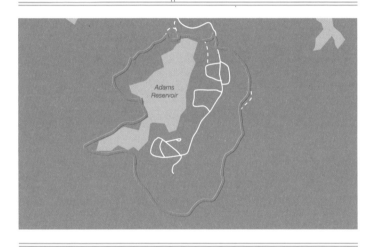

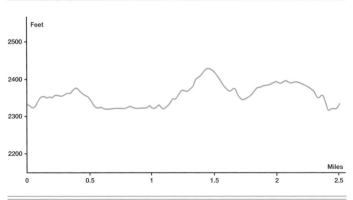

HIKE DESCRIPTION

Take a wooded stroll around scenic Adams Reservoir, situated on a mountain plateau in one of the highest elevation state parks in Vermont. Madison Brewing in the heart of historic downtown Bennington awaits you after your walk.

Located on a mountain plateau at 2,400 feet, Woodford State Park is one of the highest state parks in Vermont. Established in 1963, the park's 398-acre expanse encompasses Adams Reservoir, known for its trophy brook trout fishery. There's a large campground on the east shore of the reservoir, which was created in the early 19th century to power several sawmills.

The Reservoir Trail (also signed as the Reservoir Loop Trail and named on some trail maps as the Woodford Trail), circumnavigates Adams Reservoir. The trail officially leaves from the west side of the trailhead parking lot, but you'll make an alternate start by walking through the brown gateway to the north end of Adams Reservoir. Enjoy some quality time on the grassy promenade and the beach before you begin the counterclockwise route around the reservoir. Halfway along the west side is the narrowest part; step out on the point here to enjoy the view up and down the lake. It's one of a number of opportunities en route to get a nice water view.

Soon after, the Reservoir Trail leaves the state park and enters the Green Mountain National Forest (GMNF), which surrounds the park. After several footbridges and a path leading to the park campground, there's a sign indicating that you're now walking, for a short stretch anyway, through the George D. Aiken Wilderness, a 5,060-acre chunk of wildland that's part of GMNF. The Reservoir Trail makes a gentle ascent away from the reservoir, then meanders in a wide arc around the campground, which is well out of sight, obscured by the woods of maple, birch, beech and spruce. As the trail nears the campground road a couple miles along, the lean-to sites nearest the trail can be seen through the trees.

After the campground road, it's not long before you reach the picnic area and playground on the north end of the lake. Enjoy this last open stretch across the earthen dam before crossing the spillway, which was reconstructed in 1969, and closing the loop.

TURN-BY-TURN DIRECTIONS

1. At the parking area, avoid the official start of the Reservoir Trail (also signed en route as the Reservoir Loop Trail) and walk south to the beach area on Adams Reservoir.

2. From the beach, walk back a few yards toward the parking area, then turn left on the Reservoir Trail, which leads 500 feet to the main Reservoir Trail. Turn left here to continue.

3. At 0.1 miles and again at 0.2 miles, avoid the Atwood Loop on the left.

4. At 1.1 miles, a trail on the left leads to the park campground; continue to the right.

5. At 2.2 miles, turn right along the campground road; then ahead, turn left back onto the trail.

6. At a junction at 2.3 miles, bear right to reach the grassy earthen dam at the north end of Adams Reservoir.

7. Cross a footbridge to close the loop; then turn right to return to the trailhead.

FIND THE TRAILHEAD

From the junction of US Route 7 and VT Route 9 in downtown Bennington, drive east on VT Route 9 for 10.7 miles to the entrance of Woodford State Park on the right. Follow the park road past the campground office to the trailhead parking for the Reservoir Trail 0.2 miles from the entrance.

MADISON BREWING COMPANY PUB & RESTAURANT

Mel Madison was fresh out of college when he and his hospitality-experienced family, who had strong ties to the area, established Madison Brewing Company in 1996 in the heart of historic downtown Bennington. Located in a warm and welcoming converted storefront, Madison Brewing has grown into a regional institution, a wildly popular spot for craft beer and great food among locals and visitors alike. Old 76 Strong Ale is one of the brewery's originals and a staple among the eclectic mix of 13 brews on tap. The place's family-friendly, neighborhood tavern feel makes it the perfect spot to enjoy a fine pint, great conversation and some awesome pub grub. Burgers are big and delicious, but there are always daily specials on the full menu, so be sure to ask. Expect the unexpected!

LAND MANAGER

Woodford State Park
142 State Park Road
Bennington, VT 05201
(802) 447-7169
Info: vtstateparks.com/woodford.html
Trail map: vtstateparks.com/assets/pdf/woodford_trails.pdf

BREWERY/RESTAURANT

Madison Brewing Company Pub & Restaurant
428 Main Street
Bennington, VT 05201
(802) 442-7397
madisonbrewingco.com
Distance from trailhead: 11 miles

CAMEL'S HUMP

CLIMB ONE OF VERMONT'S HIGHEST AND MOST RECOGNIZABLE PEAKS

DUXBURY, VT

▷⋯ STARTING POINT	⋯✕ DESTINATION
MONROE TRAIL TRAILHEAD	**CAMEL'S HUMP SUMMIT**
🍺 BEER	HIKE TYPE
BANTAM DOUBLE AMERICAN IPA	**STRENUOUS**
🐾 DOG FRIENDLY	SEASON
YES (LEASH REQUIRED)	**JUNE TO OCTOBER**
$ FEES	⏲ DURATION
NO	**5 HOURS**
⛰ MAP REFERENCE	↦ LENGTH
CAMEL'S HUMP STATE PARK TRAILS GUIDE	**7.1 MILES (LOOP)**
🔍 HIGHLIGHTS	〰 ELEVATION GAIN
PRISTINE ALPINE SUMMIT, 360-DEGREE PANORAMA, LONG TRAIL	**2,625 FEET**

8.0 %
ALCOHOL
CONTENT

AMERICAN DOUBLE IPA

HAZY GOLD/ORANGE

CITRUS
TROPICAL

CITRUS
TROPICAL

BITTERNESS

SWEETNESS

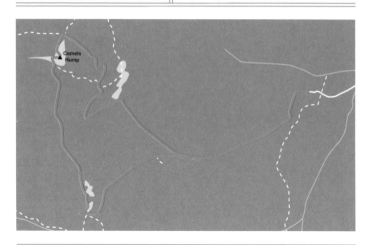

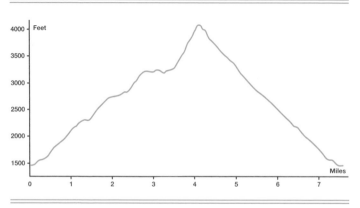

HIKE DESCRIPTION

Hike a grand circuit over Vermont's only undeveloped alpine peak for panoramic views across three states and into Canada. Then head to Waterbury for a refreshing pint and great eats at Prohibition Pig.

With its distinctive double-humped profile and conical summit pinnacle, 4,083-foot Camel's Hump is one of Vermont's highest and most recognizable peaks; it is easily visible from many points throughout the state's north-central region. It's little wonder, then, that the iconic image of Camel's Hump has been featured on the back of the state quarter since 1999. The mountain's unique shape is the result of glacial action eons ago, when powerful ice flows scoured and carved the peak into its present form, which geologists call a *roche moutonnée* or sheep's back.

Native Wabanaki called Camel's Hump "Tah-wak-be-dee-ee-wadso," which translates to "the mountain like a seat." Viewing the mountain from Lake Champlain in the early 1600s, the French explorer Samuel de Champlain called it "lion couchant," or "resting lion." The current name evolved from "Camel's Rump," which appeared on a late 18th-century map produced by the early Vermont settler Ira Allen.

While every other high peak in Vermont sports a ski area and other development, Camel's Hump features the only truly pristine alpine zone. Protection of Camel's Hump began in 1905 with a 1,200-acre

donation by the publisher and philanthropist Joseph Battell. In 1969, Vermont created a state reserve, and today, Camel's Hump State Park totals more than 21,000 acres. The top of the rocky, treeless summit, which is a National Natural Landmark, features 10 acres of fragile alpine terrain; some 5,300 acres on the mountain from the 2,500-foot level up to the peak have been granted protected status.

This circuit hike climbs Camel's Hump from the east, following the Monroe and Dean trails, and then the famous Long Trail up and over the mountain. As with any New England alpine peak, come prepared for possible harsh weather. The hike between Wind Gap and the summit ascends the rugged south ridge and features sections of steep, rocky scrambling. A series of lookouts to the east, south and west make the sweaty effort worthwhile.

The summit rocks of Camel's Hump reward hikers with a magnificent 360-degree panorama. The grand vista ranges east to the White Mountains of New Hampshire and west over the Champlain Valley and Lake Champlain to the Adirondacks in New York. Mount Mansfield, Vermont's highest point, Bolton Mountain, the Worcester Range and Jay Peak are all in view to the north, while a look southward takes in Mount Ethan Allen, Lincoln Peak, Molly Stark Mountain and many others.

TURN-BY-TURN DIRECTIONS

1. Walk west to the end of the upper lot to the trailhead kiosk, enter the woods and follow the blue blazes of the Monroe Trail.
2. Reach a fork at 1.3 miles. Here, the Monroe Trail bears right; bear left to continue on the Dean Trail, and soon after, pass the Hump Brook Tentsite.
3. Pass through Wind Gap to reach a four-way junction at 2.3 miles. To the left is the Allis Trail, while straight ahead is the southbound Long Trail. Turn right on the northbound Long Trail to begin a steep, rocky climb.
4. At 3.7 miles, the Alpine Trail enters from the right. Just ahead, enter the alpine zone high on Camel's Hump.
5. Reach the open summit of Camel's Hump (no sign) at 3.8 miles.
6. At 4 miles, arrive at Hut Clearing, where the Long Trail continues ahead to the north and the Burrows Trail departs to the left. Turn right to descend the mountain on the Monroe Trail.
7. At 4.6 miles, the Alpine Trail crosses the Monroe Trail. Continue downward on the Monroe Trail.
8. At 5.9 miles, the Monroe Trail meets the Dean Trail. Turn left on the Monroe Trail to return to the trailhead.

FIND THE TRAILHEAD

From I-89, Exit 10 in Waterbury, drive south on VT Route 100 to the rotary at the junction of US Route 2 and VT Route 100. Proceed east on US Route 2/VT Route 100 for 0.2 miles, then turn right on Winooski Street. In 0.4 miles, cross the bridge over the Winooski River and turn right on River Road. In 3.9 miles, turn left on Camel's Hump Road and drive 3.6 miles to the Monroe Trail trailhead parking lot at the end of the road.

PROHIBITION PIG RESTAURANT & BREWERY

Plenty of "fresh beer, tacos and street food" are on offer at Prohibition Pig Brewery in the heart of historic downtown Waterbury. Step inside the former schoolhouse and belly up to the beautiful wood bar or grab a table along the windows (there's also seating outdoors on the covered porch and patio) to pore over Pro Pig's extensive tap list, a diverse assortment of traditional, seasonal and contemporary beer styles. Bantam, a hazy, juicy American Double IPA, is a popular staple; enjoy it with a delicious bite from the Latin-inspired menu (oh, the Brisket Tacos, yum!). Real hungry? Check out the southeastern-style BBQ meat specialties (try the Whole Hog with cornbread and house-made pickles) in Pro Pig's restaurant right next door (same great beer) for the full experience of this lively, laid-back Stowe-area classic.

LAND MANAGER

Camel's Hump State Park
Vermont Dept. of Forests, Parks & Recreation, Essex Office
Waterbury, VT 05657
(802) 879-6565
Info and trail map: www.vtstateparks.com/camelshump.html

LONG TRAIL MANAGER

Green Mountain Club
4711 Waterbury-Stowe Road
Waterbury Center, VT 05677
(802) 244-7037
www.greenmountainclub.org

BREWERY/RESTAURANT

Prohibition Pig Brewery/Prohibition Pig Restaurant
2 Elm Street/23 South Main Street (adjacent buildings)
Waterbury, VT 05676
(802) 560-7186/(802) 244-4120
www.prohibitionpig.com
Distance from trailhead: 8 miles

ELMORE MOUNTAIN

HIKE TO A HISTORIC VERMONT FIRE TOWER FOR 360-DEGREE PANORAMIC VISTAS

LAKE ELMORE, VT

▷··· STARTING POINT	···✖ DESTINATION
END OF PARK ROAD	SUMMIT FIRE TOWER
🍺 BEER	🎲 HIKE TYPE
RIDGE RUNNER VERMONT ALE	MODERATE
🐾 DOG FRIENDLY	📅 SEASON
YES (LEASH REQUIRED)	LATE MAY TO MID-OCTOBER
$ FEES	⏱ DURATION
YES	2 HOURS 45 MIN.
⛰ MAP REFERENCE	↦ LENGTH
ELMORE STATE PARK MAP & GUIDE	4.2 MILES (LOOP)
🔍 HIGHLIGHTS	〰 ELEVATION GAIN
LAKE VIEWS, HISTORIC FIRE TOWER, PANORAMIC VISTAS	1,200 FEET

 BOLD AMBER ALE

 DARK AMBER

 MALTY

 MALT CARAMEL

BITTERNESS   **SWEETNESS**

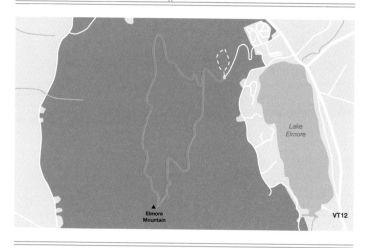

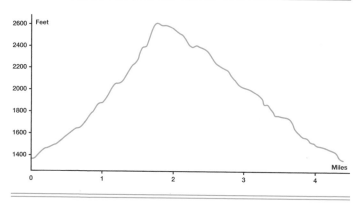

HIKE DESCRIPTION

From Elmore Mountain's historic summit fire tower, drink in the panoramic views up and down the crest of the Green Mountains. Then head for pretty Morrisville to drink up some great Rock Art Brewery brews.

The steep slopes of Elmore Mountain rise to 2,608 feet at the north end of the Worcester Range, which extends southward toward Mount Worcester, Hogback Mountain and Mount Hunger, east of Stowe and the Little River Valley. The mountain is part of Elmore State Park, a 940-acre expanse established in 1936 that includes shorefront on Lake Elmore. The sparkling lake and the little village at its north end are known as the "Beauty Spot of Vermont," and a post-hike trip to the Elmore Store on the sparkling 219-acre lake will confirm just why.

A 60-foot fire tower adorns the summit of Elmore Mountain, a remnant of a bygone era of forest fire protection and one of just 18 fire observation towers that remain standing on Vermont mountaintops. The tower,

built in 1940, is on the National Historic Lookout Register. This loop hike climbs to the tower via the Fire Tower Trail and descends by way of the Ridge Trail. The start of the Fire Tower Trail coincides with the Catamount Trail (marked with blue diamonds), a 300-mile cross-country ski route extending from Massachusetts to the Canadian border.

On the Fire Tower Trail, wooden ladders, built rock steps and steps chiseled out of the rock lead to a viewpoint overlooking Lake Elmore, where there are views of Gore and Bald mountains and a bounty of other hills. At the summit fire tower, scamper up the four flights of steps for a fantastic 360-degree panorama that takes in the crest of the Green Mountains to the west, south and north—from Camel's Hump and Mount Ethan Allen to the long high ridgeline of Mount Mansfield and on to Belvidere Mountain and Jay Peak. Vermont's Long Trail connects all of these summits on its sinuous 273-mile route from the Massachusetts state line to the Quebec border. Mount Washington and its alpine neighbors in the Presidential Range plus the rocky peaks of the Franconia Range can be seen some 60 miles to the east in New Hampshire.

From the fire tower, the Ridge Trail follows Elmore Mountain's narrow north ridge, where several outcrops amid the aromatic coniferous woods offer views northwest to the Lamoille River and the town of Morrisville, where Rock Art Brewing awaits. Partway along, a large open ledge provides one last look at Lake Elmore below—then it's on to the cool Balancing Rock precariously perched just off the trail. There's more ridge walking to do before the trail winds down Elmore's eastern slope and across several footbridges over little creeks to the finish.

TURN-BY-TURN DIRECTIONS

1. Pass around the gate and follow the gravel fire road, the route of the Fire Tower Trail.
2. At the junction at 0.3 miles, where the Ridge Trail leaves to the right, continue straight on the road.
3. At 0.6 miles, the Fire Tower Trail turns right off the road onto a footpath.
4. At 1.7 miles, reach a side trail leading 0.1 miles to the fire tower atop Elmore Mountain.
5. From the fire tower side-trail junction, continue north along the Ridge Trail.
6. At 2.2 miles, pass Balancing Rock (below you on the right).
7. At 3.9 miles, turn left on the gravel fire road to return to the trailhead.

FIND THE TRAILHEAD

In downtown Morrisville at the junction of VT Route 100 and VT Routes 12/15A, drive east on VT Routes 12/15A for 0.1 miles to a fork. Bear right to stay on VT Route 12 and drive 4.2 miles to Elmore State Park. Turn right into the park, pass the gatehouse and campground, and continue on to the trailhead parking lot in a cul-de-sac at the end of the road, 0.7 miles from VT Route 12.

ROCK ART BREWERY

Rock Art Brewery has been a mainstay in the Stowe region of north-central Vermont since its establishment in 1997. It's a true family-run operation, and the friendly Nadeaus will have you feeling right at home as soon as you walk through the door of their colorful tasting room in historic Morrisville. Rock Art brews a good variety of traditional beers, each with its own unique Vermont twist. Ridge Runner, a bold amber ale with barley wine roots, is a longtime favorite of customers among Rock Art's eight taps (plus four seltzers). Enjoy a pint or a flight outside on the porch with a view of Elmore Mountain, or in the "art gallery" indoors, which features the wonderful work of more than 50 local artists and artisans. In 2017, Rock Art was the first brewery in the U.S. to convert to 100% solar energy.

LAND MANAGER

Elmore State Park
856 VT Route 12
Lake Elmore, VT 05657
(802) 888-2982
Info and trail map: www.vtstateparks.com/elmore.html

BREWERY/RESTAURANT

Rock Art Brewery
632 Laporte Road
Morrisville, VT 05661
(802) 888-9400
rockartbrewery.com
Distance from trailhead: 5.6 miles

MOUNT MANSFIELD

EXPERIENCE THE EXTENSIVE ALPINE ZONE ON VERMONT'S HIGHEST PEAK

UNDERHILL CENTER, VT

▷⋯ STARTING POINT	⋯✕ DESTINATION
UNDERHILL STATE PARK	**MOUNT MANSFIELD SUMMIT**
🍺 BEER	🧩 HIKE TYPE
DISCO MONTAGE NEIPA	**STRENUOUS**
🐾 DOG FRIENDLY	📅 SEASON
YES (LEASH REQUIRED)	**MAY TO OCTOBER**
$ FEES	🕐 DURATION
YES	**5 HOURS 15 MIN.**
⛰ MAP REFERENCE	↦ LENGTH
UNDERHILL STATE PARK & MT. MANSFIELD STATE FOREST HIKING TRAILS	**7.8 MILES (LOOP)**
👁 HIGHLIGHTS	〜 ELEVATION GAIN
HIGH ALPINE SUMMIT, EXTENSIVE ALPINE TERRAIN, HUGE VIEWS	**2,670 FEET**

NEW ENGLAND IPA

HAZY DARK YELLOW/
LIGHT ORANGE

CITRUS
TROPICAL

JUICY CITRUS
TROPICAL FRUIT

BITTERNESS   SWEETNESS

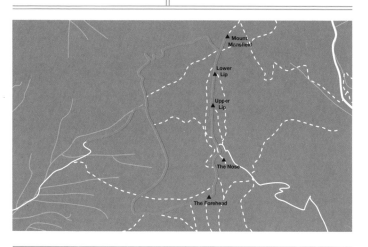

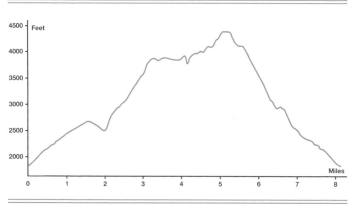

HIKE DESCRIPTION

This circuit hike over Mount Mansfield's majestic western ridges and summit crest leads through Vermont's largest alpine zone. The huge mountaintop vistas include a look toward Essex Junction, where Black Flannel Brewing awaits to quench your thirst.

Viewed from the east and west, the lofty ridgeline of 4,393-foot Mount Mansfield, Vermont's highest peak and the crown jewel of the Green Mountains, resembles an elongated human profile, with a distinct forehead, nose, upper lip, lower lip, chin and Adam's apple. The mountain rises up from the 44,444-acre Mount Mansfield State Forest, the state's largest contiguous land holding. From Underhill State Park, four trails climb Mount Mansfield's western slopes. This hike makes the ascent via the Maple Ridge Trail and descends by way of the Sunset Ridge Trail. The old CCC Road connects the two trails at the base of the mountain, while the Long Trail traverses the open country on the crest between the Forehead and the Chin.

Log ladders, carved steps, steep slabs and a deep crevice make the climb over Maple Ridge interesting, as do the views south to Camel's Hump and Bolton Mountain. The trail breaks free of the trees atop the Forehead at just under 4,000 feet at around the 3-mile mark. Some 200 acres of fragile alpine vegetation are found atop Mount Mansfield, so please watch your step as you hike the ridge of schist, gneiss and quartzite. From this point to the Chin, you're on the Long Trail, the oldest long-distance trail in the U.S. Completed in 1930, the 273-mile Long Trail predates the Appalachian Trail by seven years. The trail bypasses the communication towers on the Nose to reach the Mount Mansfield Visitor Center. The Auto Toll Road, a 4.5-mile gravel road

from VT Route 108 ends here, so you're likely to have company on the rest of the walk to the top.

From the high ridge, the westerly views over the Champlain Valley to Burlington, Lake Champlain and across to the high peaks of New York's Adirondacks are outstanding. As you stride on over the Upper Lip and Lower Lip, more terrific vistas open up, north to Belvidere and Buchanan Mountains, east to Elmore Mountain and the Worcester Range, and further on to the White Mountains of New Hampshire. The ski trails of Stowe Mountain Resort sweep down the eastern slopes to the highway, and beyond, there's the great defile of Smuggler's Notch, more ski trails, the peaks of the Sterling Range and a sea of green mountains all the way to Canada along the meandering route of the Long Trail.

The craggy summit of Mount Mansfield is unsigned, but you'll know you've reached it by the gaggle of hikers milling about. Enjoy the big panoramic view, find yourself a quiet spot off to the side and soak up the feeling of being on top of the world for a little while before sauntering down the long and winding and wonderfully wide-open Sunset Ridge. Be sure to take the short side trip to the unusual extended finger of Cantilever Rock en route.

TURN-BY-TURN DIRECTIONS

1. Begin by walking east on the CCC Road. In about 400 feet, turn right into the upper parking lot to pick up the Eagle Cut Trail.
2. The Eagle Cut Trail crosses the CCC Road three times before joining the CCC Road and following it past a group camping area to the junction with the Sunset Ridge Trail at 0.8 miles. Continue to the right (south) on the CCC Road.
3. At 2 miles, turn left to begin climbing on the Maple Ridge Trail.
4. At 3.1 miles, the Maple Ridge Trail ends at the Long Trail intersection atop the Forehead (3,940 feet); turn left (north) to follow the ridge.
5. At 3.7 miles, arrive at the Mount Mansfield Visitor Center on the left. The Auto Toll Road, parking and toilets are to the right.
6. At 4.8 miles, the Sunset Ridge Trail, your descent route, leaves to the left. Continue north on the Long Trail.
7. At 5 miles, the Long Trail reaches the summit of Mount Mansfield. To descend, retrace your steps 0.2 miles to the Sunset Ridge Trail.
8. At 6.2 miles, a side trail on the right leads 0.1 miles to Cantilever Rock.
9. At 6.9 miles, the Laura Cowles Trail enters from the left. In another 0.1 miles, join the CCC Road and turn right to follow it back to the Underhill State Park trailhead.

FIND THE TRAILHEAD

From Essex Junction, at the intersection of VT Route 289 and VT Route 15, drive east on VT Route 15. In 1.4 miles, where VT Route 128 goes straight, turn right to continue on VT Route 15 toward Jericho. In 6.1 miles, turn right on River Road and follow it for 3 miles through Underhill Center, where River Road continues as Pleasant Valley Road. After 0.7 miles on Pleasant Valley Road, turn right on Mountain Road and follow this for 2.6 miles to its end at Underhill State Park, where there is a campground and trailhead parking. (Note: Mountain Road alternates between paved and gravel surface before becoming all gravel to Underhill State Park.)

BLACK FLANNEL BREWING COMPANY

Chris Kesler opened Black Flannel Brewing & Distilling Company in the summer of 2020 in the reimagined space of a former retail outlet mall in the Burlington suburb of Essex Junction. Rooted in tradition but not limited by it, the brewery's refreshing mix of classic styles and creative experimentation will surprise and delight beer lovers. Enjoy a cold beer on the patio or in the biergarten, complete with a fantastic view of Mount Mansfield. The expansive restaurant features high ceilings, lots of stainless steel, a large solid cherry bar, beautiful stonework and, of course, great food and drink. Many of Black Flannel's talented and passionate staff are trained beer (and spirits) educators, so don't hesitate to ask questions and sample a variety of offerings. Disco Montage, a hazy, juicy beauty of a New England IPA, is the flagship brew.

LAND MANAGERS

Underhill State Park
352 Mountain Road
Underhill, VT 05490
(802) 899-3022
www.vtstateparks.com/underhill.html
Trail map: www.vtstateparks.com/assets/pdf/underhilltrails.pdf

Mt. Mansfield State Forest
Vermont Dept. of Forests, Parks and Recreation
District 3: Essex Office
111 West Street
Essex Junction, VT 05452
(802) 879-6565
fpr.vermont.gov/mt-mansfield-state-forest-0

LONG TRAIL MANAGER

Green Mountain Club
4711 Waterbury-Stowe Road
Waterbury, VT 05677
(802) 244-7037
www.greenmountainclub.org

BREWERY/RESTAURANT

Black Flannel Brewing Company
21 Essex Way
Essex Junction, VT 05452
(802) 857-5629
www.blackflannel.com
Distance from trailhead: 14 miles

MOUNT PISGAH

GET AN EAGLE'S-EYE VIEW OVER LAKE WILLOUGHBY AND WILLOUGHBY GAP

WESTMORE, VT

▷··· STARTING POINT	···✖ DESTINATION
US ROUTE 5A TRAILHEAD	THE SOUTH, WEST AND NORTH OVERLOOKS
🍺 BEER	🎲 HIKE TYPE
NEKIPA	MODERATE
🐾 DOG FRIENDLY	📅 SEASON
YES (LEASH REQUIRED)	MAY TO OCTOBER
$ FEES	🕐 DURATION
NO	2 HOURS 50 MIN.
⌂ MAP REFERENCE	↦ LENGTH
MOUNT PISGAH—WESTMORE, VT	4.2 MILES (ONE WAY)
👁 HIGHLIGHTS	〰 ELEVATION GAIN
SWEEPING CLIFFS, LAKE VIEWS, MOUNTAIN PANORAMAS	1,500 FEET

7.7 %
ALCOHOL CONTENT

NEW ENGLAND IPA

HAZY PALE GOLD

CITRUS
FRUIT

FRUITY

BITTERNESS

SWEETNESS

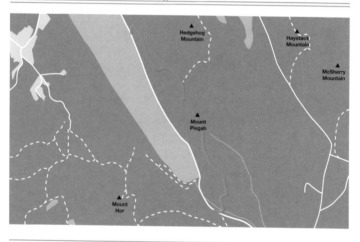

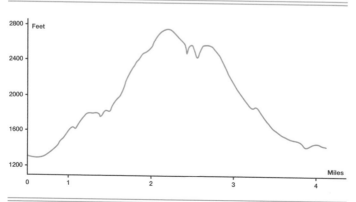

HIKE DESCRIPTION

Explore Vermont's famed Willoughby Gap on a hike to the top of the 1,500-foot cliffs of Mount Pisgah for incredible vistas over-looking Lake Willoughby. Your "next trick" is to head for a cold beer at Next Trick Brewing in West Burke.

Mount Pisgah rises to 2,751 feet and looks down on the deep, cold waters of Lake Willoughby in the rural northeastern corner of Vermont, a vast area known affectionately as the Northeast Kingdom. The mountain's precipitous cliffs drop more than 1,500 feet to the lake and, together with the steep walls of Mount Hor on the opposite side, form Willoughby Gap, an unmistakable natural landmark that's visible from many vantage points in the region.

The South Trail ascends gradually at first and then moderately, using switchbacks and rock staircases to reach Pulpit Rock on the edge of the south ridge of Mount Pisgah. Step left to get your first airy view of Lake Willoughby nearly 700 feet below. Continue the steady climb to an area of open ledges called the South Outlook, where you can look back over the Passumpsic River Valley to the ski slopes on Burke Mountain and beyond to Mount Washington and the high peaks of New Hampshire's White Mountains.

The South Trail meets the North Trail on the wooded summit of Mount Pisgah, which is a few feet left of the trail. Ahead on the North Trail, you'll soon arrive at a side trail to the West Overlook, where there's a stunning view over Lake Willoughby to the great cliffs on Mount Hor. Mount Mansfield—Vermont's highest peak—, Jay Peak, and Owl's Head across the border in Canada are also prominent.

The North Trail next reaches the side trail to the North Overlook. It's another spectacular vista that takes in the entire length of Lake Willoughby, which, at 320 feet deep, is the deepest lake entirely within the state's borders. The cliffs on Mount Pisgah and Mount Hor are part of Willoughby Cliffs Natural Area, 950 acres of special protection for the fragile alpine plants found on the cliff faces and the peregrine falcons that nest there. Willoughby State Forest protects 7,682 acres around both peaks and the lake. After the North Overlook, you'll descend steadily on the north ridge to meet the East Trail. Stay on the North Trail and follow it a couple miles down and out to VT Route 5A. The beginning trailhead is three miles south.

TURN-BY-TURN DIRECTIONS

1. The South Trail starts from the corner of the parking area to the right of the kiosk.
2. At 1.0 miles, a short spur trail on the left leads to Pulpit Rock.
3. At 1.9 miles, reach the South Overlook. Just beyond, on the summit of Mount Pisgah (2,751 feet), the South Trail ends. Continue ahead on the North Trail.
4. At 2.2 miles, a short spur trail on the left leads to the West Overlook.
5. At 2.3 miles, a spur trail on the left leads 0.1 miles to the North Overlook.
6. At a fork at 2.7 miles, the East Trail departs to the right; bear left to stay on the North Trail.
7. At 4.2 miles, reach VT Route 5A. If you've spotted a vehicle or bike here, you're all set. Otherwise, it's (usually) an easy hitch back to the starting trailhead, or a good walk of 3 miles along scenic Lake Willoughby.

FIND THE TRAILHEAD

To the starting trailhead: From I-91, Exit 23 in Lyndonville, head north through town on US Route 5. Follow US Route 5 for 9.6 miles to the junction of US Route 5 and VT Route 5A in West Burke. Bear right on VT Route 5A and follow it for 5.7 miles to trailhead parking on the right. *To the ending trailhead*: Continue north on VT Route 5A along Lake Willoughby for 3 miles to the unsigned North Trail trailhead on the right, where there is parking for several vehicles. Spot a vehicle here or plan to walk the 3 miles back along US Route 5A to the starting trailhead.

NEXT TRICK BREWING

Allan MacDonald had been a skilled homebrewer since the late 80s, and, as is so often the case, friends would always encourage him to open a brewery. "Why turn a hobby into a job?" he'd say. But when a local deal on brewing equipment was too good to pass up, the chemical engineer decided to move on to his "next trick" in life, opening Next Trick Brewing in 2017 in Vermont's rural Northeast Kingdom, where Al has owned a summer camp for ages. Housed in a renovated barn, the brewery features an intimate taproom and patio seating outside with a sweet view of Burke Mountain. Order up a juicy NEKIPA, a nod to this scenic corner of the state, and a Bavarian pretzel, and join patrons and the MacDonald family for some lively conversation.

LAND MANAGER

Willoughby State Forest
Vermont Dept. of Forests, Parks & Recreation
District 5: St. Johnsbury Office
374 Emerson Falls Road, Suite 4
St. Johnsbury, VT 05819
(802) 751-0110
fpr.vermont.gov/willoughby-state-forest
Trail map: fpr.vermont.gov/sites/fpr/files/Forest_and_Forestry/State_
Forests/Library/willoughby_trails_2019.pdf

TRAIL MANAGER

Northwoods Stewardship Center
154 Leadership Drive
East Charleston, VT 05833
(802) 723-6551
www.northwoodscenter.org/wordpress/

BREWERY

Next Trick Brewing
2370 US Route 5
West Burke, VT 05871
(802) 467-3437
nexttrickbrewing.com
Open seasonally from May to October
Distance from trailhead: 7.4 miles

SHELBURNE BAY

HIKE ALONG A BEAUTIFUL BAY ON LAKE CHAMPLAIN

SHELBURNE, VT

▷⋯ STARTING POINT	⋯✕ DESTINATION
BAY ROAD	ALLEN HILL, SHELBURNE BAY
🍺 BEER	HIKE TYPE
GREEN STATE LAGER	EASY
🐾 DOG FRIENDLY	📅 SEASON
YES (LEASH REQUIRED)	YEAR-ROUND
$ FEES	🕐 DURATION
NO	1 HOUR 20 MIN.
🗺 MAP REFERENCE	↦ LENGTH
SHELBURNE BAY PARK	2.6 MILES (LOOP)
👁 HIGHLIGHTS	〰 ELEVATION GAIN
BAY VIEWS, ROCKY BLUFFS, SHADY WOODS, GRASSY MEADOWS	160 FEET

PILSNER

BRIGHT GOLDEN

CRISP CRACKER
SLIGHLTY MALTY
HONEY

CRISP AND CLEAN
LIGHT HONEY
LIGHT HOPS

BITTERNESS

SWEETNESS

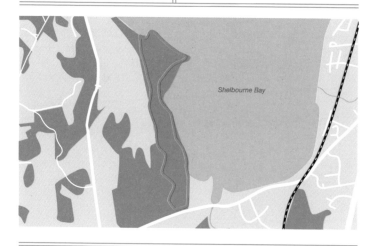

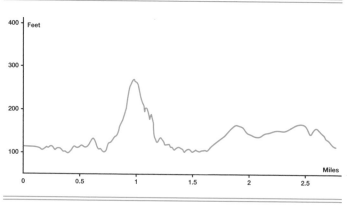

HIKE DESCRIPTION

Follow the trails of this municipal park along the wind-swept shores of Shelburne Bay on Lake Champlain. Later on, break free of gravitational forces with good brews and eats at Zero Gravity in Burlington.

Shelburne Bay is a large bay on the east side of Lake Champlain in the town of Shelburne, a few miles south of the city of Burlington. Lake Champlain, 120 miles long and 14 miles wide, is one of the largest freshwater lakes in the U.S. and forms a natural boundary between the Green Mountains of Vermont and the Adirondack Mountains of New York. Shelburne Bay Park is a 104-acre municipal park owned and managed by the Town of Shelburne that features over a mile of scenic shoreline, shady woods, limestone bluffs and grassy meadows. Three trails thread through the park: the Clarke Trail and the Allen Hill Trail wind along the shore of Shelburne Bay, while the Shelburne Recreation Path passes through the interior. This hike follows all three paths for a pleasant loop.

Look right as you stroll over the gravel drive toward the woods ahead to see where the La Platte River empties into the bay and the state of Vermont operates a public boat launch. The Clarke Trail closely follows the lakeshore for the first 0.75 miles, providing ample opportunities for views up and down the pretty bay. Just north of the parking lot, note

the reddish rocks; these are Monkton Quartzite and are more than 500 million years old. A little further on, the dock is part of the town's mooring area that serves as many as 65 boaters. Pad through shady, fragrant woods of cedar, pine and hemlock beyond to reach the Allen Hill Trail and the next leg of the walk.

The Allen Hill Trail climbs over 220-foot Allen Hill, the highest ground on Shelburne Point. There's a log on top to sit on before you move along to tackle the wooded outcrops ahead. Several ledges offer nice looks back along the bay to the sailboats and motorboats in the mooring area. Then the trail rounds the rocky headland to meet the north end of the Clarke Trail and then the Shelburne Recreation Path. There's beach access to the right, so do wander over to the water to get a lovely last look at the bay. The boats moored here are part of the Lake Champlain Yacht Club, which was founded in 1887.

The hardened gravel Shelburne Recreation Path leads along the western edge of the park back to the trailhead. If you're still itching for more, just across the road from the boat launch parking lot is the La Platte River Marsh Natural Area owned by The Nature Conservancy. There you'll find a really sweet nearly 2-mile out-and-back hike along the river.

TURN-BY-TURN DIRECTIONS

1. From the Bay Road parking area, walk north on the park road to the next parking area and kiosk. Stay right and enter the woods beyond to follow the Clarke Trail.
2. At 0.4 miles, reach the mooring docks on Shelburne Bay.
3. At a four-way junction at 0.9 miles, bear right to continue on the Allen Hill Trail.
4. At 1.5 miles, the Clarke Trail enters from the left, while beach access is to the right. Just beyond is the Shelburne Recreation Path; turn left to follow it back to Bay Road in a little over a mile.

FIND THE TRAILHEAD

From I-89 in South Burlington, take Exit 13 onto I-189 and drive west for about 2.5 miles to US Route 7. Turn left (south) on US Route 7 and travel 2.9 miles. Then turn right on Bay Road and follow it for 1.3 miles to Shelburne Bay Park and the trailhead parking on the right.

ZERO GRAVITY CRAFT BREWERY

The gravitational pull of Zero Gravity will most assuredly draw you into its Pine Street tasting room, opened in 2015, where you'll enjoy a "beautiful and balanced" selection of classic beers and "what's new." The former industrial building has been transformed into a really cool and comfortable community space, complete with vintage lights from an old schoolhouse and gymnasium, an ever-popular shuffleboard table, and a covered patio and beer garden outdoors—all a perfect fit for Burlington's south end arts district. Green State Lager, an

easy-drinking pilsner, is a house favorite, as is the bright and juicy Cone Head IPA. Drink up and chow down with a fried chicken sandwich and dirty fries, both specialties of the brewery's sister restaurant, Great Northern, which shares the space. Dogs and kids are welcome.

LAND MANAGER/TRAIL MANAGER

Shelburne Parks & Recreation Dept.
Shelburne, VT
(802) 985-9551
Info and trail map: shelburnevt.org/Facilities/Facility/Details/Shelburne-Bay-Park-14

Shelburne Bike & Pedestrian Paths Committee
(802) 497-0898

BREWERY/RESTAURANT

Zero Gravity Craft Brewery
716 Pine Street
Burlington, VT 05401
(802) 497-0054
www.zerogravitybeer.com
Distance from trailhead: 5.2 miles

SNAKE MOUNTAIN

ENJOY CLIFFTOP VIEWS OF THE ADIRONDACKS AND LAKE CHAMPLAIN

ADDISON, VT

▷··· STARTING POINT	···✕ DESTINATION
MOUNTAIN ROAD	**SNAKE MOUNTAIN SUMMIT**
🍺 BEER	HIKE TYPE
HEART OF LOTHIAN SCOTTISH ALE	**MODERATE**
🐾 DOG FRIENDLY	📅 SEASON
YES (LEASH REQUIRED)	**MAY TO OCTOBER**
$ FEES	🕐 DURATION
NO	**2 HOURS 40 MIN.**
⛰ MAP REFERENCE	↦ LENGTH
SNAKE MOUNTAIN WILDLIFE MANAGEMENT AREA	**4.1 MILES (LOOP)**
👁 HIGHLIGHTS	∿ ELEVATION GAIN
RURAL FARMLANDS, LAKE VIEWS, HIGH MOUNTAIN PROFILES	**1,200 FEET**

 SCOTTISH
ALE

 DARK BROWN

 EARTHY
CARAMEL
CHOCOLATE

 MALTY SWEET
CARAMEL
CHOCOLATE

BITTERNESS

SWEETNESS

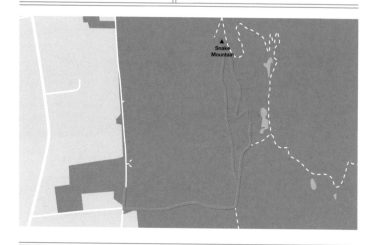

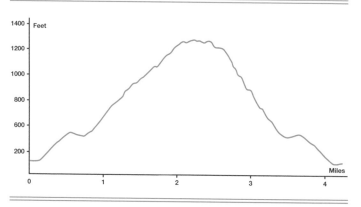

HIKE DESCRIPTION

Drink in the grand view of Lake Champlain and New York's Adirondacks from atop the huge cliffs on Snake Mountain. Then drop in for a brew at Drop-In Brewing in Middlebury.

The isolated mass of Snake Mountain rises dramatically from the farmlands of the bucolic Champlain Valley. From atop the sheer cliffs on the 1,287-foot summit, hikers can enjoy beautiful vistas ranging west to Lake Champlain and the high peaks of the Adirondacks in New York. Snake Mountain Wildlife Management Area protects 1,215 acres around the mountain, while The Nature Conservancy's Willmarth Woods Natural Area preserves 81 acres on its southwestern edge.

The trail, part of the old carriage road to the top, rises gradually through the deciduous forest. A mile into the walk, you'll turn along another old road and continue climbing. The moderate ascent finally levels off at an intersection near the top of the peak. Note the footpath on your left marked by a small rock cairn; this is your descent route. Fix the junction in your memory, as this unmarked path is not included on the official trail map. Continue to the top of Snake Mountain and the huge ledges at the old hotel overlook. The true summit and an old stone foundation are just to the right.

The west-facing view from the clifftop is extraordinary, reaching far out over the farms and fields to the blue waters of Lake Champlain, one of the largest lakes in the U.S. and part of the boundary between Vermont and New York. On the far side of the lake, your view is dominated by the Adirondack Mountains, a jumble of high and wild peaks topped by 5,344-foot Mount Marcy, New York's highest summit.

Snake Mountain was once known as Grand View Mountain, so named for the hotel built on its summit in 1874. The proprietor, Jonas N. Smith, thinking the name Snake Mountain was bad for business, changed it to the more marketable Grand View Mountain. Smith also built a 68-foot observation tower and a carriage road (the present trail route) to the summit. The Grand View Hotel closed in 1925 and eventually burned down, the carriage road was destroyed by heavy rains during a 1927 flood, and the tower failed to survive a hurricane in 1938.

On the return trip, go back to the four-way intersection and bear right onto that unmarked footpath. You'll descend gradually to Red Rock Pond, now mostly grown in. The rocky spine beyond offers a few more views before you duck into the trees for the steady descent back to the old carriage road and out to the trailhead.

TURN-BY-TURN DIRECTIONS

1. From the trailhead parking area, walk right (south) on Mountain Road for 600 feet to its junction with Willmarth Road. At the trail sign, turn left into the woods.

2. At 0.8 miles, reach a T-junction. Turn left to follow the wide track uphill.

3. At a somewhat obscure fork 1 mile, stay right to continue on the old carriage road. (The path on the left is the base of your descent route.)

4. Just beyond the ridge crest at 2 miles, reach a four-way junction. Notice the footpath and small rock cairn on the left; this is your descent route. For now, however, continue straight ahead.

5. At 2.1 miles, reach the open west-facing ledges on top of Snake Mountain on the left.

6. On the return trip from the summit ledges, retrace your steps 0.1 miles to the four-way junction, then bear right onto the footpath to descend.

7. At 3.2 miles, the footpath merges with the old carriage road; bear right to return to the Mountain Road trailhead.

FIND THE TRAILHEAD

From the rotary in downtown Middlebury at the junction of VT Route 125 and VT Route 30, follow VT Route 125 west for 8.2 miles. At the T-intersection of VT Route 22A and VT Route 125, turn right on VT Routes 22A/125. In 0.4 miles, VT Route 125 turns off to the left; continue north on VT Route 22A for another 3.7 miles and then turn right on Willmarth Road. In 0.6 miles, turn left on Mountain Road. Trailhead parking for Snake Mountain is 0.1 miles ahead on the left.

DROP-IN BREWING COMPANY

With years of brewing experience in the US and abroad, UK native Steve Parkes realized his long-held dream of owning his own brewery in 2012, when he opened Drop-In Brewing in an old plumbing supply building just south of downtown Middlebury. Dedicated to making quality beer available to everyone every day at a reasonable price, the affable Parkes encourages beer enthusiasts to "drop in" to the brewery for an enjoyable drinking experience. The small taproom, its walls festooned with beer memorabilia from across the country, is a museum of sorts, while the beer garden outside is a fine spot for a brew on a sunny day. English- and European-style beers are Parke's specialty; popular among them is the year-rounder Heart of Lothian, a smooth, sessionable Scottish Ale. Visit Grapevine Grille next door for cheesesteaks, wraps and sandwiches.

LAND MANAGER

Vermont Fish & Wildlife Dept.
District 3: Essex District Office
111 West Street
Essex Junction, VT 05452
(802) 878-1564
Info and trail map: vtfishandwildlife.com/node/155

BREWERY

Drop-In Brewing Company
610 US Route 7 South
Middlebury, VT 05753
(802) 989-7414
dropinbrewing.com
Distance from trailhead: 10 miles

MOUNT TOM
AND THE POGUE

WANDER THE MANAGED WOODLANDS OF A HISTORIC ESTATE

WOODSTOCK, VT

▷⋯ STARTING POINT	⋯✕ DESTINATION
BILLINGS FARM & MUSEUM VISITOR CENTER	**THE POGUE, MOUNT TOM (SOUTH PEAK)**
🍺 BEER	🔢 HIKE TYPE
LONG TRAIL ALE	**MODERATE**
🐾 DOG FRIENDLY	📅 SEASON
YES (LEASH REQUIRED)	**MAY TO OCTOBER**
$ FEES	🕐 DURATION
NO	**2 HOURS 40 MIN.**
⛰ MAP REFERENCE	↦ LENGTH
WALK WOODSTOCK	**4.7 MILES (ONE-WAY)**
🔍 HIGHLIGHTS	〜 ELEVATION GAIN
HISTORIC CARRIAGE ROADS, MOUNTAIN POND, CLIFFTOP VIEWS	**675 FEET**

5.0 %
ALCOHOL
CONTENT

GERMAN-STYLE ALTBIER

DEEP AMBER

CARAMEL
EARTHY

FULL-BODIED, SMOOTH
CARAMEL
ROASTED

BITTERNESS   SWEETNESS

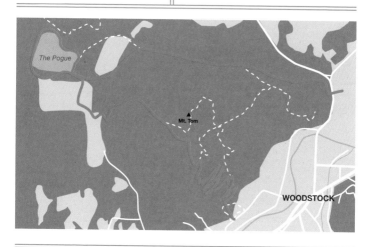

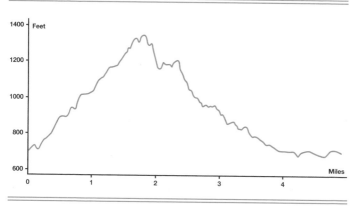

HIKE DESCRIPTION

Follow old carriage roads and winding footpaths on Mount Tom leading to a pleasant pond and clifftop vistas. Visit Long Trail Brewing after your hike for a cold Long Trail Ale.

From the huge open ledges high on the southeast slopes of Mount Tom, hikers can enjoy a wonderful view over historic downtown Woodstock. Mount Tom is the central natural feature of the former Marsh estate, now a 600-acre conservation landscape known as the Marsh-Billings-Rockefeller National Historic Park. Opened in 1998, the park is a model of conservation and stewardship and its name honors several of its environmentally conscious former owners.

George Perkins Marsh grew up on the estate in the shadow of Mount Tom in the early 1800s. As a young man, Marsh became increasingly concerned about the rampant deforestation of the Vermont woods and the poor agricultural methods used by farmers, and later published *Man and Nature or Physical Geography as Modified by Human Behavior*, an important book that laid the foundation for the modern conservation movement in the U.S.

Frederick Billings and his wife Julia purchased the land in 1869. Profoundly impacted by Marsh's work, Billings established a managed forest and progressive dairy farm, a showcase for sustainable management practices, and developed a system of carriage roads and trails. Julia Billings's daughter, Mary French, married Laurance Spelman Rockefeller, the son of oil tycoon John D. Rockefeller Jr., in 1934. The couple later inherited the estate and managed it until 1992, when it was donated to the National Park Service.

The Carriage Barn Visitor Center near the start of this hike is worth a visit, and you may want to take a tour of the George Perkins Marsh Boyhood Home, which, built in 1805, is the park's architectural centerpiece. The Mountain Road leads to a circuit around the scenic pond known as the Pogue, while the Mount Tom Road threads past pretty pastures to the aforementioned South Peak Overlook. The Faulkner Trail then descends via 14 switchbacks through Faulkner Park, a "place of respite and healthy exercise" created by Marianne Faulkner in memory of her husband, Edward Daniels Faulkner.

TURN-BY-TURN DIRECTIONS

1. From the kiosk near the front of the museum, walk to Elm Street and cross it.
2. At the junction, "Gardens" are to the left and "Trails" are to the right; go right on Mountain Road.
3. At 0.25 miles, stay straight to pass the Forest Center and the Woodshed Exhibit.
4. Follow Mountain Road to the Pogue at 1.4 miles, avoiding all trails and roads to the left and right en route. Turn right to circle the Pogue via the Pogue Loop.
5. Back at the Mountain Road junction at 2.1 miles, turn right to follow Mountain Road.
6. At 2.2 miles, turn right on Mount Tom Road, and over the next mile, avoid all trails and roads diverging to the left and right.
7. At 3.2 miles, reach the South Peak Overlook on Mount Tom. Descend via the switchbacks of the Faulkner Trail. Pass the Upper Link, a stone bridge and the Lower Link en route.
8. At the base of the Faulkner Trail at 4.4 miles, reach a kiosk. Turn right to follow the paved path out to Mountain Avenue. If you've spotted a vehicle here, great! Otherwise, walk the mile back to the starting trailhead via Mountain Avenue, Riverside Street and Elm Street.

FIND THE TRAILHEAD

To the starting trailhead: In downtown Woodstock at the junction of US Route 4/VT Route 12 (Central Street) and VT Route 12 (Elm Street) (about 11 miles west of I-89 Exit 1), turn north on Elm Street (VT Route 12). Drive 0.4 miles, then turn right on Old River Road, and then right again into the parking area for Billings Farm & Museum Visitor Center.
To the ending trailhead: From the center of Woodstock at the junction of US Route 4/VT Route 12 (Central Street) and VT Route 12 (Elm Street), continue west on US Route 4 for 0.1 miles, then turn right on Mountain Avenue. Follow Mountain Avenue for 0.3 miles to parking along the right side of the road at Faulkner Park.

LONG TRAIL BREWING COMPANY

The Long Trail threads a scenic route along the crest of Vermont's Green Mountains for 273 miles, from Massachusetts to Canada. The famous long-distance hiking path—completed in 1930, it's the nation's oldest—was the inspiration for Long Trail Ale back in 1989, at the trail-blazing start of Vermont's craft beer movement. Today, the venerable hiking trail and Long Trail Brewing, with its flagship German-style alt-bier, are well-loved institutions in the Green Mountain State. "Take A Hike" and then enjoy a cold one at the brew pub on the beautiful Ottauquechee River, where you'll find twelve taps pouring a variety of Long Trail beers, plus classic pub fare with a Vermont twist. Grab a pint and a table on the outdoor patio or wander down to the rippling river to dip your toes and enjoy the mountain views.

LAND MANAGER

Marsh-Billings-Rockefeller National Historical Park
54 Elm Street
Woodstock, VT 05091
(802) 457-3368
Info and trail map: www.nps.gov/mabi/

BREWERY/RESTAURANT

Long Trail Brewing Company
5520 U.S. Route 4
Bridgewater Corners, VT 05035
(802) 672-5011
longtrail.com
Distance from trailhead: 8.9 miles

WINDMILL RIDGE

HIKE TO THE PINNACLE, THE SCENIC HIGHPOINT ON THE 26-MILE LONG WINDMILL RIDGE

WESTMINSTER, VT

▷⋯ STARTING POINT	⋯✕ DESTINATION
WINDMILL HILL ROAD	**THE PINNACLE**
🍺 BEER	🀰 HIKE TYPE
WHETSTONER SESSION IPA	**MODERATE** 🥾
🐾 DOG FRIENDLY	📅 SEASON
YES (LEASH REQUIRED)	**APRIL TO NOVEMBER**
$ FEES	🕐 DURATION
NO (DONATIONS REQUESTED)	**2 HOURS 15 MIN.**
⛰ MAP REFERENCE	↦ LENGTH
WHPA WINDMILL RIDGE NATURE RESERVE & TRAIL	**4.0 MILES (LOOP)**
🔎 HIGHLIGHTS	〰 ELEVATION GAIN
MOUNTAIN VIEWS, RIDGETOP CABIN, INTERPRETIVE TRAIL	**500 FEET**

INDIA PALE ALE

HAZY GOLD

DANK
CITRUS
FLORAL

BRIGHT
CITRUS-FORWARD

BITTERNESS

SWEETNESS

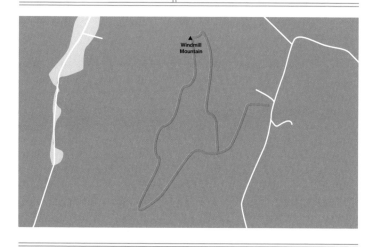

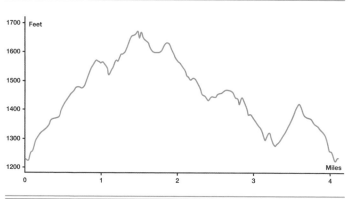

HIKE DESCRIPTION

Take a wandering walk through the woods of the Windmill Ridge Nature Reserve. Then wander south to Brattleboro and Whetstone Station for a cold brew and a scenic view over the Connecticut River.

From the modest 1,683-foot summit of the Pinnacle in rural Westminster West in southeastern Vermont, hikers are rewarded with a terrific vista westward to the crest of the Green Mountains, where the high peaks of Mount Snow, Stratton Mountain, Equinox Mountain and Dorset Mountain are all on show. In fact, the view reaches from Mount Greylock in northern Massachusetts all the way to lofty Killington Peak, a range of about 70 miles. The Pinnacle is the high point and crown jewel of Windmill Ridge, which extends some 16 miles north to south through portions of the towns of Rockingham, Athens, Westminster, Brookline, Putney and Dummerston.

This hike climbs easily to the Pinnacle via the Holden Trail, scampers along the ridgeline on the Pinnacle Trail, then descends the mountain by way of the Headwaters Trail before rejoining the Holden Trail for the last section back to the trailhead. The Pinnacle Cabin, a log lean-to built in 1964 by the former landowner as a family retreat, adorns the top of the mountain at the big viewpoint. Both the cabin steps and the granite bench out front are fabulous places to relax and enjoy the far-reaching view over the lovely Vermont countryside.

"A Walk Through Time" is a self-guided trail tour of the Holden, Pinnacle and Headwaters hiking loop that you'll want to download in advance and take along on your walk as a pleasant hiking companion. The brochure, available at windmillhillpinnacle.org/pages/resources.html, matches the 16 interpretive station posts en route that showcase the rich and fascinating natural and cultural history of the lands on and around the Pinnacle.

When a young local fellow named Jamie Charles Latham died in a tragic accident in 1991, his family and friends decided to establish a fitting memorial for this outdoor-loving soul and embarked on an ambitious mission to permanently protect the Pinnacle, which was then privately owned. The Windmill Hill Pinnacle Association was born in 1992, and its members and supporters have worked tirelessly ever since to purchase lands and secure easements along the length and breadth of Windmill Ridge. Today, some 2,700 acres of wildlife habitat across six towns, from Grafton to Townshend, have been protected, and an interconnected system of 26 miles of trails—known as the Windmill Ridge Nature Reserve & Trail—is now in place for use by the recreating public; a rather extraordinary feat accomplished in a short timeframe. Bravo, dedicated volunteers!

TURN-BY-TURN DIRECTIONS

1. Pass between the kiosk and gate to begin on the Holden Trail, which is marked with red dots.
2. At 0.5 miles, where the Headwaters Trail (blue dots) goes straight, turn right to continue on the Holden Trail.
3. At 1.3 miles, reach a T-junction atop Pinnacle Ridge. Turn left onto the Pinnacle Trail and follow the white dots.
4. At 1.4 miles, reach the summit of the Pinnacle (1,683 feet), the Pinnacle Cabin and a big view westward. From the Pinnacle, continue south on the Pinnacle Trail.
5. At 1.6 miles, the Cascade Trail departs to the right; continue straight on the Pinnacle Trail.
6. At 2.7 miles, leave the ridge to the left to follow the Headwaters Trail (blue dots).
7. Merge with the Holden Trail at 3.5 miles and follow this out to the trailhead.

FIND THE TRAILHEAD

From I-91, Exit 4 in Putney, turn north on US Route 5 and proceed into Putney village. At the junction of Main Street (US Route 5) and Kimball Hill Road, turn left on Kimball Hill Road, which soon morphs into Westminster Road and then Westminster West Road. Drive 6.9 miles to Westminster West village, then turn left on West Road, which quickly turns to dirt. In 0.9 miles, turn right on Windmill Hill Road North (sign: The Pinnacle-Holden Trail). Proceed 1.2 miles to reach the parking lot for Pinnacle Hill on the right.

WHETSTONE STATION RESTAURANT AND BREWERY

Longtime Brattleboro innkeepers Tim and Amy Brady and business-man David Hiler opened Whetstone Station in an abandoned building at the south end of downtown in 2012. Overlooking the wide and beau-tiful Connecticut River, the brewery has become a wildly popular go-to spot for brews, food and fun in a comfortable, low-key atmosphere. Grab a cold pint of the flagship Whetstoner Session IPA and head for the sunny upper patio deck, aka the biergarten, to mingle with new and old friends and enjoy the amazing view over the river—replete with boaters, canoeists and kayakers—to the slopes of Wantastiquet Moun-tain in New Hampshire (for the record, the VT–NH state line runs right through Whetstone Station). Dig into the Steak Tips and Station Fries while you kick back and ponder another beer. Be sure to also check out Whetstone's newest downtown location at River Garden Marketplace when you visit.

LAND MANAGER

Windmill Hill Pinnacle Association
35 Sleepy Valley Road
Athens, VT 05143
(802) 376-8365
Info and trail map: windmillhillpinnacle.org

BREWERY/RESTAURANT

Whetstone Station Restaurant and Brewery
36 Bridge Street
Brattleboro, VT 05301
(802) 490-2354
www.whetstonestation.com
Distance from trailhead: 21 miles

NEW HAMPSHIRE

NORTHWOOD MEADOWS

TAKE A WALK AROUND A SCENIC RESERVOIR

NORTHWOOD, NH

▷⋯ STARTING POINT	⋯✗ DESTINATION
US ROUTES 202/4 & NH ROUTE 9 TRAILHEAD	**MEADOW LAKE LOOP**
🍺 BEER	🗺 HIKE TYPE
GLASS DDH IPA	**EASY** 🚶
🐾 DOG FRIENDLY	📅 SEASON
YES (LEASH REQUIRED)	**YEAR-ROUND**
$ FEES	🕐 DURATION
NO	**1 HOUR 30 MIN.**
🗻 MAP REFERENCE	↦ LENGTH
NORTHWOOD MEADOWS AREA	**2.9 MILES (LOOP)**
🔎 HIGHLIGHTS	〰 ELEVATION GAIN
PRETTY LAKE, PLEASANT WOODS, WETLANDS, SWIMMING	**90 FEET**

DOUBLE DRY-HOPPED IPA

GOLDEN/HAZY

PEACH, APRICOT
MANGO
CITRUS

STONEFRUIT, TROPICAL
CITRUS
PINE

BITTERNESS   SWEETNESS

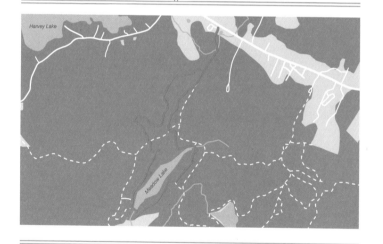

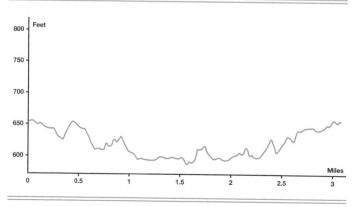

HIKE DESCRIPTION

Circumnavigate beautiful Meadow Lake in the heart of Northwood Meadows State Park. Then head just down the road to Northwoods Brewing for a family-brewed pint and some scratch-made pizza or a fresh-baked cruller.

Northwood Meadows State Park is 675 acres of woods and wetlands in a wide valley surrounding beautiful Meadow Lake. The small reservoir is a source of the Lamprey River, which meanders through the state for 49 miles before emptying into Great Bay on the New Hampshire seacoast. The park is surrounded by several thousand acres of conservation land, notably the Forest Peters Wildlife Management Area (456 acres) and the Guptill-Lamprey Pasture Conservation Area (101 acres). Volunteers from the Friends of Northwood Meadows State Park help maintain the park's trails.

This hike combines the Huckins Orchard Trail and the Lake Trail for a pleasant walk around Meadow Lake. You'll begin on the gravel Dashingdown Road, then strike off on the Huckins Orchard Trail, which contours across a hillside before winding through a shady ravine of hemlocks. One mile along, cross the NALMC Trail to reach Meadow Lake via the Lake Trail. The acronym NALMC stands for Northwood Area Land Management Collaborative, a partnership of public and private landowners in Northwood that has been working cooperatively since 2006 to conserve land in the area in an effort to protect valuable wildlife habitat and water resources from further fragmentation.

The Lake Trail leads quickly to the lake area, where a picnic table and huge log tepee beckon from the nearby woods. Not far along, the trail reaches a sandy stretch of shoreline; on a warm summer day, this would be a nice spot for a swim. Fragrant white pines and cedars dominate the forest canopy as you saunter along the west side of Meadow Lake to the earthen dam at its south end. The picnic table here is a good place to pause and enjoy the fine view up the lake.

A man named M. Edward Burtt began purchasing land in this part of Northwood in the 1960s. Over the years, Burtt developed his property into a recreation area of sorts, with boulder-lined gravel roads, walking trails and a 30-acre pond. Burtt called it Betty Meadows, a nod to the historical name of the wetlands and the Betty family who once lived on the land. In the 1990s, Burtt transferred his lands to the state of New Hampshire for the purpose of creating Northwood Meadows State Park. Around the same time, the Peters family holdings became a wildlife management area. These two properties plus Carl Wallman's 211-acre Harmony Hill Farm to the west form the core of the mostly contiguous NALMC conservation lands.

The Lake Trail continues south from the dam to a bench overlooking Betty Meadows before turning north again up the east side of Meadow Lake. There is a picnic table halfway along the lake and another at its north end. After merging with the NALMC Trail, you'll join the Universal Access Trail for the walk to Dashingdown Road and then out to the highway.

TURN-BY-TURN DIRECTIONS

1. From the orange gate at the park entrance, hike south on Dashingdown Road, passing an information kiosk after about 100 feet.
2. At 0.25 miles, turn right on the Huckins Orchard Trail.
3. At 1.0 miles, cross the NALMC Trail, then turn right on the unsigned Lake Trail.
4. At 1.2 miles, a spur on the left leads to Meadow Lake.
5. At 1.4 miles, reach the earthen dam at the south end of Meadow Lake.
6. At 1.5 miles, reach a bench overlooking Betty Meadows.
7. At 2.2 miles, a spur trail to the left leads to Meadow Lake.
8. At 2.3 miles, turn left on the NALMC Trail, and in 50 feet, turn right on the Universal Access Trail to return to the trailhead.

FIND THE TRAILHEAD

In Northwood, at the junction of NH Route 43, US Route 202/NH Route 9 and US Route 4, travel west on US Routes 4/202 and NH Route 9 for 2.8 miles, then turn left into Northwood Meadows State Park. Trailhead parking is to the right.

NORTHWOODS BREWING CO.

Jeff Fenerty and his family opened Northwoods Brewing in a big red barn-like building in rural Northwoods in 2018. The brewery complements the family's restaurant next door, Johnson's Seafood & Steak, a classic stop along US Route 1 since its dairy bar days in the 1940s. At Northwoods they believe that "beer should take you somewhere," so settle into the comfy taproom and let a pint of good brew transport you to a favorite place in the great New Hampshire outdoors. Many of the twelve beers on tap follow a fly-fishing theme, like the flagship Glass, a juicy DDH IPA. For Fenerty, an ardent angler, a "glass day" is when the water on the trout pond is like a mirror, just perfect for wetting a hand-tied fly. Enjoy your "glass" day with a sourdough pizza or a glazed cruller (or both?) from the brewery's bake shop.

LAND MANAGER

Northwood Meadows State Park
755 First NH Turnpike
Northwood, NH 03261
(603) 485-1031
Info and trail map: https: www.nhstateparks.org/visit/state-parks/northwood-meadows-state-park

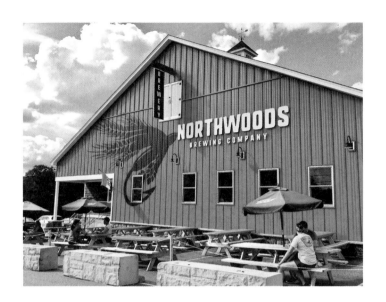

BREWERY/RESTAURANT

Northwoods Brewing Company
1334 1st NH Turnpike
Northwood, NH 03261
(603) 942-6400
northwoodsbrewingcompany.com
Distance from trailhead: 2.8 miles

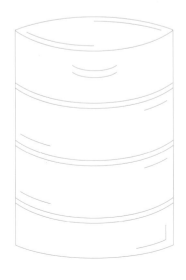

MOUNT CARDIGAN

SCAMPER OVER TREELESS GRANITE SLOPES TO AN HISTORIC SUMMIT FIRE TOWER

ORANGE, NH

▷⋯ STARTING POINT	⋯✖ DESTINATION
CARDIGAN MOUNTAIN STATE PARK	**MOUNT CARDIGAN SUMMIT**
🍺 BEER	🀫 HIKE TYPE
NEWFOUND NUTBROWN ALE	**MODERATE** 🚶
🐾 DOG FRIENDLY	📅 SEASON
YES (LEASH REQUIRED)	**MAY TO OCTOBER**
$ FEES	🕐 DURATION
YES	**1 HOUR 25 MIN.**
⛰ MAP REFERENCE	⊢ LENGTH
MT. CARDIGAN STATE PARK & FOREST, WEST SIDE HIKING TRAILS	**3.3 MILES (LOOP)**
👁 HIGHLIGHTS	〰 ELEVATION GAIN
HISTORIC FIRE TOWER, SWEEPING GRANITE SLOPES, BIG VIEWS	**1,150 FEET**

5.4 % ALCOHOL CONTENT — NUTBROWN ALE

DARK BROWN

MALTY TOASTED

CARAMEL-SWEET

BITTERNESS

SWEETNESS

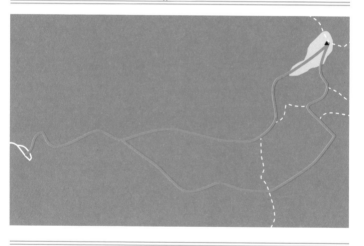

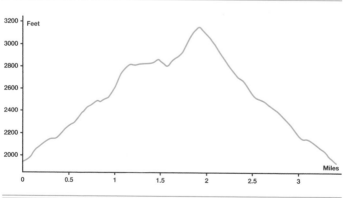

HIKE DESCRIPTION

Delight in the incredible expanse of treeless granite ledges atop Mount Cardigan. Then celebrate the day's big views with a cold pint on the square at Shackett's Brewing in Bristol.

Established in 1918 with 700 acres, Cardigan Mountain State Park today consists of 5,655 acres across the towns of Orange and Alexandria in west-central New Hampshire. The heart of this wildland area is Mount Cardigan, which rises to 3,155 feet and is topped by a historic fire tower. The summit and high ridges on Cardigan are a veritable sea of treeless granite ledges, the result of devastating forest fires in 1855.

This loop hike follows the West Ridge Trail, the South Ridge Trail and a short section of the Clark Trail on the ascent, then descends Cardigan via the West Ridge Trail. As you climb, the northern hardwood forest of beech, maple and birch gives way to spruce and fir, and then, on the upper slopes exposed to the harsh weather, to subalpine fragile heath vegetation and the stunted and twisted trunks of birch, spruce and fir known as *krummholz*.

The hike breaks out of the woods at around the 1-mile mark and remains mostly in the open for the next mile. The views from Rimrock are outstanding and include Camel's Hump, Killington and Mount

Ascutney to the west in Vermont, and Ragged Mountain, Mount Kearsarge and Mount Sunapee to the south. The rock wall windbreak on the South Peak is a nice spot to pause for a bit to enjoy the view north to Mount Washington, Mount Chocorua and the Tripyramids, among many other peaks. And, of course, there's an impressive view of the fire tower perched atop Cardigan's rocky dome.

From the old fire lookout's cabin, it's a phenomenal scramble straight up moderate-to-steep granite slabs to the summit and a 360-degree vista. Far beyond the bald peak of Firescrew Mountain, the high peaks of Washington, Lafayette and Moosilauke all stand out to the north. To the northeast, across Lake Winnipesaukee, you'll see Mount Roberts and Mount Shaw, and in Vermont to the west there are a multitude of peaks along the high crest of the Green Mountains.

Descending from the peak, the West Ridge is wide open for another wonderful 0.5 miles, so follow the large rock cairns marking the route and enjoy the epic views a little longer before dipping down into the trees for the remainder of the day's journey.

TURN-BY-TURN DIRECTIONS

1. The West Ridge Trail begins across the parking lot loop road 50 feet from the picnic pavilion.
2. At 0.5 miles, turn right on the South Ridge Trail.
3. At Rimrock at 1.1 miles, cross the Skyland Trail to continue on the South Ridge Trail.
4. At 1.4 miles, reach Cardigan's South Peak.
5. At 1.5 miles, reach Hurricane Gap and the Hurricane Gap Trail on the right; continue straight ahead on the South Ridge Trail.
6. At 1.6 miles, the Ranger Cabin Trail enters from the left; turn right to stay on the South Ridge Trail.
7. At the warden's cabin at 1.7 miles, turn left on the Clark Trail and climb at a moderate to steep grade over open ledges.
8. At 1.8 miles, turn right on the West Ridge Trail and reach the fire tower on the summit of Mount Cardigan in another 100 feet.
9. From Cardigan's summit, descend via the West Ridge Trail, following large rock cairns over open ledges.
10. Pass the Skyline Trail on the left at 2.3 miles, then pass the South Ridge Trail on the left at 2.8 miles on the way back to the trailhead.

FIND THE TRAILHEAD

In Canaan, at the intersection of US Route 4 and NH Route 118, turn north on NH Route 118. In 0.5 miles, turn right on Cardigan Mountain Road/Orange Road (large sign: Cardigan State Park). In another 3.3 miles, enter Mount Cardigan State Forest (sign), and 0.1 miles beyond, bear left to stay on Cardigan Mountain Road. In 0.6 miles, reach the trailhead parking lot.

SHACKETT'S BREWING COMPANY

You'll find Shackett's Brewing Company, established in 2014, nestled among the shops around pretty Central Square in the heart of Bristol village. From the street-level front door, amble down the stone steps into the taproom, a warm and comfortable space of exposed brick walls, community tables and big windows looking out over the New-found River. Six of Shackett's fine brews are always on tap, in addition to a couple of guest taps. Jon Shackett, owner, head brewer and Bristol native, is partial to his Newfound Nutbrown Ale, but you're sure to find your own favorite among the rotating selection of artisanal ales, seasonal brews and experimental batches. For munchies there's free popcorn and a selection of light pub fare. Plans are in place to build a large outdoor deck overlooking the rushing river below; look for it on your next visit.

LAND MANAGER

Cardigan Mountain State Park
658 Cardigan Mountain Road
Orange, NH 03741
(603) 227-8745
Info and trail map: www.nhstateparks.org/visit/state-parks/cardigan-mountain-state-park

BREWERY

Shackett's Brewing Company
26 Central Square
Bristol, NH 03222
(603) 217-7730
www.shackettsbrewing.com
Distance from trailhead: 26 miles

MOUNT KEARSARGE

HIKE A FIGURE-EIGHT LOOP OVER A VERITABLE SEA OF MOUNTAINTOP GRANITE

WILMOT, NH

▷⋯ STARTING POINT	⋯✗ DESTINATION
WINSLOW STATE PARK PICNIC AREA	**KEARSARGE SOUTH FIRE TOWER**
🍺 BEER	🁢 HIKE TYPE
LONG BROTHERS AMERICAN IPA	**MODERATE**
🐾 DOG FRIENDLY	📅 SEASON
YES (LEASH REQUIRED)	**MAY TO OCTOBER**
$ FEES	🕐 DURATION
YES	**2 HOURS 30 MIN.**
⛰ MAP REFERENCE	↦ LENGTH
MT. KEARSARGE HIKING TRAILS	**3.6 MILES (LOOP)**
🔍 HIGHLIGHTS	〜 ELEVATION GAIN
HISTORIC FIRE TOWER, SWEEPING GRANITE LEDGES, BIG VIEWS	**1,450 FEET**

AMERICAN IPA

CLEAR LIGHT ORANGE

CATTY
PUNGENT

BITTER HOP BITE
CLEAN
CRISP

BITTERNESS

SWEETNESS

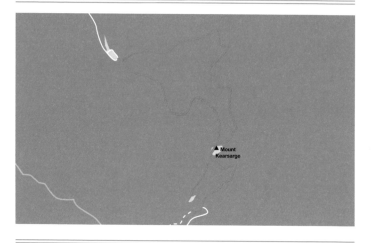

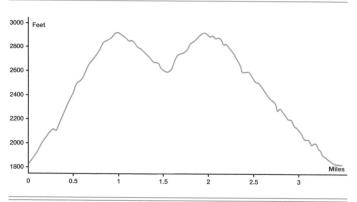

HIKE DESCRIPTION

Hikers will be flying high on this fabulous figure-eight loop over the sweeping granite ledges on Mount Kearsarge, which is topped by an historic fire tower. After your hike, enjoy good food and drink in the shadow of the mountain at the Flying Goose Pub.

Mount Kearsarge is an isolated mountain mass, known as a monadnock, rising to an elevation of 2,937 feet on the town line between Wilmot and Warner in south-central New Hampshire. The name Kearsarge is thought to be a derivation of the native Penacook name for the peak, *Carasarga*, meaning "notch-pointed mountain of pines." The mountain is surrounded by conservation lands, including Winslow State Park, where the hike begins and ends, on the northwest slope, and Rollins State Park on the southern slopes.

This hike makes a figure-eight loop up and over Mount Kearsarge and back, utilizing all four trails on the mountain: The Winslow Trail (up) and the Barlow Trail (down) on the Winslow side and the Rollins Trail (down) and the Lincoln Trail (up) on the Rollins side. The Winslow Trail and the Lincoln Trail are part of the Sunapee-Ragged-Kearsarge Greenway, a 75-mile circuit hike that connects the three major summits of the trail's name. Winslow State Park is named for a 19th-century hotel, the Winslow House, which once stood where the trailhead picnic area is today. Only a cellar hole remains. The hotel was named for Admiral John Winslow, who commanded the USS Kearsarge during the Civil War.

Open ledges on the upper section of the Winslow Trail yield fabulous westerly views to Pleasant Lake, the village of New London, Lake Sunapee and the ski trails on Mount Sunapee. To the north are Mount Cardigan, Smarts Mountain and Mount Cube. Amid the veritable sea of granite bedrock on top of the mountain stands the Kearsarge South Fire Tower. Closed to the public, the 27-foot tower has stood on this spot since 1913, one of only 16 such towers remaining in New Hampshire. Looking south from the summit, the vista takes in Mount Monadnock, Pack Monadnock, Crotched Mountain, the central Massachusetts hills and even, on a good day, the Boston skyline. To the north are the lofty White Mountains, while to the west is the crest of Vermont's Green Mountains. It's an extraordinary spot worth spending some time at.

When you're ready to move on, wander across the open ledges to the obvious subsidiary summit, then descend a short distance to the Rollins Trail. This wide path winds in a delightful manner down to the "Garden" at the parking area for the 3.5-mile auto road (circa 1873) that snakes up the mountain from the tollhouse base in Warner. Look for the bronze marker dedicated to Frank West Rollins, whom the park is named after. Rollins served as Governor of New Hamphsire from 1901 to 1903 and was a co-founder of the Society for the Protection of New Hampshire Forests. The Lincoln Trail, steeper and rockier than the Rollins Trail, will guide you back to the top of Kearsarge. The Barlow Trail descends to the north and features a number of ledge views before the path swings west to its end.

TURN-BY-TURN DIRECTIONS

1. Enter the woods at the upper left end of the picnic area parking lot, and in 200 feet, reach a fork where the Barlow Trail departs to the left and the Winslow Trail departs to the right. Bear right to follow the Winslow Trail.
2. At 1.0 miles, the Barlow Trail joins from the left. In 250 feet, reach the top of Mount Kearsarge and its summit fire tower (closed to the public).
3. From the summit tower, follow the Rollins Trail across the open slabs and past a large rock cairn to a junction at 1.1 miles, where the Lincoln Trail continues straight ahead; turn left to follow the Rollins Trail.
4. At 1.6 miles, reach a picnic area and parking area at the upper terminus of the 3.5-mile auto road that winds up the Warner side. At the southwest end of the lot, re-enter the woods and begin climbing on the Lincoln Trail.
5. At a T-junction at 1.65 miles, turn right to continue on the Lincoln Trail toward the summit of Kearsarge.
6. At 2.1 miles, join the Rollins Trail for the 0.1-mile walk over open ledges to the summit fire tower.
7. From the fire tower, descend via the Winslow Trail, and in 250 feet, bear right on the Barlow Trail.
8. At 3.5 miles, turn right on the Winslow Trail to reach the picnic area parking lot just ahead.

FIND THE TRAILHEAD

From I-89, Exit 10 in Sutton, turn right on North Road. In 0.4 miles, turn left on Kearsarge Valley Road. In 3.0 miles, turn right on Kearsarge Mountain Road. In another 1.6 miles, bear right to stay on Kearsarge Mountain Road. Continue 1.2 miles to the entrance gate of Winslow State Park. A picnic area and trailhead parking are 0.3 miles ahead at the end of the road.

FLYING GOOSE BREW PUB & GRILLE

Tom Mills has operated The Flying Goose at the four corners of NH Routes 114 and 11 in rural, picture-perfect New London since 1993. Today, the casual, family-friendly place is managed by his three kids and continues to serve up great beer, great food and, of course, a great view of Mount Kearsarge. Braumeister Rik Marley ("I brew everything") has been happily producing the good stuff at Flying Goose since 2007, including his ever-popular West Coast–style Long Brothers American IPA, the pub's "best selling beer by a country mile." The cozy taproom, festooned with fun and funky paraphernalia collected over the years, is a comfortable spot to enjoy a brew and one of Flying Goose's famous burgers, like the favorite PB & Sriracha with cheddar and bacon on a pub roll.

LAND MANAGERS

Winslow State Park
475 Kearsarge Mountain Road
Wilmot, NH 03287
(603) 526-6168
Info and trail map: www.nhstateparks.org/visit/state-parks/winslow-state-park

Rollins State Park
1066 Kearsarge Mountain Road
Warner, NH 03278
(603) 456-3808
www.nhstateparks.org/visit/state-parks/rollins-state-park

BREWERY/RESTAURANT

Flying Goose Brew Pub & Grille
40 Andover Road
New London, NH 03257
(603) 526-6899
www.flyinggoose.com
Distance from trailhead: 6.6 miles

MOUNT MOOSILAUKE

CLIMB NEW HAMPSHIRE'S WESTERNMOST 4,000-FOOT ALPINE PEAK

BENTON, NH

▷⋯ STARTING POINT	⋯✕ DESTINATION
HIKER PARKING, RAVINE LODGE ROAD	**MOUNT MOOSILAUKE SUMMIT**
🍺 BEER	🏯 HIKE TYPE
PIG'S EAR BROWN ALE	**STRENUOUS** 🚶
🐾 DOG FRIENDLY	📅 SEASON
YES (LEASH REQUIRED)	**MAY TO OCTOBER**
$ FEES	🕐 DURATION
NO	**5 HOURS 20 MIN.**
⌖ MAP REFERENCE	↦ LENGTH
WHITE MOUNTAIN NATIONAL FOREST MAP & GUIDE	**8.2 MILES (LOOP)**
🔎 HIGHLIGHTS	〰 ELEVATION GAIN
HIGH ALPINE PEAK, 360-DEGREE VIEWS, APPALACHIAN TRAIL	**2,450 FEET**

 BROWN ALE

 CARAMEL BROWN

 NUTTY

 COFFEE
NUTTY
CHOCOLATE

BITTERNESS   SWEETNESS

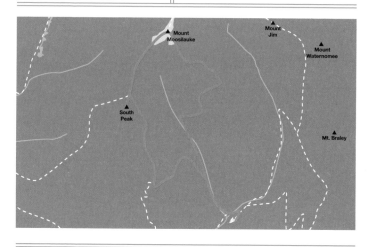

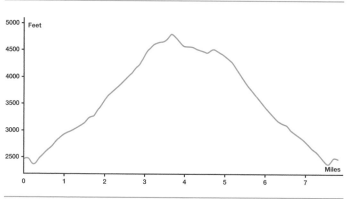

HIKE DESCRIPTION

Climb to what many seasoned hikers consider the finest alpine summit in the White Mountains. Descend into Woodstock after your trek for great food and drink at the lively Woodstock Inn Brewery.

Mount Moosilauke is the tenth highest and the most westerly of the 48 peaks over 4,000 feet in the White Mountain National Forest, which sprawls across more than 750,000 acres in northern New Hampshire and over the state line into Maine. The 4,802-foot Moosilauke, features an extensive alpine zone and far-reaching panoramic vistas ranging from the Kinsman Range, Franconia Range and Presidential Range in the White Mountains to Vermont's Green Mountains and beyond to the Adirondacks in New York.

This hike ascends Mount Moosilauke from the south via the Gorge Brook Trail, the easiest (a relative term; it's still a strenuous hike) and most popular route up the mountain. The Gorge Brook Trail begins near Moosilauke Ravine Lodge, a large log structure owned by Dartmouth College and operated by the Dartmouth Outing Club. The beautiful new lodge opened in 2017, replacing the old building that stood on the same site from 1938 to 2016. The lodge is open to the public except during special events, so be sure to check it out after your hike. The college owns 4,600 acres on the southern and eastern flanks of Moosilauke, and its students, faculty, staff and alumni have enjoyed its slopes for generations.

From the treeless, windswept summit, you'll follow the Moosilauke Carriage Road across the high, vista-rich ridgeline to a spur leading to the 4,523-foot South Peak, a worthwhile side trip for a great look back to the main summit. This section of the Carriage Road is part of the

Appalachian Trail (AT), which extends for 2,192 miles along the crest of the Appalachian Mountains from Georgia to Maine. The carriage road was constructed in the 1870s to serve the Tip Top House on the mountain's summit. The old hotel is long gone, but the rocks outlining part of its former shape remain. The descent continues on the Carriage Road, then follows the Snapper Trail, an old ski trail, back to the Gorge Brook Trail to complete a fine circuit of about 8 miles.

Moosilauke hikers should be well prepared for possible harsh weather in the open areas above the timberline. Take care to follow the trail markers and not to stray from the rocky path, as the vegetation in the alpine zone is very fragile. On the Gorge Brook Trail climb, be sure to heed the "last sure water" sign at 3,300 feet, where the trail leaves the brook at the Ross McKenney Forest memorial plaque. The name Moosilauke is derived from the Abenaki language and means "bald place." The reason for this name will become crystal clear once you're on top and enjoying the incredible 360-degree view (provided the weather cooperates, of course).

TURN-BY-TURN DIRECTIONS

1. From the hiker parking, walk north on the gravel road past Moosilauke Ravine Lodge to the turnaround at the end of the road at 0.25 miles. Continue ahead 100 yards, turn left, and soon after, turn left again (follow signs "to Gorge Brook Trail").

2. At 0.45 miles, after passing behind several Ravine Lodge bunkhouses, reach an information kiosk and a footbridge over Baker River. The Gorge Brook Trail begins here. At the other end of the bridge, turn left.

3. At 0.5 miles, where the Hurricane Trail continues straight, turn right to stay on the Gorge Brook Trail.

4. At a fork at 1.0 miles, the Snapper Trail heads left; bear right to continue on the Gorge Brook Trail.

5. At 1.8 miles, pass the Ross McKenney Forest memorial plaque.

6. At 4.0 miles, reach the alpine summit of Mount Moosilauke. From here, continue south on the Moosilauke Carriage Road (also the route of the Appalachian Trail).

7. At 4.9 miles, reach a three-way junction: The Glencliff Trail (AT) leaves to the right, a 0.2-mile spur to the south peak of Mount Moosilauke goes straight and the Carriage Road goes left. Take the spur to the south peak; then return and continue on the Carriage Road.

8. At 6.4 miles, turn left on the Snapper Trail.

9. At 7.3 miles, turn right on the Gorge Brook Trail and retrace your steps to the hiker parking on the Ravine Lodge Road, about 1 mile ahead.

FIND THE TRAILHEAD

From I-93, Exit 32 in North Woodstock, drive west on NH Route 112. In about 0.5 miles, reach the junction of US Route 3 in downtown North Woodstock. Continue straight ahead on NH Route 112. In 2.6 miles, turn left onto NH Route 118 and drive 7.1 miles to Ravine Road. Turn right on Ravine Road and proceed 1.4 miles to hiker parking on the right. Please parallel park here and walk to the Ravine Lodge turn-around and trailhead 0.25 miles ahead at the end of the road.

WOODSTOCK INN BREWERY

Situated in the heart of North Woodstock, not far from famed Franconia Notch, Woodstock Inn Brewery bills itself as a basecamp of sorts where adventurous visitors are encouraged to "Eat. Drink. Stay. Repeat." Family owned and operated since it opened in 1982 as a small inn and restaurant, Woodstock Inn added a brewery in 1995, and today this lively, eclectic spot is one of the most popular hangouts in the White Mountains. The super drinkable Pig's Ear Brown Ale is the brewery's original creation and its flagship beer among a diverse menu of mountain-themed brews. Enjoy a flight or a pint and some excellent eats (steaks and burgers are specialties) outdoors, either streetside or on the patio, or in one of four comfy indoor areas: The Main Bar, Dam Bar, Brew Pub and Tap Room.

LAND MANAGER

White Mountain National Forest
Pemigewasset Ranger District
71 White Mountain Drive
Campton, NH 03223
(603) 536-6100
www.fs.usda.gov/main/whitemountain/home
Trail map: amcstore.outdoors.org/products/white-mountain-national-forest-map-guide

BREWERY/RESTAURANT

Woodstock Inn Brewery
135 Main Street
North Woodstock, NH 03262
(603) 745-3951
www.woodstockinnbrewery.com
Distance from trailhead: 11 miles

MOUNT ROBERTS

HIKE THE MOST POPULAR PEAK IN THE CASTLE IN THE CLOUDS CONSERVATION AREA

MOULTONBOROUGH, NH

▷⋯ STARTING POINT	⋯✕ DESTINATION
SHANNON POND	**MOUNT ROBERTS SUMMIT**
🍺 BEER	HIKE TYPE
BLACK SHEEP PILS	**MODERATE**
🐾 DOG FRIENDLY	SEASON
YES (LEASH REQUIRED)	**MAY TO OCTOBER**
$ FEES	⏱ DURATION
NO	**3 HOURS 20 MIN.**
🗺 MAP REFERENCE	↦ LENGTH
CASTLE IN THE CLOUDS	**5.3 MILES (ROUND TRIP)**
👁 HIGHLIGHTS	〰 ELEVATION GAIN
LAKE AND MOUNTAIN VIEWS, COOL GEOLOGY, HISTORIC CASTLE	**1,350 FEET**

GERMAN-STYLE PILSNER

PALE YELLOW

FLORAL

LIGHT
CRISP
CLEAN

BITTERNESS

SWEETNESS

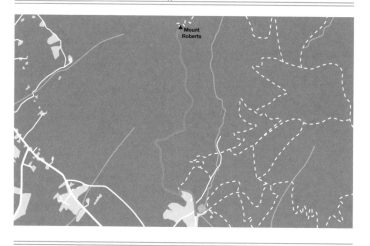

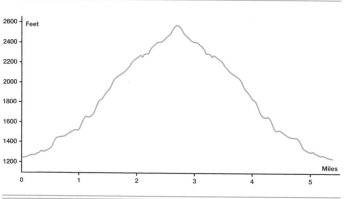

HIKE DESCRIPTION

Meander through the old Castle in the Clouds estate and enjoy outstanding views from Mount Roberts that range from the White Mountains to Lake Winnipesaukee. Head for Hobbs Tavern for cold beer and hot wings after your ascent.

Mount Roberts rises to 2,582 feet in the Ossipee Mountains just north of beautiful Lake Winnipesaukee in east-central New Hampshire. The Ossipee Mountains are the remnants of a 125-million-year-old volcanic ring-dike complex that extends across the towns of Moultonborough, Tuftonboro, Ossipee and Sandwich. The circular Ossipee ring-dike was formed when the magma chamber of an ancient caldera, or volcanic crater, collapsed. Nine miles in diameter, the distinctive geologic formation is clearly defined on satellite images and topographic maps.

Mount Roberts is the westernmost summit in the Castle in the Clouds Conservation Area (CCCA), a 5,246-acre chunk of mountainous land owned and managed by the Lakes Region Conservation Trust. Founded

in 1979, the LRCT has conserved more than 25,000 acres across 145 properties. A 30-mile system of trails connects Mount Roberts with Faraway Mountain, Turtleback Mountain, Bald Knob, Mount Shaw and Black Snout to the east.

Visit Shannon Pond for a lovely view of Mount Roberts before striking off on the Mount Roberts Trail, which climbs at a mostly moderate grade through the predominantly oak woods on the mountain's south ridge. Between the one- and two-mile marks of the hike you'll come upon a series of open ledges, some quite extensive, that yield incredible views, especially of Lake Winnipesaukee, which dominates the landscape to the south. Twenty-one miles long and with an area of 69 square miles, this sprawling lake is New Hampshire's largest. Looming over the lake's south shore are the peaks of the Belknap Range, including Belknap Mountain—the highest—and its neighbor, Gunstock Mountain, the home of the popular ski area of the same name. The easterly view features Mount Shaw, which at 2,790 feet is the highest among the six summits of the CCCA.

A pile of rocks and a sign amid the scrub oaks marks the top of Mount Roberts. The panorama to the north is extraordinary and reaches across a long series of peaks in the 4,000-6,000-foot range: Mounts Whiteface and Passaconaway in the Sandwich Range, Mount Carrigain in the Pemigewasset Wilderness, Mount Lafayette in the Franconia Range, Mount Washington in the Presidential Range and Wildcat in the Carter-Moriah Range. Linger awhile with lunch and enjoy.

Back at the base of Mount Roberts, the Castle in the Clouds estate is definitely worth a visit. Tickets are required. The Castle, also known as the Lucknow Mansion, is owned and operated by the Castle Preservation Society. The 16-room Arts and Crafts–style mansion was built in 1914 by Thomas Plant, a shoe industry magnate, and his wife, Olive.

TURN-BY-TURN DIRECTIONS

1. From the main hiker parking lot, walk along the road past the gate into the Castle in the Clouds property.
2. At the road junction at 0.1 miles, turn left, then pass the riding stables to pick up the Mt. Roberts Trail.
3. At 0.4 miles, the Settlement Trail leaves to the right; bear left to continue on the Mt. Roberts Trail.
4. At 2.65 miles, reach the summit of Mount Roberts.
5. Retrace your steps to Shannon Pond and the main hiker parking lot.

FIND THE TRAILHEAD

From the junction of NH Route 109 and NH Route 25 just north of Moultonborough village, turn east on NH Route 109 and drive 2.2 miles. Where NH Route 109 goes right, continue straight on NH Route 171 for another 0.5 miles. Turn left on Ossipee Park Road and drive 1.3 miles to the trailhead parking for Castle in the Clouds Conservation Area on the right.

HOBBS BREWING COMPANY

Hobbs Brewing opened its tap room in 2020 in a brick-red barn style structure in Ossipee on the eastern edge of the scenic Lakes Region. The long, polished concrete bar is front and center as you enter the welcoming space, which combines stainless-steel fixtures and old pine boards for an industrial-meets-nature vibe. "There's a little something for everyone here," says Ash Fischbein, Hobbs's co-owner and co-founder—so pull up a stool, relax and enjoy one of the eight rotating beers on tap, like the Black Sheep Pilsner or the Lake Life Pale Ale. Hungry? Head 11 miles north to West Ossipee and Fischbein's original 2014 venture, Hobbs Tavern, a casual family-friendly spot in a beautifully restored 1885 Victorian farmhouse, part of the old Hobbs family sheep farm. It serves great food and the same great beer.

LAND MANAGERS

Lakes Region Conservation Trust
156 Dane Road
Center Harbor, NH 03226
(603) 253-3301
Info and trail map: lrct.org

Castle in the Clouds
455 Old Mountain Road (NH Route 171)
Moultonborough, NH 03254
(603) 476-5900
www.castleintheclouds.org

BREWERY & BREWERY/RESTAURANT

Hobbs Brewing Company
765 Route 16
Ossipee, NH 03864
(603) 539-3795
hobbsbeer.com
Distance from trailhead: 17 miles

Hobbs Tavern
2415 White Mountain Highway
West Ossipee, NH 03890
(603) 539-2000

MOUNT WASHINGTON

TAKE AN ABOVE-TREELINE RAMBLE AROUND THE SUMMIT OF NEW ENGLAND'S HIGHEST PEAK

SARGENT'S PURCHASE, NH

▷⋯ STARTING POINT	⋯✕ DESTINATION
COW PASTURE, MT. WASHINGTON AUTO ROAD	**MOUNT WASHINGTON SUMMIT LOOP**
🍺 BEER	HIKE TYPE
AS YOU WISH NEIPA	**STRENUOUS**
🐾 DOG FRIENDLY	📅 SEASON
YES (LEASH REQUIRED)	**LATE MAY TO LATE OCTOBER**
$ FEES	🕐 DURATION
YES	**4 HOURS**
⛰ MAP REFERENCE	↦ LENGTH
WHITE MOUNTAIN NATIONAL FOREST MAP & GUIDE	**6.1 MILES (LOOP)**
👁 HIGHLIGHTS	〰 ELEVATION GAIN
HIGH MOUNTAIN SUMMIT, EXTENSIVE ALPINE ZONE, HIKER HUT	**1,750 FEET**

NEW ENGLAND IPA

HAZY PALE AMBER/
ORANGE

ORANGE
PASSION FRUIT
PINEAPPLE

LIGHT BITTER
CITRUS
RESIDUAL HOPS

BITTERNESS

SWEETNESS

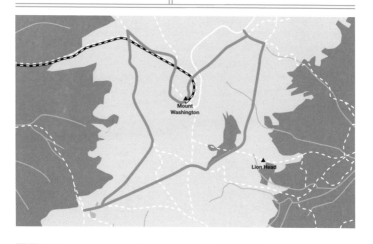

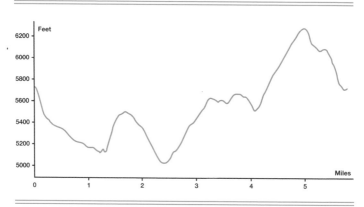

HIKE DESCRIPTION

"Get rad" on an awesome ramble through the incredible alpine zone on the slopes of Mount Washington's summit cone. "Then drink beer" at Ledge Brewing far below in the Mount Washington Valley.

Mount Washington is the crown jewel of the White Mountains of New Hampshire, and at a lofty 6,288 feet in elevation, it is the highest peak in New England—or anywhere in the northeastern US—for that matter. Circus showman P.T. Barnum once called Mount Washington the "Second Greatest Show on Earth" for the extraordinary panorama from its rocky summit, a view that extends as far as 130 miles to Massachusetts, Vermont, New York, Quebec, Maine and the Atlantic Ocean. As you might expect, the mountain's considerable elevation makes it a natural attraction.

The top of Mount Washington buzzes with human activity—a bustling scene worthy of any amusement park. Dozens of trails lure countless adventurers up the mountain's flanks, as does the Mt. Washington Cog Railway, which chugs up to the peak from the west, while the Mt. Washington Auto Road, the access route for this hike, winds 8 miles up from the east. The summit is dotted with communications towers and structures including the Sherman Adams Summit Building, which houses a visitor center, weather observatory, museum, cafeteria, gift shop and even a post office!

Mount Washington is at the heart of the Presidential Range, amid an incredible expanse of treeless alpine terrain. Rather than ascend some 4,000 feet from far below, this hike follows a fully exposed high-elevation route that begins and ends above 5,000 feet, nearly circumnavigating the mountain's

summit cone before reaching the top. During the day's hike, you'll follow a series of trails: The Huntington Ravine Trail, the Alpine Garden Trail, the Tuckerman Ravine Trail, the Tuckerman Crossover, the Crawford Path, the Westside Trail, the Gulfside Trail and the Nelson Crag Trail.

Do watch your step and stick to the rocks as the vegetation is very fragile in the alpine zone. About halfway along, you'll arrive at the Lakes of the Clouds Hut. Operated by the Appalachian Mountain Club, it's one of eight high-mountain huts in the White Mountains along the Appalachian Trail between Franconia Notch and Carter Notch. The hut is a great place to duck into, relax a while and mingle with other outdoor travelers.

The mountain is notorious for having some of the worst weather in the world, so hikers should be well prepared with warm, weatherproof clothing, a day pack full of proper gear, and good shoes. Be sure to check the weather in advance; it's reported directly from the meteorologists atop the peak at the Mount Washington Observatory (www.mountwashington.org). If the forecast is good, go; if not, save this hike for another day, as you don't want to miss a thing on the "Rooftop of New England."

TURN-BY-TURN DIRECTIONS

1. The Huntington Ravine Trail begins on the south side of the Mt. Washington Auto Road.
2. At 0.1 miles, cross the Nelson Crag Trail, then descend.
3. At 0.3 miles, turn right to follow the Alpine Garden Trail.
4. At 1.3 miles, cross the Lion Head Trail and continue.
5. At 1.6 miles, turn right on the Tuckerman Ravine Trail and climb.
6. Reach Tuckerman Junction at 1.8 miles. Continue straight ahead on the Tuckerman Crossover across Bigelow Lawn.
7. At 2.1 miles, the Tuckerman Crossover crosses the Davis Path. Continue straight ahead on the Tuckerman Crossover.
8. At 2.6 miles, reach the junction with the Crawford Path. Turn left to follow the Crawford Path and reach the AMC's Lakes of the Clouds Hut at 2.7 miles.

9. From the Lakes of the Clouds Hut, retrace your steps on the Crawford Path and continue on it, ascending the slopes of Mount Washington's summit cone.
10. At 3.5 miles, the Crawford Path meets the Westside Trail. Turn left to follow the Westside Trail on a contouring route.
11. At 4.4 miles, soon after crossing the tracks of the Mt. Washington Cog Railway, the Westside Trail meets the Gulfside Trail. Turn right to follow the Gulfside Trail on the north side of the tracks.
12. At 4.9 miles, where the Great Gulf Trail leaves to the left, bear right to continue on the Gulfside Trail. You will soon cross over the railway tracks.
13. At 5.1 miles, turn left on the Crawford Path and follow it to the summit.
14. At 5.3 miles, reach the summit buildings atop Mount Washington. Mount Washington's true summit is marked by a signed rock pile between the old Tip Top House and the Sherman Adams Summit Building.
15. To descend, follow the Nelson Crag Trail from the front or east side of the Sherman Adams Summit Building. The trail crosses the Cog Railway tracks and then the Auto Road to reach the junction with the Huntington Ravine Trail at 6.0 miles. Turn left to quickly reach the Cow Pasture trailhead parking lots.

FIND THE TRAILHEAD

The entrance to the Mt. Washington Auto Road is opposite the Glen House on NH Route 16, about 8 miles south of the junction of US Route 2 and NH Route 16 in Gorham, and about 15 miles north of the junction of US Route 302 and NH Route 16 in Glen. Proceed to the tollbooth, then drive the narrow, winding Mt. Washington Auto Road up the east side of Mount Washington for 6.5 miles to the "Cow Pasture" and trailhead parking (small lots on both sides of the road) for the Huntington Ravine Trail. Advance reservations for the Auto Road are recommended.

Mt. Washington Auto Road
1 Mount Washington Auto Road
Gorham, NH 03581
(603) 466-3988
mt-washington.com

LEDGE BREWING COMPANY

When locals Silas Miller and Ian Ferguson teamed up to create Ledge Brewing, Ian tapped his high school friend, the talented professional Cody Floyd, to be their head brewer. It was Cody who coined the name "Ledge" for the many granite ledges scattered about the beautiful Mt. Washington Valley, airy destinations where you can kick back and enjoy the view. At Ledge Brewing, which opened in 2020, patrons can

"Get Rad, Then Drink Beer" amid the outdoorsy mountain vibe of the spacious former model-train museum. Ledge Brewing sports an adventurous lineup of "really solid, sessionable beers"; among the ten rotating taps you'll find everything from lagers and farmhouse-inspired saisons to ales, IPAs and more. Food trucks on weekends, live music and a beer garden add extra flavor to this hopping hangout.

LAND MANAGERS

White Mountain National Forest
Androscoggin Ranger District
300 Glen Road
Gorham, NH 03581
(603) 466-2713
www.fs.usda.gov/whitemountain
Trail map: amcstore.outdoors.org/products/white-mountain-national-forest-map-guide

Mt. Washington State Park
1598 Mt. Washington Auto Road
Sargent's Purchase, NH 03846
(603) 466-3347
www.nhstateparks.org/visit/state-parks/mt-washington-state-park

BREWERY

Ledge Brewing Company
15 Town Hall Road
Intervale, NH 03860
(603) 307-1070
www.ledgebrewing.com
Distance from Mt. Washington Auto Road base: 16 miles

NORTH AND MIDDLE SUGARLOAF

ENJOY BIG MOUNTAIN VIEWS FROM SUGARLOAF'S HUGE GRANITE LEDGES

BETHLEHEM, NH

▷⋯ STARTING POINT	⋯✗ DESTINATION
ZEALAND ROAD	**NORTH AND MIDDLE SUGARLOAF SUMMITS**
🍺 BEER	⊞ HIKE TYPE
PRETENTIOUS HOPPER NEIPA	**MODERATE** 🚶
🐾 DOG FRIENDLY	📅 SEASON
YES (LEASH REQUIRED)	**MAY TO OCTOBER**
$ FEES	🕐 DURATION
YES	**2 HOURS 20 MIN.**
⊠ MAP REFERENCE	↦ LENGTH
WHITE MOUNTAINS NATIONAL FOREST MAP & GUIDE	**3.5 MILES (ROUND-TRIP)**
🔍 HIGHLIGHTS	〰 ELEVATION GAIN
SWEEPING GRANITE LEDGES, FAR-REACHING MOUNTAIN VIEWS	**1,100 FEET**

NEW ENGLAND IPA

HAZY ORANGE

TROPICAL FRUIT
HOPPY

JUICY ORANGE, PINEAPPLE
ORANGE, MANGO
PINE

BITTERNESS   SWEETNESS

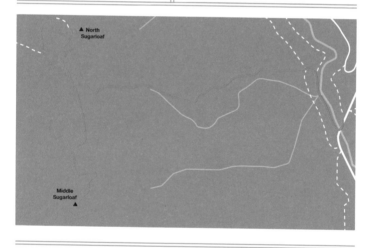

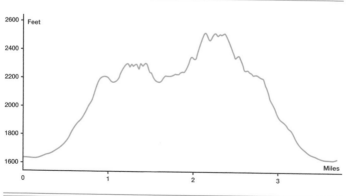

HIKE DESCRIPTION

Climb to the shapely twin peaks of North and Middle Sugarloaf for outstanding views of the Presidential and Franconia ranges. Afterwards, you might find yourself getting a little reckless with the awesome beer and food at Rek'-lis Brewing.

North Sugarloaf and Middle Sugarloaf are twin peaks rising to around 2,500 feet on the western edge of the vast 750,000-acre White Mountain National Forest, which sprawls across northern New Hampshire and into Maine. The extensive open ledges on the two summits reward hikers with outstanding panoramic views of the surrounding high peaks. Each of the Sugarloafs has a conical shape and steep slopes; the name refers to the conical shape of the sugarloaf, the form that refined sugar was sold in until granulated sugar and sugar cubes were introduced in the late 19th century.

At the beginning of this hike, the Sugarloaf Trail coincides with the Trestle Trail along the Zealand River. This is the route of the former Zealand Valley Railroad, a logging line used to haul timber out of the Zealand Valley in the late 1800s. The wood was brought to sawmills and charcoal kilns in the village of Zealand, which was built and owned by the lumber baron J.E. Henry. Little remains of the once bustling company community, now the site of Zealand Campground.

Leaving the Zealand River, the Sugarloaf Trail climbs westerly at a moderate but steady grade to a col between North and Middle Sugarloaf. Early on you'll pass by some huge boulders; known as glacial

erratics, these rocks were deposited by glaciers eons ago. At the col, a low point between the peaks, head for the ledges atop North Sugarloaf. The view is outstanding, taking in North Twin, Mount Hale and the Willey Range to the south; Mounts Eisenhower, Monroe, Washington, Jefferson and Adams in the Presidential Range to the northeast; and Mounts Martha and Deception to the north.

Returning to the col, you'll continue on to Middle Sugarloaf and its extensive open granite ledges. Scramble up a wooden ladder to reach the east ledges, then amble on to the south ledges. The views are similar to those from the other peak, but the sea of open granite is simply amazing and enhances the far-reaching vistas tenfold. Wander around at will and enjoy every bit of this glorious mountaintop perch.

Looking west, you can now see Burke Mountain in Vermont, and beyond to the crest of the Green Mountains, which includes lofty Mount Mansfield (Vermont's highest) and Camel's Hump. Mount Washington looms large to the northeast; at 6,288 feet, it's the highest mountain not only in New England, but also in the entire northeastern US. Look closely and you'll see the route of the Cog Railway that has been chugging to its rocky, windswept summit since 1869.

TURN-BY-TURN DIRECTIONS

1. From the trailhead kiosk, walk across the bridge, then turn right into the woods on the Sugarloaf Trail, which coincides with the Trestle Trail.
2. At 0.2 miles, turn left to continue on the Sugarloaf Trail.
3. At the col at 0.9 miles, turn right toward North Sugarloaf.
4. At 1.3 miles, reach the summit ledges on North Sugarloaf (2,310 feet). Retrace your steps back to the col.
5. At the col again at 1.6 miles, head south on the Sugarloaf Trail toward Middle Sugarloaf.
6. At 2.0 miles, reach the east ledges atop Middle Sugarloaf (2,539 feet).
7. At 2.2 miles, reach the south ledges on Middle Sugarloaf.
8. Retrace your steps to the col and descend to the trailhead.

FIND THE TRAILHEAD

From Twin Mountain (Carroll), at the junction of US Route 3 and US Route 302, drive east on US Route 302 for 2.2 miles. Turn right into Zealand Recreation Area and continue on Zealand Road for 0.9 miles to trailhead parking for the Sugarloaf Trail on the right.

REK'-LIS BREWING COMPANY

Ian Dowling and Marlaina Renton, passionate outdoors people with a love for mountain biking, backcountry skiing and good beer, are the dynamic duo behind the wildly popular Rek'-Lis Brewing Company (opened in 2016) in the mountain town of Bethlehem. If it's busy (and it usually is), put your name in for a table, then head to the "brew shed"

for a pint. Pretentious Hopper, a play on the name of the original trend-setting New England IPA, is the big seller among the eclectic selection of draft beers. With "Rek'-Lis abandon," enjoy a wander around this "adult playhouse," which features a beautiful beer garden, a maze of funky rooms and decks, regular live music and lots of games. Rek'-Lis Brewing—an adventure in great brews, delicious food and good fun—is an experience you won't soon forget.

LAND MANAGER

White Mountain National Forest
Pemigewasset Ranger District
71 White Mountain Drive
Campton, NH 03223
(603) 536-6100
www.fs.usda.gov/main/whitemountain/home
Trail map: amcstore.outdoors.org/products/white-mountain-national-forest-map-guide

BREWERY/RESTAURANT

Rek'-Lis Brewing Company
2085 Main Street
Bethlehem, NH 03574
(603) 991-2357
www.reklisbrewing.com
Distance from trailhead: 11 miles

PISGAH RIDGE

MEANDER THROUGH NEW HAMPSHIRE'S LARGEST STATE PARK

WINCHESTER, NH

▷⋯ STARTING POINT	⋯✕ DESTINATION
KILBURN TRAILHEAD, NH ROUTE 63	**PISGAH MOUNTAIN LOOP**
🍺 BEER	🏁 HIKE TYPE
KEENE KOLSCH	**STRENUOUS**
🐾 DOG FRIENDLY	📅 SEASON
YES (LEASH REQUIRED)	**APRIL TO NOVEMBER**
$ FEES	🕐 DURATION
YES	**4 HOURS 45 MIN.**
⛰ MAP REFERENCE	↦ LENGTH
PISGAH STATE PARK	**8.6 MILES (LOOP)**
🔍 HIGHLIGHTS	〰 ELEVATION GAIN
MATURE FORESTS, MOUNTAIN VIEWS, WILDERNESS CHARACTER	**950 FEET**

KOLSCH

STRAW YELLOW

LIGHT MALT
DELICATE FLORAL

CRISP, DRY, LIGHT
BREADY
MALTY

BITTERNESS

SWEETNESS

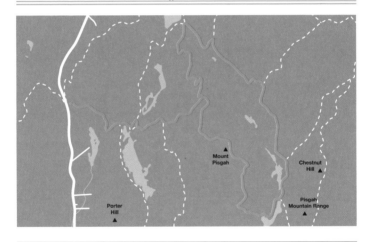

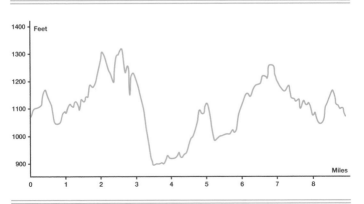

HIKE DESCRIPTION

Journey through Pisgah State Park, one of the wildest, least developed chunks of state-owned land in New England. Then wander into beautiful downtown Keene for cold beers and delicious food at Elm City Brewing.

Pisgah State Park spans the towns of Chesterfield, Hinsdale and Winchester in the rural southwest corner of New Hampshire. At 13,361 acres—a whopping 21 square miles—it is the largest property in the state park system, encompassing an entire watershed just north of the Ashuelot River within which there are seven ponds and reservoirs, four mountain ridges, numerous wetland areas, as well as plenty of wildlife. This hike follows six trails—Kilburn Road, the Kilburn Loop Trail, the Pisgah Ridge Connector, the Pisgah Ridge Trail, the Reservoir Trail and the Baker Pond Trail—in whole or in part as it tracks a lollipop loop through the western reaches of Pisgah State Park.

The multi-summited ridgeline of Pisgah Mountain tops out at just 1,329 feet, but don't let the moderate elevation fool you, as there are ups and downs enough to total nearly 1,000 feet on this walk in the woods. Take it in stride and enjoy your journey through one of the wildest, least developed chunks of state-owned land in New England. Posted maps here and there along the hiking route will help keep you on track.

The predominant forest cover in Pisgah State Park is hemlock, pine, beech and oak. It's around Pisgah Ridge that you'll walk through amazing stands of stately woods that are more than 200 years old, with some specimens close to 300 years of age. It's here, too, that the remoteness of the place might start to sink in, giving you that "out

there" feeling of solitude. And in a state where stone walls are seemingly everywhere, you could also find yourself asking, "Why are there no stone walls here?" The answer is that, unlike most of the region in the mid- to late-1800s, this forestland was never cleared for agriculture. It was instead managed sustainably by the Dickinson family, who eschewed clear-cutting in favor of single-tree selective harvesting, and thereby preserved much of what you see today.

On the long, granite Pisgah Ridge, as you walk through the pitch pines and red pines, blueberries and huckleberries, you will come upon a number of ledge viewpoints with fine vistas over the impressive unbroken forest. The bulk of Mount Monadnock (3,165 feet), perhaps New Hampshire's most climbed peak, figures large in the east, while to the west are Mounts Snow, Hogback, Haystack and Olga in Vermont. Tom Wessels, an ecologist and professor at Antioch New England University in nearby Keene, has described the eastward view from Pisgah Mountain as "the most wilderness summit view I have seen anywhere in New England," akin to the view from the Whites, the Adirondacks (NY) and the Greens (VT). Now that's a ringing endorsement.

TURN-BY-TURN DIRECTIONS

1. Begin at the kiosk and orange gate and walk east on Kilburn Road, a forest road.
2. At a junction at 0.65 miles, the Kilburn Road becomes the Kilburn Loop Trail; bear left to continue on the Kilburn Loop Trail.
3. At 0.85 miles, bear right to stay on the Kilburn Loop Trail and cross a footbridge.
4. At 0.9 miles, where the John Summers Trail goes right, stay left on the Kilburn Loop Trail.
5. At a Y-junction at 1.2 miles, where the Kilburn Loop Trail goes right, bear left on the Pisgah Ridge Connector toward the Pisgah Ridge Trail.
6. At 1.7 miles, reach the Pisgah Ridge Trail; turn right to follow the loop counterclockwise.
7. At 3.65 miles, after several ups and downs and viewpoints along Pisgah Ridge, reach the Reservoir Trail at the north end of Pisgah Reservoir. Turn left (north) to follow the wide track of the Reservoir Trail.
8. At 4.1 miles, where the Parker Trail goes right, bear left to stay on the Reservoir Trail.
9. At 4.8 miles, where the North Ponds Trail goes right, bear left to stay on the Reservoir Trail.
10. At 5.5 miles, where the Reservoir Trail continues straight ahead, turn left on the Baker Pond Trail.
11. At 5.9 miles, reach a four-way intersection. Here, the Baker Pond Trail heads north and the Town Forest Trail heads west. Turn left (south) on the Pisgah Ridge Trail.
12. At 7.0 miles, close the loop around Pisgah Mountain and turn right to retrace your steps back to the Kilburn Trailhead via the Pisgah Ridge Connector, the Kilburn Loop Trail and Kilburn Road.

FIND THE TRAILHEAD

From the intersection of NH Route 9 and NH Route 63 in Chesterfield, 9 miles west of Keene, turn south on NH Route 63 and drive 4.4 miles to the Kilburn Road Trailhead parking area on the left.

ELM CITY BREWING COMPANY

Debra Rivest opened Keene's first brewery in 1995 in the renovated historic Faulkner & Colony Woolen Mill on the edge of downtown. The tall stack of the 1838 structure, an unmistakable landmark adorned with the letters F & C, still looms large over Elm City Brewing. The front patio area, shaded by graceful silver maples, greets you upon arrival, while inside, the brewpub features warm wood and brick in the sunroom, cozy bar and main dining room. You'll find "No Crap on Tap" at

Elm City, says Rivest of the traditional menu of beers—from German lagers and Belgian Dubbels to American IPAs and English porters, plus the contemporary New England IPA's, sours, seasonals and small-batch brews. Enjoy your choice of brew with a plate of locally sourced, scratch-made delights created by the talented kitchen team.

LAND MANAGER

Pisgah State Park
520 Old Chesterfield Road
Winchester, NH 03470
(603) 239-8153
Info and trail map: www.nhstateparks.org/visit/state-parks/pisgah-state-park

BREWERY/RESTAURANT

Elm City Brewing Company
The Colony Mill
222 West Street
Keene, NH 03431
(603) 355-3335
www.elmcitybrewing.com
Distance from trailhead: 15 miles

THE SWEET TRAIL

AMBLE THROUGH A MIX OF COASTAL CONSERVATION LANDS NEAR THE GREAT BAY ESTUARY

DURHAM, NH

▷⋯ STARTING POINT	⋯✗ DESTINATION
LONGMARSH ROAD	**GREAT BAY ESTUARY**
🍺 BEER	HIKE TYPE
FULL CLIP NEIPA	**MODERATE**
🐾 DOG FRIENDLY	SEASON
YES (LEASH REQUIRED)	**YEAR-ROUND**
$ FEES	🕐 DURATION
NO	**2 HOURS 45 MIN.**
⛰ MAP REFERENCE	↦ LENGTH
THE CY AND BOBBIE SWEET TRAIL TRAIL MAP & GUIDE	**5.3 MILES (ONE-WAY)**
🔎 HIGHLIGHTS	〜 ELEVATION GAIN
PONDS, WETLANDS, SALT MARSHES, WILDLIFE, BAY VIEWS	**190 FEET**

NEW ENGLAND IPA

HAZY GOLD

PINEAPPLE
PEACH
CITRUS

CITRUS
TROPICAL

BITTERNESS

SWEETNESS

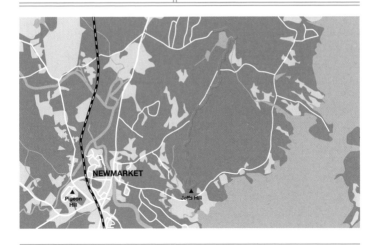

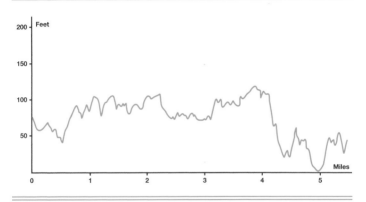

HIKE DESCRIPTION

 Enjoy a sweet stroll on the Sweet Trail through a mosaic of protected coastal lands adjacent to Great Bay. Then put on a happy face with a good brew at Stoneface Brewing.

Great Bay is an enormous tidal estuary in southeastern New Hampshire spanning more than 6,000 acres. Dominated by the twice-daily tides, the estuary drains three major rivers—the Lamprey, Squamscott and Winnicut—while four others feed the system en route to the Piscataqua River and the Gulf of Maine. The Great Bay Estuary, formed by the mixing of melting glaciers and sea water eons ago, is ecologically significant because of its abundance of critically important wildlife habitats.

In the mid-1970s, Durham Point on Great Bay was proposed as the site of the world's largest oil refinery, a project planned and bankrolled by shipping and oil magnate Aristotle Onassis and which would have operated a pipeline extending out to the seacoast at Isle of Shoals. Recognizing and reacting to the potential destruction of this fragile and invaluable ecosystem, a well-organized grassroots campaign worked tirelessly to defeat the proposal. Thanks to the votes of more than 1,000 Durham residents in 1974, the project was crushed.

The refinery fight reignited and galvanized support for the Great Bay Estuary, and this led to the formation of the Great Bay Resource Protection Partnership, a coalition of local, state and national partners that has been working to protect land and encourage stewardship and recreation in the region since 1994. This extraordinary collaboration

has resulted in the conservation of more than 10,000 acres in the Great Bay watershed. Among its accomplishments was the creation of the Sweet Trail in 2007.

The Sweet Trail, named for longtime conservation advocates Cyrus and Bobbie Sweet of nearby New Castle, NH, threads a wonderful 5-mile route through a mosaic of protected public and private properties, from Long Marsh in Durham to Lubberland Creek in Newmarket. Marked by blue and white diamonds bearing the GBRPP logo, this walk is rich with the natural delights of upland forests, marshes, beaver ponds, creeks, salt marshes, and bird and animal life aplenty.

Near the trail's end, granite benches ring a large, round marker dedicated to Cy and Bobbie Sweet for "the inspiration to connect people and nature, the leadership to join the land to the sea, the support to link conservation lands together with this trail, and the vision of hope for the next generation, that they too may enjoy the beauty of Great Bay."

TURN-BY-TURN DIRECTIONS

1. Walk 100 feet along Longmarsh Road to a kiosk and red gate; pass around the gate and continue straight ahead.
2. At 0.5 miles, turn sharply right off the old road and onto the Sweet Trail.
3. At 1.25 miles, cross the gravel Dame Road.
4. At 1.9 miles, reach Dame Road again, with a garden of stones and several interpretive signs on the left and a parking lot on the right.
5. At 2.2 miles, the trail reaches Dame Road once more; turn left to follow it.
6. At 2.5 miles, turn left off Dame Road and into Lubberland Creek Preserve.
7. At 3.8 miles, avoid Chanell Loop ahead; turn right to stay on the Sweet Trail.
8. At 3.9 miles, reach Jeff's Hill Loop and turn right. For the next 0.4 miles, the Sweet Trail and Jeff's Hill Loop coincide.
9. At a four-way intersection at 4.4 miles (right leads to the Lubberland Creek Preserve trailhead parking lot; left is Jeff's Hill Loop), continue straight.
10. At 4.5 miles, cross paved Bay Road.
11. At 4.8 miles, arrive at the salt marshes of the Great Bay estuary and the end of the Sweet Trail. Retrace your steps to Bay Road and turn left to reach the Lubberland Creek Preserve trailhead and the end of the walk.

FIND THE TRAILHEAD

Starting trailhead: From the US Route 4/NH Route 108 interchange in Durham, drive south on NH Route 108 for 2 miles, then turn left on Longmarsh Road and proceed. In 0.9 miles, the road turns to dirt, and in another 0.3 miles, there's a small, unsigned dirt parking lot on the left. *Ending trailhead:* From the junction of Longmarsh Road and NH Route 108, drive south on NH Route 108 2.4 miles to Newmarket, then turn left on Bay Road. In 1.1 miles, pass The Nature Conservancy's Great Bay office. Continue another 0.3 miles to trailhead parking on the left at TNC's Lubberland Creek Preserve. (Spot a vehicle here or arrange for a taxi or rideshare at the end of your hike to transport you back to the starting trailhead.)

STONEFACE BREWING CO.

Stoneface Brewing's name is a tip of the hat to New Hampshire's state icon, the Old Man of the Mountains, the 40-foot granite profile of a human face that stood high on Cannon Mountain overlooking Franconia Notch until it collapsed in 2003. It's fun nostalgia for owner Pete Beauregard, who grew up in the Old Man's shadow and went on to

open Stoneface Brewing in 2014. "We brew the beer we like to drink," says Beauregard, whose tap menu includes the popular IPA and Full Clip NEIPA and a host of other great brews, as well as regular experimental batches. Enjoy a pint in the casual, family-friendly atmosphere of the funky tasting room or sit outside under the big tent. Satisfy the munchies with something delish from the full kitchen, like the popular smash burger, Philly cheese steak or killer wings.

TRAIL MANAGER

Great Bay Resource Protection Partnership
(603) 868-6112
Info and trail map: www.greatbaypartnership.org

BREWERY/RESTAURANT

Stoneface Brewing Co.
436 Shattuck Way
Newington, NH 03801
(603) 427-9801
www.stonefacebrewing.com
Distance from trailhead: 9 miles

MAINE

ACADIA NATIONAL PARK

EXPERIENCE THE SCENIC HEART OF MAINE'S BELOVED NATIONAL PARK ON THIS POND AND MOUNTAIN HIKE

BAR HARBOR, ME

▷··· STARTING POINT	··✕ DESTINATION
JORDAN POND	**SARGENT MOUNTAIN AND PENOBSCOT MOUNTAIN**
🍺 BEER	HIKE TYPE
FLAT HAT AMERICAN PALE ALE	**MODERATE**
🐾 DOG FRIENDLY	📅 SEASON
YES (LEASH REQUIRED)	**MAY TO OCTOBER**
💲 FEES	🕐 DURATION
YES	**3 HOURS 45 MIN.**
⛺ MAP REFERENCE	↦ LENGTH
PURCHASE AT PARK VISITOR CENTERS OR TOWN SHOPS	**6.4 MILES (LOOP)**
🔎 HIGHLIGHTS	〰 ELEVATION GAIN
PRETTY LAKE, HIDDEN POND, GRANITE CLIFFS, MOUNTAIN VIEWS	**1,200 FEET**

AMERICAN PALE ALE

STRAW
UNFILTERED

BREADY, GRASSY
FLORAL
EARTHY

CRISP
LIGHT

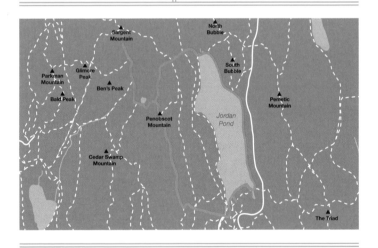

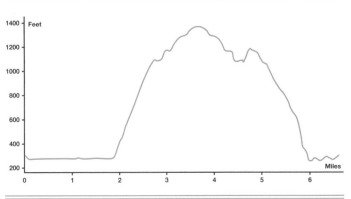

HIKE DESCRIPTION

Sample some of Acadia's finest sights on a walk along Jordan Pond and a climb of Sargent and Penobscot mountains. Then head into bustling Bar Harbor to sample the fine beers and eats at Atlantic Brewing's Midtown brewpub.

Acadia National Park protects a spectacular 51,000-acre chunk of Maine's eastern coastline, with the bulk of the acreage—some 31,000 acres—on Mount Desert Island. Scoured and shaped by the action of powerful glaciers eons ago, the 80,000-acre island, the state's largest, is divided into distinct east and west halves by Somes Sound, a natural *fjard*. Blue Hill Bay to the west and Frenchman Bay to the east bookend the island.

A jumble of 26 pink-granite mountains range across MDI, with eight peaks exceeding 1,000 feet in elevation. At 1,528 feet, Cadillac Mountain is the highest summit. The island also features 26 pretty lakes and ponds, 41 miles of rugged shoreline, and an abundance of wildlife. More than 125 miles of hiking trails and walking paths, 45 miles of non-motorized carriage roads and the 27-mile Park Loop Road offer countless ways for visitors to enjoy the park.

Permanent protection for lands on MDI began with the establishment of Sieur de Monts National Monument in 1916. Congress redesignated this as Lafayette National Park three years later, and in 1929, the name was changed to Acadia. In 1604, Samuel de Champlain, the French explorer, described the island's mountains as "destitute of trees, as there are only rocks on them," and subsequently named the place *Isle de Monts Deserts* or "Island of Barren Mountains," an apt description of this natural wonder of the Maine coast.

This scenic walk leads you into the heart of Acadia National Park on the east side of MDI to Jordan Pond, the park's deepest and second-largest lake. The hike follows five fabulous footpaths—the Jordan Pond Path, the Deer Brook Trail, the Penobscot Mountain Trail, the Sargent South Ridge Trail and the Spring Trail—and along the way you'll cross several of the park's historic carriage roads.

The route along the east side of the pond offers outstanding views of the steep walls of South Bubble and Jordan Cliffs before climbing along Deer Brook and then on to tiny Sargent Mountain Pond. From the wide-open ridgetops of Sargent Mountain (1,367 feet) and Penobscot Mountain (1,243 feet), you'll enjoy amazing panoramic vistas east and west across the island, north to the mainland hills and south to the Gulf of Maine and a multitude of islands.

Tea and popovers with creamery butter and strawberry jam on the grassy lawn at Jordan Pond House—where you can relax and view much of the hike you just completed—are a wonderfully traditional way to conclude this fine circuit (before heading into Bar Harbor for a beer, of course)!

TURN-BY-TURN DIRECTIONS

1. Begin at the kiosk at the west end of the parking lot, walk down the boat ramp drive to the pond and turn right on the Jordan Pond Path.
2. Follow the Jordan Pond Path around the south, east and north sides of the pond, passing the Bubble & Jordan Ponds Path, the Jordan Pond Carry and the Bubbles Trail, and the Bubbles Divide Trail en route.
3. At 1.8 miles, leave Jordan Pond and turn right on the Deer Brook Trail.
4. In a prominent notch at 2.7 miles, turn right on the Penobscot Mountain Trail.
5. At 2.8 miles, reach Sargent Mountain Pond.
6. At 2.9 miles, turn right on the Sargent South Ridge Trail.
7. At 3.6 miles, reach the summit of Sargent Mountain, passing the Hadlock Brook Trail and the Maple Spring Trail en route.
8. To continue, retrace your steps to the notch at the Deer Brook Trail junction at 4.5 miles via the Sargent South Ridge Trail and the Penobscot Mountain Trail. Continue ahead on the Penobscot Mountain Trail.
9. At 4.6 miles, reach the summit of Penobscot Mountain.
10. At a fork at 5.5 miles, turn left on the Spring Trail and descend to the east.
11. Cross a carriage road, pass the Jordan Cliffs Trail, pass the Asticou & Jordan Pond Path and finally cross another carriage road to reach Jordan Pond House at 6.1 miles.
12. Follow the path along Jordan Pond House out to Jordan Pond at 6.2 miles. Turn right to reach the boat ramp drive and then the trailhead parking lot.

FIND THE TRAILHEAD

By car: From the junction of ME Route 3 and ME Route 233 in Bar Harbor, travel west on ME Route 233 for about 1 mile, then turn right into Acadia National Park and proceed to the Park Loop Road. Turn left (south) on the two-way section of the Park Loop Road and drive 5 miles to the Jordan Pond trailhead and boat launch parking lot on the right. *By bus*: From late June through mid-October, Acadia visitors may use the free Island Explorer shuttle bus (a park entrance pass is required) to reach Jordan Pond, which is served by routes 4 and 5. Visit exploreacadia.com for schedule information.

ATLANTIC BREWING COMPANY, MIDTOWN

Bar Harbor is the gateway to Acadia National Park, and Atlantic Brewing's Midtown location is your portal to great brews and delish pub fare. The family-owned, modern brewery has a northern European feel to it, with lots of exposed metal, big glass windows and a large polished concrete bar to cozy up to. There's also a beer garden on the roof, which is a sweet spot to hang out on a nice summer day. The Real Ale and Blueberry Ale are longtime classics, but you might also want to try the Flat Hat American Pale Ale, a cold, crisp, refreshing light beer. A portion of Flat Hat sales helps support water quality research at Jordan Pond in the park, so you can drink beer and do good. Enjoy your brew with a Midtown Classic Burger, one of the best anywhere!

LAND MANAGER

Acadia National Park
Hulls Cove Visitor Center
25 Visitor Center Road
Bar Harbor, ME 04609
(207) 288-3338
General info and entrance pass (required) info: www.nps.gov/acad
Trail maps: A variety of maps are available at shops around MDI and at park concessions.

BREWERY/RESTAURANT

Atlantic Brewing Company-Midtown
52 Cottage Street
Bar Harbor, ME 04609
(207) 288-2326
www.atlanticbrewing.com/midtown
Distance from trailhead: 6.8 miles

BANGOR CITY FOREST & ORONO BOG

EXPLORE A RARE RAISED PEAT BOG AND WALK THROUGH A BIG, BEAUTIFUL MUNICIPAL FOREST

BANGOR AND ORONO, ME

▷⋯ STARTING POINT	⋯✕ DESTINATION
TRIPP DRIVE TRAILHEAD	**ORONO BOG, EAST-WEST LOOP**
🍺 BEER	🗺 HIKE TYPE
CATCHPHRASE NEIPA	**MODERATE**
🐾 DOG FRIENDLY	📅 SEASON
CITY FOREST: YES (LEASH REQUIRED); BOG WALK: NO	CITY FOREST: YEAR-ROUND; BOG WALK: MAY TO LATE NOVEMBER
$ FEES	🕐 DURATION
CITY FOREST: NO; BOG WALK: DONATIONS APPRECIATED	**2.5 HOURS**
⌂ MAP REFERENCE	↦ LENGTH
ROLAND PERRY CITY FOREST, ORONO BOG BOARDWALK	**5.0 MILES (LOOP)**
🔎 HIGHLIGHTS	〰 ELEVATION GAIN
STATELY PINE TREES, RAISED PEAT BOG, OLD RAILROAD BED	**30 FEET**

NEW ENGLAND IPA

LIGHT GOLD
SLIGHTLY HAZY

CITRUS
MELON
SLIGHTLY DANK

CITRUS
MELON
BREADY

BITTERNESS   SWEETNESS

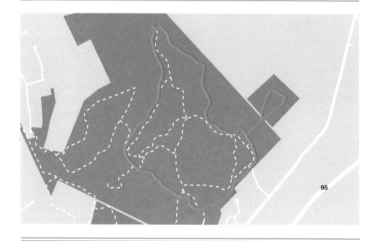

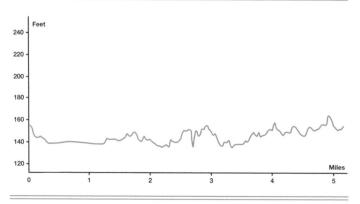

HIKE DESCRIPTION

Explore a fascinating peat bog on a beautiful boardwalk and wander through the tall pines of Bangor's city forest. Cap off your adventure with brews and Chinese and Asian cuisine at Bangor Beer Co.

Just minutes from the hubbub of the Bangor Mall area and Interstate 95 is a surprisingly wild 686-acre block of land known as the Bangor City Forest—or more officially, the Roland F. Perry City Forest, in honor of the former city forester who cared for Bangor's parks and woodlands from 1964 to 2006. Nine miles of trails wend through these big woods, which are popular with walkers, hikers, runners and mountain bikers alike.

Adjacent to the city forest is the Orono Bog, a 616-acre expanse of raised peat bog that is home to a wide array of northern bog plants, from small-leaved cranberry, bog rosemary and Labrador tea to leatherleaf and a host of evergreen shrubs and dwarf conifer trees. The bog is accessed from the city forest via a beautiful 4-foot-wide, 4,200-foot-long floating boardwalk that makes a lollipop loop.

This hike follows the entire East-West Loop Trail, which extends to all corners of the Bangor City Forest on its 4-mile circuit. A quarter-mile into the hike, you'll bear east to enjoy a stroll through the largely wide-open bog landscape. The boardwalk passes through a number of different ecological zones, from mixed-wooded fen to conifer-wooded fen to wooded-shrub heath and moss lawn. Seven interpretive stations offer a wealth of information about this fascinating landscape, which was designated a National Natural Landmark in 1974.

The Bangor City Forest is managed not only for recreation and as wildlife habitat but as a demonstration forest as well, and on this pleasant route you'll pass through impressive stands of white pine, red pine and white spruce. Partway along, be sure to take the short side-trip to visit the old Veazie Railroad Bed, part of the former 12-mile public railway that carried people and goods between Bangor and Milford from 1836 to 1869.

TURN-BY-TURN DIRECTIONS

1. The East-West Loop Trail starts at map post 1 on the northeast side of the parking area.
2. At a cabin and kiosks at 0.3 miles, turn right on the Orono Bog Boardwalk, a 1-mile lollipop loop.
3. At 1.3 miles, back at the cabin/kiosks, turn right to continue on the East-West Loop Trail, immediately passing map post 2.
4. At map post 3 at 1.6 miles, pass the Deer Trail.
5. At map post 4 at 2.2 miles, pass the Rabbit Trail.
6. At map post 5 at 2.6 miles, reach a four-way junction with Main Road; turn right and walk 150 feet to see the old Veazie Railroad Bed. Double back to the intersection, then turn right to continue on the East-West Loop Trail.
7. At map post 6 at 3.0 miles, the Rabbit Trail forks to the left; bear right to continue.
8. At 3.9 miles, pass map post 7 and the Moose Trail.
9. At 4.3 miles, cross the Arboretum Trail and pass map post 8.
10. At 4.4 miles, pass the Deer Trail and map post 9.
11. At 4.5 miles, cross Main Road at map post 10.
12. At map post 11 at 4.9 miles, where the Bog Trail forks left, bear right and continue back to trailhead.

FIND THE TRAILHEAD

From I-95, Exit 187 in Bangor, drive west on Hogan Road for 0.6 miles. Then turn right on Stillwater Avenue and proceed 1.6 miles to Tripp Drive on the left. Turn here and continue 0.3 miles to the trailhead parking at the end of the road.

BANGOR BEER CO.

Oriental Jade, one of Bangor's most popular eateries, was established in 1979 by the Lo family. Find "the Jade," as it is affectionately referred to by locals, in a far corner of the sprawling Bangor Mall parking lot, and you'll also have found the adjoining Bangor Beer Company. Opened by the Lo family in 2017, the decor of the brewery's comfortable tasting room is a bit of Brooklyn in Bangor, a mix of

hipster, eclectic, nostalgic and casual. Catchphrase, a sessionable New England IPA with a creamy body, is Bangor Beer's flagship brew among the twelve taps, which feature everything from other regulars like Juri (a DDH NEIPA) and Odd Ball (an American Stout) to limited releases and surprise brews. Got the munchies? Order up tasty Chinese, Asian and American delights from right next door.

LAND AND TRAIL MANAGERS

Bangor Parks & Recreation Dept.
647 Main Street
Bangor, ME 04401
(207) 992-4490
Info and trail map: www.bangormaine.gov/trails

Orono Bog Boardwalk
Jim Bird, Boardwalk Project Director
james.bird@maine.edu
Info and trail map: umaine.edu/oronobogwalk

BREWERY/RESTAURANT

Bangor Beer Co.
330 Bangor Mall Boulevard
Bangor, ME 04401
(207) 947-6960
www.bangorbeerco.com
Distance from trailhead: 2.9 miles

FOREST CITY TRAIL

CONNECT A HOST OF PORTLAND'S URBAN GREEN SPACES ON ITS MINI VERSION OF THE APPALACHIAN TRAIL

PORTLAND, ME

▷⋯ STARTING POINT	⋯✗ DESTINATION
STROUDWATER RIVER	**PRESUMPSCOT RIVER**
🍺 BEER	🚏 HIKE TYPE
ISHMAEL COPPER ALE	**MODERATE-STRENUOUS**
🐾 DOG FRIENDLY	📅 SEASON
YES (LEASH REQUIRED)	**YEAR-ROUND**
$ FEES	🕐 DURATION
NO	**6 HOURS**
⛰ MAP REFERENCE	↦ LENGTH
PORTLAND TRAILS: TRAILS, PARKS & OPEN SPACES	**10.7 MILES (ONE-WAY)**
🔍 HIGHLIGHTS	〰 ELEVATION GAIN
URBAN WILDS, GREEN SPACES, RIVERS, WATERFALLS, HISTORY	**400 FEET**

COPPER ALE

COPPER PENNY

WHOLE WHEAT TOAST
MOLASSES

MALTY, TOASTY
SWEET,
EARTHY

BITTERNESS   SWEETNESS

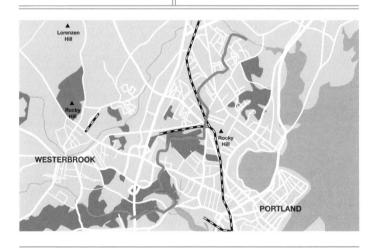

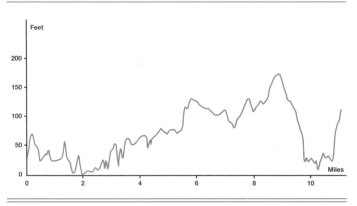

HIKE DESCRIPTION

 Visit a wide variety of woods, waters and waysides on this wonderful long walk through the city of Portland. When you're through, reward yourself with a beer and a bite at Rising Tide Brewing.

The Forest City Trail follows a serpentine route across Portland, from the southwest corner of the city near Westbrook to its northern margin on the boundary with Falmouth. This 10-mile hike across Maine's largest city combines numerous trails as it connects a diverse natural landscape and many sites that reveal a wealth of human history, taking hikers from the quiet of the wild places and green spaces to the sights and sounds of urban streets and residential neighborhoods.

The trail is the vision of Tom Jewell, a Portland native, attorney, trails advocate and one of the founders of Portland Trails. For years, Jewell led regular walks the length of the trail route; he eventually decided to formalize the increasingly popular trek, which is affectionately considered Portland's own mini version of the Appalachian Trail. The Forest City Trail was waymarked with blazes, signs and information kiosks, and was officially opened to the public in 2011.

Portland Trails is a nonprofit urban land trust that has been building trails and linking open spaces, neighborhoods and schools for both recreation and transportation purposes since 1991. The Forest City Trail forms the spine of the Portland Trails network, which has grown to more than 70 miles. The land trust produces both a paper and a digital map; one or the other is a must for navigating the many twists and turns along the Forest City Trail.

From the Blueberry Road trailhead at the hike's southern end, the Forest City Trail follows the winding corridor of the placid Stroudwater River. Next comes the Fore River Sanctuary, which features a stroll through the salt marshes along the remains of historic Cumberland and Oxford Canal, and then a wooded romp to cascading Jewell Falls, Portland's only natural waterfall. Further on is Evergreen Cemetery and its pleasant mature woods and pretty duck ponds. The hike later traverses Oat Nuts Park before reaching roaring Presumpscot Falls in the Presumpscot River Preserve. Between these highlights, the trail meanders through the wooded patches and neighborhoods of Stroudwater, Nasons Corner, Sagamore Village, Morrills Corner and North Deering.

TURN-BY-TURN DIRECTIONS

(Note: this is an abbreviated list of turns)

1. From the end of Blueberry Road, veer right over broken pavement to several brick buildings, where an information kiosk marks the start of the Stroudwater Trail and the Forest City Trail.
2. At River's Edge Drive at 1.3 miles, turn left along Congress Street; at 1.8 miles, turn left off Congress Street and onto the footpath into Fore River Sanctuary.
3. At Hillcrest Avenue at 3.5 miles, turn left along Brighton Avenue.
4. At Rowe Avenue at 3.6 miles, cross Brighton Avenue, turn left along it, and at 3.7 miles, turn right on Lomond Street (dirt).
5. At the end of Woodvale Street at 4.6 miles, enter Evergreen Cemetery.
6. At College Avenue at 5.7 miles, turn left along Stevens Avenue.
7. At 6.1 miles, cross Forest Avenue and proceed along Allen Avenue.
8. At 6.7 miles, turn left off Allen Avenue into the campus of Portland Arts & Technology High School.
9. At the corner of Skylark Avenue at 7.5 miles, cross Washington Avenue and turn left; at 7.6 miles, turn right onto the Shalom Trail.
10. At 7.8 miles, cross Auburn Street and enter the grounds of Harrison Lyseth Elementary School.
11. At the corner of Bramblewood Drive at 8.3 miles, cross Summit Street and turn left along it.
12. At 8.7 miles, turn right into Oat Nuts Park at the silver gate and kiosk.
13. At 9.3 miles, a side trail on the left leads to trailhead parking at the end of Overset Road. Just ahead, enter the Presumpscot River Preserve.
14. At 10 miles, reach the base of Presumpscot Falls and the end of the Forest City Trail. Retrace your steps from this point to the trailhead parking at Overset Road.

FIND THE TRAILHEAD

Starting trailhead: From I-95/Maine Turnpike, Exit 46 in Portland, turn left on Skyway and proceed to Congress Street. Turn right and drive 0.2 miles, then turn left on Blueberry Road and follow it 0.2 miles to its end, where there is trailhead parking. *Ending trailhead:* From I-95/Maine Turnpike, Exit 53 in West Falmouth, turn right on Auburn Street (ME Routes 26/100) and drive 1.0 miles to Summit Street. Turn left on Summit Street, and in 0.4 miles, turn left on Curtis Road. In 0.3 miles, turn right on Overset Road and follow it 0.1 miles to the trailhead parking at its end. You'll want to spot a vehicle here or arrange for a taxi or rideshare at the end of your hike.

RISING TIDE BREWING COMPANY

Established by Portland originals Nathan and Heather Sanborn, Rising Tide Brewing's tasting room has been an anchor of the city's East Bayside neighborhood since 2012. Rising Tide is characterized by "creative flavors, quality, consistency and a love for all things outdoors," and you'll feel right at home at this casual, comfortable hangout, whether you choose to sit inside the big bay doors of the former truck maintenance facility or outside on what's affectionately called the "tar patio." Rising Tide serves up 14 "balanced, approachable, easy drinking and dynamic beers," most with nautical-themed names and all with brightly colored, eye-catching graphics. The popular copper ale, Ishmael—a nod to the seafaring character in Herman Melville's *Moby-Dick*—is Rising Tide's original beer and remains a genuine crowd pleaser. Enjoy yours with a delish bite of elevated pub fare from the in-house kitchen, The Galley.

LAND MANAGER

Portland Trails
305 Commercial Street
Portland, ME 04101
(207) 775-2411
Info and trail map: trails.org

BREWERY/RESTAURANT

Rising Tide Brewing Company
103 Fox Street
Portland, ME 04101
(207) 370-2337
risingtidebrewing.com
Distance from trailhead: 4.8 miles

MONHEGAN ISLAND

HIKE A RUGGED ISLAND 10 MILES OUT TO SEA

MONHEGAN ISLAND, ME

▷··· STARTING POINT	···✕ DESTINATION
MONHEGAN WHARF	**WHITE HEAD**
🍺 BEER	🔳 HIKE TYPE
ISLAND FARM DOUBLE IPA	**EASY-MODERATE**
🐾 DOG FRIENDLY	📅 SEASON
YES (LEASH REQUIRED)	**APRIL TO OCTOBER**
$ FEES	🕐 DURATION
YES	**1 HOUR 40 MIN.**
⛰ MAP REFERENCE	↦ LENGTH
MONHEGAN ASSOCIATES TRAIL MAP	**3.1 MILES (LOOP)**
🔍 HIGHLIGHTS	〰 ELEVATION GAIN
BOLD OCEAN CLIFFS, SHIPWRECK, LIGHTHOUSE, MUSEUM	**300 FEET**

 DOUBLE IPA

 LIGHT AMBER/ORANGE

 PINE
CITRUS
CANDY-LIKE

 CARAMEL
CITRUS
PINE

BITTERNESS | SWEETNESS

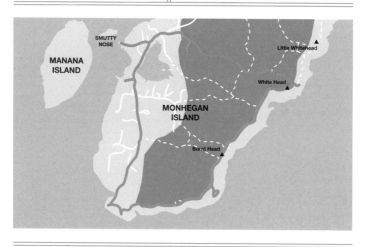

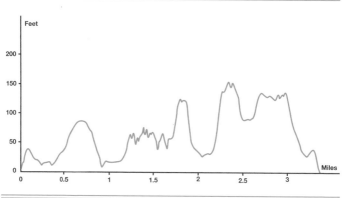

HIKE DESCRIPTION

Enjoy a salty ferry ride to Monhegan Island 10 miles off the Maine coast for a spectacular clifftop hiking loop and great brews at the small-batch Monhegan Brewing Company.

Monhegan Island, roughly 1.75 miles long and 0.75 miles across, is heavily forested with spruce and fir, and its rugged shorelines are dominated by cliffs of gabbro, an igneous rock of volcanic origin. On the island's west side is a snug harbor and a compact village of about 75 year-round residents. The balance of the island is preserved in an undeveloped state and managed by Monhegan Associates. Well-known as an artists' colony for more than 100 years, this incredibly beautiful island has been preserved through the foresight and dedication of many; today, its unspoiled scenery inspires thousands of visitors.

From the wharf, stroll uphill past the charming Island Inn, then amble along Main Street with its collection of shops, eateries and cottages. From Monhegan House, the island's only public restrooms are 150 feet to the left up Horns Hill Road. Continue on Lobster Cove Road to Monhegan Brewing Company. Sample a brew now or return afterward to enjoy the cool "Trap Room." Lobster Cove Road narrows to a footpath that leads out to a meadow at Lobster Point. Head left to the lifesaving ring hanging on a post atop the rocks, then on to the rusted wreckage of the *D.T. Sheridan*, a 110-foot tug that ran aground in dense fog in November 1948.

Monhegan's 9 miles of trails are numbered 1 through 18, and you're now on the Cliff Trail (1), which leads around the outer edge of the island. The trail's short ups and downs en route are numerous, but for

each new incline you're rewarded with bold ocean vistas. Occasionally the Cliff Trail splits, and the alternative path (1A), takes an easier interior route.

The Cliff Trail leads around Christmas Cove to a huge slab known as Gull Rock; make the short side-scramble to its top for an up-close-and-personal look at the churning ocean. Burnt Head is visible to the north, and soon enough you're climbing to its open ledges. After circling around Gull Cove, hike on to the grassy ledges atop White Head, 155 feet above the Gulf of Maine. From this vantage point, there's a great view north up the rocky coast to Black Head. To the east, there's nothing but the Atlantic Ocean between you and Europe. Relax for a while, enjoy the scenery and keep an eye out for shore and sea birds, porpoises and seals.

Head inland for the village on the White Head Trail (7) to reach Lighthouse Hill, the Monhegan Lighthouse (built in 1824) and the Monhegan Museum of Art & History. Housed in the former lightkeeper's house, the museum is a wonderful showcase of the island's natural and human history. Browse the grounds, then settle down on a bench to enjoy the tremendous view over the village, which is just a few minutes' walk below you.

TURN-BY-TURN DIRECTIONS

1. From the wharf, walk uphill on the gravel lane past the Island Inn.
2. In 0.1 miles, turn right on Main Street and proceed through the village.
3. At the Monhegan House intersection at 0.5 miles, go straight on Lobster Cove Road.
4. At 0.7 miles, arrive at Monhegan Brewing Company.
5. At 1.0 miles, reach Lobster Point and the wreck of the *D.T. Sheridan*. The Cliff Trail (1) starts here.
6. At 1.4 miles, pass Gull Rock (spur to top of rock).
7. At 1.7 miles, the Underhill Trail (3) enters from the left.
8. At 1.8 miles, reach the top of Burnt Head and the Burnt Head Trail (4).
9. At Gull Cove at 2.0 miles, the Gull Cove Trail (5) enters from the left.
10. At 2.2 miles, reach the top of White Head.
11. From White Head, follow the White Head Trail inland, passing the Red Ribbon Trail (9) and the Alder Trail (6) en route.
12. At 2.7 miles, reach the Monhegan Museum, just 0.4 miles from the wharf.

FIND THE TRAILHEAD

From the junction of US Route 1 and ME Route 131 in Thomaston, drive south on ME Route 131 for 14.2 miles to Port Clyde and the Monhegan Boat Line ferry terminal. A staff member will direct you to a parking spot on the dock. The boat line offers year-round service to Monhegan Island, located 10 miles offshore, via the Laura B or Elizabeth Ann; sailing time is about an hour each way. No cars are allowed on the island. Tickets may be purchased at the office at the dock, but advance reservations are recommended (info, schedules, tickets: monheganboat.com, (207) 372-8848).

MONHEGAN BREWING COMPANY

Opened in 2013, Monhegan Brewing is owned and operated by year-round island residents Mary and Matt Weber, with the help of Mary's father, Danny McGovern, a pioneer in the Maine brewing community who taught them the art and science of producing great beer. The brewery's unique outdoor "Trap Room" is an enclosure of 400 lobster traps stacked five-high, complete with picnic tables and canopies. Come winter, Matt works as a lobsterman, and those same traps are put to use fishing the waters around Monhegan Island. Relax and enjoy a pour of "craft beer 10 miles out to sea" from the five rotating taps; there's also a seltzer tap, and for the kids, there's non-alcoholic root beer and ginger beer. BYO lunch or grab a yummy bite—think fried seafood, po' boys and bahn-mi sandwiches—from the food truck.

LAND MANAGER

Monhegan Associates, Inc.
monheganassociates.org
A trail map is available online. You can also obtain one at the Monhegan Boat Line ticket office (nominal fee) where you can also get a free copy of *A Visitors Guide to Monhegan Maine*. Trail maps are also available at many shops on the island.

BREWERY

Monhegan Brewing Company
1 Boody Lane
Monhegan, ME 04852
(207) 596-0011
monheganbrewing.com
Open seasonally from April to October
Distance from wharf/trailhead: 0.7 miles (on trail)

MOXIE BALD MOUNTAIN

HIKE THE APPALACHIAN TRAIL TO ONE OF MAINE'S FINEST SUMMIT VIEWS

BALD MOUNTAIN TOWNSHIP, ME

▷··· STARTING POINT	···✕ DESTINATION
TROUTDALE ROAD	**MOXIE BALD SUMMIT**
🍺 BEER	🔲 HIKE TYPE
BIG MAMA BLUEBERRY ALE	**STRENUOUS**
🐾 DOG FRIENDLY	📅 SEASON
YES	**MAY TO OCTOBER**
$ FEES	🕐 DURATION
NO	**4 HOURS 45 MIN.**
⛰ MAP REFERENCE	↦ LENGTH
APPALACHIAN TRAIL—MOXIE BALD	**9.4 MILES (ROUND TRIP)**
👁 HIGHLIGHTS	〜 ELEVATION GAIN
HUGE SUMMIT VIEWS, SCENIC LAKES, APPALACHIAN TRAIL	**1,700 FEET**

BLONDE ALE

GOLDEN

SUBTLE HOPS
BLUEBERRY

MALTY
BLUEBERRY

BITTERNESS   SWEETNESS

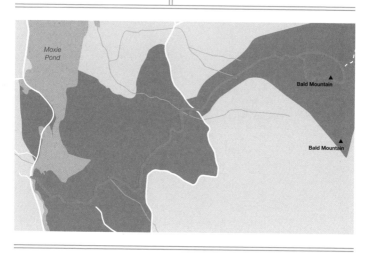

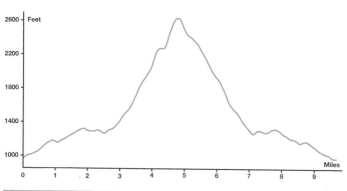

HIKE DESCRIPTION

Hike the Appalachian Trail to the huge granite ledges atop Moxie Bald for one of the finest panoramas in the entire state of Maine. Quench your thirst post-hike with a Big Mama Blueberry Ale at Kennebec River Brewery.

Moxie Bald Mountain rises to 2,630 feet in remote Bald Mountain Township. It is the highest point along the Appalachian Trail between the Kennebec River and the village of Monson. The mountaintop's extensive open granite ledges offer hikers extraordinary views in every direction, plus plenty of delicious wild blueberries (Maine's official state fruit) in high summer.

From Troutdale Road at the south end of Moxie Pond, rock-hop across Baker Stream and follow the AT's white paint blazes into the woods beyond. It's a pleasant couple of miles over gently rising terrain to Bald Mountain Brook and then, just beyond, to Bald Mountain Brook Lean-to. This three-sided log shelter is meant for overnight camping, but it's a great place for a break for day hikers. After the shelter, you'll begin climbing Moxie Bald in earnest.

Beyond the Summit Bypass (part of your descent route), the AT follows a mossy ledge wall, then passes through a cool slab rock cave and passageway. After the trail breaks out of the trees, you'll follow rock cairns over the sweeping granite slabs. Be sure to turn around often to appreciate the views over Moxie Pond to Moxie, Pleasant Pond and Mosquito mountains and far beyond, to the peaks of the Bigelow Range and Mount Abraham. As you gaze west nearly to the Canadian border (50 miles away), Number Six and Number Five mountains and Coburn and Boundary Bald mountains come into the picture.

A trail sign marks the top of Moxie Bald, a good spot to enjoy lunch. Note the metal footings of the old 1919 fire lookout tower, which stood on top until it was removed by the Maine Forest Service in 1994. It was one of 144 towers erected in Maine and staffed by watchmen to guard against forest fires. The panorama north toward Moosehead Lake includes Big Moose, Little and Big Spencer, Baker and Number Four mountains. It spans 60 miles northwest across the 100-Mile Wilderness to mile-high Katahdin (Maine's highest point). If you've come on a sunny day, it's easy to see why the vista from Moxie Bald is so revered.

From the summit, cross more open ground before descending to the north. Pristine Bald Mountain Pond comes into view as you navigate the wide ledges to the Summit Bypass in a small clearing. Take the Summit Bypass (blue blazes) down to rejoin the AT in 0.5 miles, then follow the AT back to Troutdale Road.

TURN-BY-TURN DIRECTIONS

1. From Troutdale Road, begin by rock-hopping across Baker Stream and following the AT's white blazes.
2. At 2.5 miles, pass a side trail on the right to Bald Mountain Lean-to, and 0.1 miles ahead, another side trail to the shelter.
3. At 2.8 miles, the AT crosses a gravel logging road.
4. At 4 miles, reach a fork where the Summit Bypass goes left; bear right to stay on the AT.
5. At 4.6 miles, a short spur on the left leads to the summit of Moxie Bald.
6. At 5.0 miles, in a small clearing, reach a junction with the upper end of the Summit Bypass. Turn left on the blue-blazed Summit Bypass to descend.
7. At 5.5 miles, rejoin the AT and retrace your steps back to Troutdale Road.

FIND THE TRAILHEAD

From US Route 201 in The Forks, just before the highway crosses the Kennebec River, turn east on Lake Moxie Road and follow it for 5.3 miles to Moxie Pond. Turn right on Troutdale Road and follow it along Moxie Pond. At 12.9 miles, reach a small parking area on the right; the sign for the AT and Moxie Bald is on the left.

KENNEBEC RIVER BREWERY

Refreshingly cold and delicious traditional beers are on tap at Kennebec River Brewery (KRB) in a beautiful open-timbered log lodge at Northern Outdoors in The Forks, Maine's only whitewater rafting and adventure resort with its own brewery. To Jim Yearwood, the Vice President of Northern Outdoors who founded the brewery in 1996, the communal tables, comfy couches and fieldstone fireplace feel like a throwback to a friendly neighborhood pub. KRB doesn't distribute, so you'll have to enjoy their unfiltered beers onsite or take home a fresh growler. The Magic Hole IPA and Big Mama Blueberry Ale, both named after fierce rapids on the Kennebec River, are bestsellers among the seven regular taps and the brewer's choice. Enjoy a pint and something tasty from the full menu of hearty pub fare while you're thinking about booking a wet and wild river-rafting trip.

TRAIL MANAGER

Maine Appalachian Trail Club
www.matc.org
Trail map: www.mainetrailfinder.com/trails/trail/appalachian-trail-mox-ie-bald

BREWERY/RESTAURANT

Northern Outdoors
Kennebec River Brewery
1771 US Route 201
The Forks, ME 04985
(207) 663-4466
www.northernoutdoors.com/kennebec-river-brewery
Distance from trailhead: 18 miles

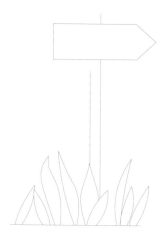

OLD SPECK MOUNTAIN

SCALE LOFTY OLD SPECK, MAINE'S FIFTH-HIGHEST MOUNTAIN

GRAFTON TOWNSHIP, ME

▷⋯ STARTING POINT	⋯✕ DESTINATION
GRAFTON NOTCH	**OLD SPECK MOUNTAIN SUMMIT**
🍺 BEER	🎲 HIKE TYPE
C-SURPLUS IPA	**STRENUOUS**
🐾 DOG FRIENDLY	📅 SEASON
YES (LEASH REQUIRED)	**MAY TO OCTOBER**
💲 FEES	🕐 DURATION
YES	**5 HOURS**
🗺 MAP REFERENCE	↦ LENGTH
GRAFTON NOTCH STATE PARK AND MAHOOSUC PUBLIC LANDS	**7.8 MILES (ROUND-TRIP)**
🔎 HIGHLIGHTS	〰 ELEVATION GAIN
SUMMIT TOWER, HUGE CLIFFS, BIG VIEWS, APPALACHIAN TRAIL	**2,700 FEET**

INDIA PALE ALE

HAZY GOLD

ORANGE
PINEAPPLE
MANGO

CREAMY, ORANGE
PINEAPPLE
MANGO

BITTERNESS   SWEETNESS

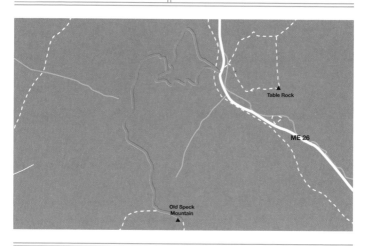

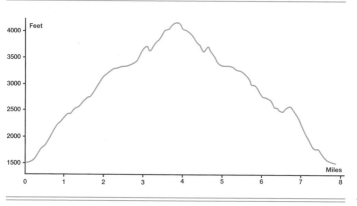

HIKE DESCRIPTION

Climb the observation tower atop Old Speck for panoramic views; then scamper across the lip of 700-foot Eyebrow Cliff overlooking Grafton Notch. Complete your adventure with a cold beer at Steam Mill Brewing in Bethel.

Old Speck rises nearly 2,700 feet above Grafton Notch, topping out at a lofty 4,270 feet in elevation. Situated in Grafton Township a scant 3 miles east of the New Hampshire state line, the mountain is the highest in the wild Mahoosuc Range and the fifth-highest peak in Maine. Old Speck's predominant feature is the Eyebrow, a massive 700-foot cliff.

The Old Speck Trail, also the route of the Appalachian Trail, climbs switchbacks beside tumbling Cascade Brook to arrive at ledges with a good view of the upper reaches of Old Speck. Note the large alternating swaths of exposed rock and tree cover from many slides over the ages. This speckled appearance is the source of the mountain's name, tweaked to distinguish it from other similarly named mountains in the region. The wavy metamorphic bedrock on Old Speck is estimated to be 420 million years old. The Old Speck Trail passes the Eyebrow Trail, then continues to ascend the mountain over a series of wooded knobs

to meet the Mahoosuc Trail on the 4,000-foot summit ridge. The Mahoosuc Trail is an easy 0.3-mile saunter through dense conifers to the top of Old Speck.

Climb Old Speck's 36-foot observation tower for a huge 360-degree vista. Look west to see deep into Mahoosuc Notch, famously known as the most difficult mile on the entire 2,192-mile AT. The profiles of Mahoosuc Arm, Fulling Mill Mountain and Goose Eye are clearly defined, and beyond you can see as far as New Hampshire's Carter-Moriah Range, the Wildcats and Mount Washington with its northern Presidential Range neighbors. Cast an eye over the U-shaped valley of Grafton Notch for a look at the Baldpates, Sunday River Whitecap and Puzzle Mountain. Surveying the domain before you, consider that the 3,191 acres of Grafton Notch State Park are surrounded by the Mahoosuc Public Lands—31,764 acres of extraordinary wild terrain, a third of which is specially designated as an ecological reserve.

From the Old Speck summit, retrace your steps down to the Eyebrow Trail junction; then follow orange blazes along the precipitous lip of Eyebrow Cliff, where several breaks in the trees allow looks out over the airy expanse to the trailhead parking lot far below. The descent of the Eyebrow is relatively short but steep and features a series of iron rungs, ladders, handrails and cables to assist hikers. Take your time and enjoy this exciting section, because after leveling out below, it's just a few minutes back to the trailhead.

TURN-BY-TURN DIRECTIONS

1. From the trailhead kiosk, proceed south on the white-blazed Old Speck Trail/AT, and in 450 feet, turn left (to the right is the orange-blazed Eyebrow Trail).
2. At 1 mile, the Eyebrow Trail enters from the right; bear left to continue on the Old Speck Trail/AT.
3. At 3.5 miles, reach a T-junction on the Old Speck summit ridge; turn left to follow the Mahoosuc Trail (blue blazes).
4. At 3.8 miles, reach the wooded 4,170-foot peak of Old Speck Mountain and its observation tower.
5. From the Old Speck summit, retrace your steps on the Mahoosuc Trail, and at 4.1 miles, turn sharply right on the Old Speck Trail/AT to descend.
6. At 6.6 miles, turn left to follow the Eyebrow Trail (orange blazes).
7. At 7.2 miles, continue the descent via a series of iron rungs, ladders, handrails and cables (this section is about 0.1 miles long).
8. At 7.7 miles, merge with the Old Speck Trail/AT 0.1 miles shy of the trailhead.

FIND THE TRAILHEAD

From the junction of US Route 2 and ME Route 26 in Newry (about 6 miles east of Bethel), turn north on ME Route 26 (Bear River Road). In 8.5 miles, enter Grafton Notch State Park, and at 12.2 miles, turn left into the large "Hiking Trails" parking lot.

STEAM MILL BREWING

Steam Mill Brewing takes its name from the Steam Mill section of Bethel, the location of an old steam mill in the mid-1900s and the neighborhood where friends Scott Fraser and Brent Angevine began homebrewing after college. Years later, when the pair of locals opened their brewery and taproom in downtown Bethel in 2018, it was the realization of a long-held dream. Using locally sourced ingredients, Steam Mill produces a diverse lineup of refreshing brews with names inspired by local landmarks, such as the C-Surplus IPA, Alder River Red and Goose Eye Mountain Ale. By 2021, the popular brewery had outgrown its original space and moved to a larger venue near the Sunday River ski resort. The new brewpub features expanded indoor seating, a large bar, a beer garden, "elevated pub food," and, of course, the same great beer.

LAND MANAGERS

Grafton Notch State Park
1941 Bear River Road
Newry, ME 04938
In season: (207) 824-2912
Off season: (207) 624-6080
Info and trail map: www.maine.gov/graftonnotch

Mahoosuc Public Lands
Maine Bureau of Parks and Lands
Western Public Lands Office
Farmington, ME 04938
(207) 778-8231
www.parksandlands.com

BREWERY/RESTAURANT

Steam Mill Brewing
96 Sunday River Road
Bethel, ME 04217
(207) 824-1149
www.steammillbrew.com
Distance from trailhead: 15 miles

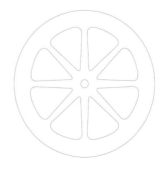

QUODDY HEAD

EXPLORE THE EASTERNMOST POINT OF LAND IN THE US

LUBEC, ME

▷⋯ STARTING POINT	⋯✗ DESTINATION
TRAILHEAD PARKING	**HIGH LEDGE, GREEN POINT**
🍺 BEER	HIKE TYPE
QUODDY HEAD RED	**MODERATE**
🐾 DOG FRIENDLY	📅 SEASON
YES (LEASH REQUIRED)	**MAY TO OCTOBER**
$ FEES	🕐 DURATION
YES	**2 HOURS 15 MIN.**
🗺 MAP REFERENCE	↦ LENGTH
QUODDY HEAD STATE PARK	**4.2 MILES (LOOP)**
👁 HIGHLIGHTS	〰 ELEVATION GAIN
LIGHTHOUSE, BOLD OCEAN CLIFFS, SANDY BEACH, PEAT BOG	**180 FEET**

RED ALE

BURNT ORANGE/
RED

FLORAL

MALTY
PINE NOTES

BITTERNESS

SWEETNESS

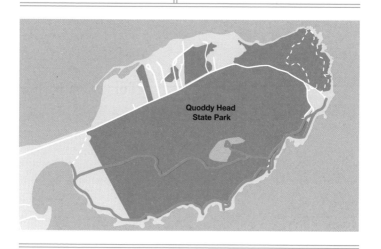

Quoddy Head
State Park

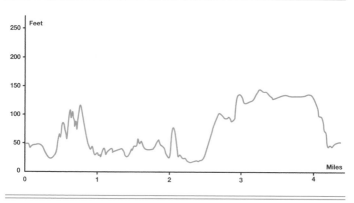

HIKE DESCRIPTION

Make a grand loop around rugged Quoddy Head, the easternmost point of land in the US, capped by a visit to its iconic candy-striped lighthouse. Then enjoy a post-hike Quoddy Head Red at Lubec Brewing in salty downtown Lubec.

Quoddy Head State Park encompasses 541 acres of prime real estate on West Quoddy Head in Lubec, the easternmost point of land in the continental US. Established in 1962, the park is best known for its iconic red-and-white-striped lighthouse standing tall on the shore of the Grand Manan Channel. "Quoddy" is a Passamaquoddy term meaning "fertile and beautiful."

Before you begin your hike, be sure to visit West Quoddy Head Light, built in 1858. The lighthouse isn't generally open to the public, but the former lightkeeper's quarters are open as a museum and visitor center that capture the colorful history of the light station. Save the museum for later; now stroll back to the trailhead kiosk and head west on the Coastal Trail.

At Gulliver's Hole, the narrow chasm in the rocks far below produces a thunderous roar when the tides—which range as much as 24 feet here—are just right. The next stop is High Ledge, a grassy perch 150 feet above the ocean, where rugged cliffs, cobble beaches, steep headlands and hilly bumps dominate the view. From this point and numerous others along the way, you'll be treated to grand views across the channel to the impressive 400-foot columnar basalt cliffs on Grand Manan Island, part of New Brunswick, Canada. At Green Point, the broad clifftop yields another outstanding vista of the bold Quoddy coastline. In late summer, be on watch for humpback, minke and finback whales cavorting offshore.

The Coastal Trail journeys on and, swinging around a cobble cove and a jumble of rocks, reaches Carrying Place Cove and the Thompson Trail. Before continuing on the Thompson Trail, take the path through Minzy Field to the cove and its long, arching, sandy beach, a great spot for lunch and some beachcombing. The cove is so named because it was once a canoe portage site for Native Americans crossing the narrow peninsula from the ocean to Lubec Flats.

The Thompson Trail leads over a gentle rise to the Bog Trail; take this short detour to West Quoddy Head Bog, the easternmost open peatland in the US. The Bog Trail's boardwalk explores the 7-acre, nearly circular expanse, and interpretive signs tell the fascinating story of how the bog, once a pond formed by glaciers, has evolved over 8,000 years through a slow process of plant accumulation and decay. Return to the main trail and follow the Inland Trail back to the lighthouse area.

TURN-BY-TURN DIRECTIONS

1. Begin at the trailhead kiosk and walk left to reach the lighthouse.
2. From the lighthouse, retrace your steps to the kiosk and continue ahead on the Coastal Trail.
3. At 0.6 miles, reach a view of Gulliver's Hole.
4. At 0.7 miles, arrive at High Ledge.
5. At 1.0 miles, a spur on the left leads to Green Point.
6. At 2.2 miles, reach the junction with the Thompson Trail and a side trail to Carrying Place Cove. Explore the cove, then return to the junction to continue on the Thompson Trail.
7. At 3.4 miles, turn left on the Bog Trail, a lollipop loop. After visiting the bog, return to the trail junction and turn left on the Inland Trail.
8. At 4 miles, the Inland and Coastal trails merge for a short distance. Ahead, bear left to follow the Inland Trail back to the parking area in another 0.2 miles.

FIND THE TRAILHEAD

From the junction of US Route 1 and ME Route 189 in Whiting, drive east on ME Route 189 toward Lubec. In 10 miles, turn right on South Lubec Road. In 4.6 miles, enter Quoddy Head State Park. Where the road forks (straight ahead leads to parking for the lighthouse), bear right and continue 0.1 miles to the large trailhead parking lot.

LUBEC BREWING COMPANY

Nuclear-physicist-turned-brewer Gale White fell in love with the Maine coast while on vacation and never looked back, and in 2014, he opened Lubec Brewing on the downtown Lubec waterfront. Overlooking Lubec Narrows and the international bridge to Campobello Island in New Brunswick, the easternmost brewery in the US is a welcoming place where everybody is a friend. Find a comfy spot in the tasting room or the corner beer garden and enjoy a pint and some salty conversation with locals and visitors alike, as well as the affable White and his wife, chief beer taster McGinley Jones. The flagship Quoddy Head Red, with its sultry red-haired mermaid logo, is an easy drinking red ale and one of a handful of classic German-style beers regularly on tap, each inspired by an interesting local story worth asking about.

LAND MANAGER

Quoddy Head State Park
973 South Lubec Road
Lubec, Maine 04652
May 15-October 15: (207) 733-0911
October 16-May 14: (207) 941-4014
Info and trail map: www.maine.gov/quoddyhead

BREWERY

Lubec Brewing Company
41 Water Street
Lubec, ME 04652
(207) 733-4555
Facebook: Lubec Brewing Company
Distance from trailhead: 6 miles

TUMBLEDOWN MOUNTAIN

VENTURE TO AN ALLURING ALPINE TARN AND SWEEPING 700-FOOT CLIFFS

TWP 6 NORTH OF WELD, ME

▷⋯ STARTING POINT	⋯✗ DESTINATION
BROOK TRAIL TRAILHEAD, BYRON ROAD	**TUMBLEDOWN WEST PEAK**
🍺 BEER	🏔 HIKE TYPE
STOP. HAMMOCK TIME CREAM ALE	**STRENUOUS**
🐾 DOG FRIENDLY	📅 SEASON
YES (LEASH REQUIRED)	**MAY TO OCTOBER**
$ FEES	⏲ DURATION
NO	**3 HOURS 15 MIN.**
⛰ MAP REFERENCE	⊢ LENGTH
MOUNT BLUE STATE PARK AND TUMBLEDOWN PUBLIC LANDS	**6.2 MILES (LOOP)**
🔎 HIGHLIGHTS	〰 ELEVATION GAIN
ALPINE TARN, DRAMATIC CLIFFS, MOUNTAIN VIEWS, SWIMMING	**1,800 FEET**

 CREAM ALE

 LIGHT YELLOW

 CITRUSY

 CRISP
LEMONY NOTES

BITTERNESS   SWEETNESS

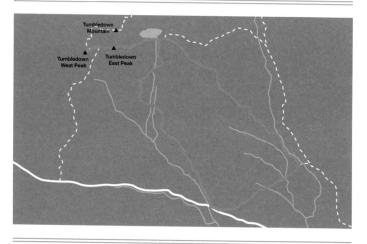

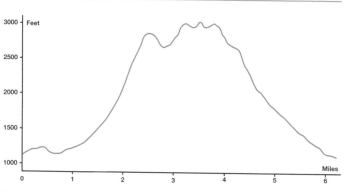

HIKE DESCRIPTION

Climb to a stunning alpine tarn and then scamper along an airy ridge above sweeping 700-foot cliffs to Tumbledown's west summit for extraordinary views. Celebrate your ambition later on with a thirst-quenching brew at Ambition Brewing in Wilton.

Hemmed in by craggy alpine summits, Tumbledown Pond is easily one of the prettiest—and most popular—hiking destinations in western Maine. Just west of the windswept tarn, Tumbledown Mountain's 700-foot south-facing cliffs fall away in dramatic fashion, emphasizing the beauty and allure of this high and wild place. The state of Maine owns or holds conservation easements on some 22,000 acres around the mountain, an expanse known collectively as Tumbledown Public Lands. Add the 8,000 acres of neighboring Mount Blue State Park and you've got a real recreation bonanza.

From the Brook Trail trailhead kiosk, the Little Jackson Connector heads northeast for a mile to meet the Parker Ridge Trail, which climbs at a mostly moderate grade. Once above the treeline, there are broad

views south to Webb Lake, Mount Blue, Bald Mountain and Saddleback Wind. At the crest of the Parker Ridge Trail, you'll enjoy views of the remarkable Tumbledown cliffs, the west and main peaks of Tumbledown, and Little Jackson and Big Jackson mountains, all four over 3,000 feet in elevation.

The Parker Ridge Trail continues a few hundred feet down to Tumbledown Pond, sometimes referred to as Crater Lake because its bowl looks much like the crater of an ancient volcano. But it was the powerful glaciers of the last ice age that were responsible for gouging out the depression that would eventually become the pond. A great swimming hole on a hot summer day, Tumbledown Pond is a well-used and very fragile place, so please be a good steward and practice Leave No Trace.

From Tumbledown Pond, the Tumbledown Ridge Trail follows a rather exposed route to the ridgetop above, then descends steeply into a notch to meet the upper end of the Loop Trail, a gnarly hike that navigates a chimney-like fissure known as Fat Man's Misery via iron rungs. Continuing straight ahead, some scrambling leads to the 3,068-foot west peak of Tumbledown. The view north from Tumbledown's summit takes in everything from Old Blue and Bemis mountains to Saddleback and Mount Abraham. In the foreground is the higher main peak of Tumbledown; trail-less, it's a difficult bushwhack.

Retrace your steps to Tumbledown Pond, then descend via the Brook Trail. Steep and rough with lots of rocks and roots at first, the path eventually becomes more moderate before returning to the trailhead on Byron Road.

TURN-BY-TURN DIRECTIONS

1. From the parking area, cross Byron Road to the trailhead kiosk. Beyond, where the Brook Trail continues straight, bear right to follow the Little Jackson Connector.
2. At 1.0 miles, turn left to follow the Parker Ridge Trail.
3. At 2.7 miles, the Pond Link Trail leaves to the right; continue to the left on the Parker Ridge Trail.
4. At 2.8 miles, the Brook Trail merges from the left; 50 feet beyond, reach Tumbledown Pond. Turn left to follow the Tumbledown Ridge Trail.
5. At 3.4 miles, in a prominent notch, the Loop Trail enters from the left; continue straight ahead on the Tumbledown Ridge Trail.
6. At 3.6 miles, reach the west peak of Tumbledown Mountain at 3,068 feet.
7. Retrace your steps on the Tumbledown Ridge Trail to Tumbledown Pond and the Brook Trail.
8. At 4.5 miles, descend the mountain via the Brook Trail.

FIND THE TRAILHEAD

From the junction of ME Routes 156 and 142 in the village of Weld (14 miles north of US Route 2 in Wilton via ME Route 156), travel north on ME Route 142. In 2.4 miles, turn left on West Side Road and follow it for 0.5 miles. Where the paved West Side Road bears sharply left, continue straight ahead on the gravel-surfaced Byron Road. Follow this for 3.8 miles to the Brook Trail trailhead parking area on the left.

AMBITION BREWING

Ambition Brewing, the "best and smallest brewery" in Wilton (pop. 3,900), produces a nice variety of drinkable beers, including a British-influenced bitter and brown, favorites of co-owner and long-time hobby brewer Jeff Chaisson. Chaisson wanted a new adventure, and so Ambition Brewing was born in 2019. With the help of his business partner, Josh Michaud, he's ambitiously working to revitalize this former mill town. The tap room on Main Street, with its cozy neighborhood pub feel, is a great place to relax and enjoy a flight or a pint and some friendly banter with local folks and visitors alike. "Stop. Hammock Time," a cream ale, is the flagship brew among a dozen offerings on tap. Enjoy your beer with a bite of modern pub grub (think wraps, sandwiches, pizza and wing) from the small but terrific kitchen.

LAND MANAGERS

Tumbledown Public Lands
Maine Bureau of Parks and Lands
Western Public Lands Office
Farmington, ME 04938
(207) 778-8231
Info and trail map: www.parksandlands.com, "Find Parks and Lands,"
"Mt. Blue State Park"

BREWERY

Ambition Brewing
295 Main Street
Wilton, ME 04294
(207) 516-1466
www.ambitionbrews.com
Distance from trailhead: 21 miles

VAUGHAN WOODS

WANDER OVER THE OLD CARRIAGE ROADS AND STONE ARCH BRIDGES OF A HISTORICAL HOMESTEAD

HALLOWELL, ME

▷··· STARTING POINT	···✕ DESTINATION
LITCHFIELD ROAD	**CORNICHE TRAIL LOOP**
🍺 BEER	🏁 HIKE TYPE
ALEWIFE PALE ALE	**EASY**
🐾 DOG FRIENDLY	📅 SEASON
YES (LEASH REQUIRED)	**YEAR-ROUND**
$ FEES	🕐 DURATION
NO (DONATIONS APPRECIATED)	**1 HOUR 10 MIN.**
⛰ MAP REFERENCE	↦ LENGTH
VAUGHAN WOODS MAP	**2.1 MILES (LOOP)**
🔍 HIGHLIGHTS	〜 ELEVATION GAIN
HISTORIC CARRIAGE ROADS, STONE BRIDGES, MATURE WOODS	**200 FEET**

ENGLISH PALE ALE

 RICH AMBER

 TOFFEE
EARTHY
PINEY

 BITTERSWEET

BITTERNESS   SWEETNESS

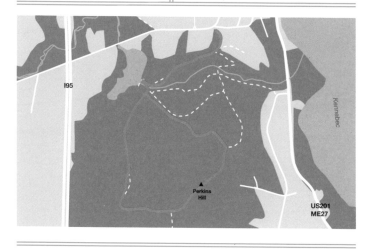

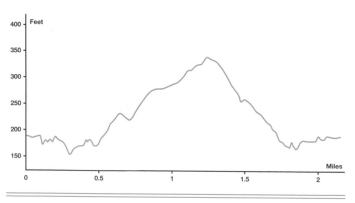

HIKE DESCRIPTION

Enjoy a pleasant stroll through the natural beauty and rich history of Vaughan Woods. Then saunter into Hallowell for a tall, cold glass of English-style brew at The Liberal Cup.

The Vaughan Woods & Historic Homestead, an idyllic 197-acre nature preserve, is situated on a hillside above the Kennebec River in Hallowell. Cared for by members of the Vaughan family for more than two centuries and now managed by the Kennebec Land Trust, the property features 3 miles of old carriage roads, winding footpaths, incredible stone bridges and tall trunks of white pine and hemlock.

This hike combines the Corniche Trail ("corniche" is French for "road on a cliff") and the Corniche Trail Loop for a wonderful 2-mile stroll along the scenic ravine of Vaughan Brook to pretty Cascade Pond and then over wooded Perkins Hill. Meander slowly and savor the beauty and history of this very special place as if you had nowhere to go and all day to get there (your only commitment is to a cold beer at The Liberal Cup in town when you're done, of course).

In 1761, the land that is Vaughan Woods was granted to Benjamin Hallowell by the Kennebec Proprietors. In 1797, Hallowell's grandson, Benjamin Vaughan, moved from England to Hallowell to settle the land, transforming it into an agricultural showcase of orchards and cattle. Following Vaughan's death, however, much of the land was sold off. The woods were cleared for pasture and farming, and the beautiful

ravine was lined with industry (a wire mill, a sandpaper factory and a glue factory, among others) powered by the regular flow of water from the Stickney and Page Dam on Cascade Pond, which was built in 1871.

By the late 1880s, grandson William Warren Vaughan had begun to revitalize the family estate, buying back much of the property around Vaughan Brook and seeing to it that the mills were dismantled. His plan was to create a "pleasure ground" with carriage roads, stone arch bridges, a ski run and a tea house. The carriage road, built in 1911, was designed to carry a horse and carriage—and later on, those newfangled automobiles—alongside the ravine, across the Driving Bridge and on up to the Tea House, a rustic gazebo that stood for more than 40 years. In the 1930s, the Vaughan family maintained a swimming beach on the pond for local kids.

The Vaughan family maintained the property for public access for over 100 years, and in 1991 donated a conservation easement on the land to the Kennebec Land Trust. In 2002, the Vaughans established the nonprofit Vaughan Woods & Historic Homestead to forever protect this remarkable spot.

TURN-BY-TURN DIRECTIONS

1. The trail begins at the kiosk, passes through a meadow, then bears right into the woods beyond. Over the next 0.25 miles on the old carriage road, you'll cross three stone arch bridges.
2. At 0.4 miles, reach the beautiful stone Driving Bridge over Vaughan Brook and a junction. Take the rock steps on the right up to the top of the old dam on Cascade Pond (aka Vaughan's Reservoir).
3. Retrace your steps to the Driving Bridge and walk across it to a fork. Bear right here to follow the Corniche Trail Loop counterclockwise through the lovely woods on Perkins Hill.
4. Avoiding the unmarked trail to the right to Hall-Dale High School and then the Rice Pines Trail, arrive at a pasture and a junction at 1.5 miles, where the Lower Rice Pines Trail heads off to the right. Continue on the Corniche Trail Loop.
5. Close the Corniche Trail Loop at 1.7 miles. Bear right over the Driving Bridge to continue back out to the trailhead.

FIND THE TRAILHEAD

From I-95, Exit 109 in Augusta, turn east on Western Avenue (US Route 202 and ME Routes 100/17/11). At the rotary circle in about 1.5 miles, take the first exit onto State Street (ME Route 27 and US Route 201). Follow this south for 2 miles to the Liberal Cup on Water Street (your post-hike brewery). Continue to the next corner and turn right on Central Street. Three blocks ahead, turn left on Middle Street and follow it to the end in another 0.6 miles at its junction with Litchfield Road. The parking spaces for the trailhead are along the stone wall just across the road.

THE LIBERAL CUP PUBLIC HOUSE & BREWERY

Opened in 2000, The Liberal Cup on historic Water Street has become an institution in beautiful downtown Hallowell. Owner Geoff Houghton dreamed of opening an English-style pub and this place is the real deal, complete with a warm wood-and-brick interior, a casual atmosphere and plenty of good food and drink. Settle in at the beautiful old tree slab of a bar and enjoy some friendly banter with the mug-clubbers and the rest of the happy crowd while you hoist an Alewife Ale or Bug Lager, the two flagship brews. Curious about the name The Liberal Cup? When you grab hold of that 20-ounce pint glass . . . well, you'll know exactly where the brewery gets its name. Dig into a plate of the Cup's tasty pub fare and you'll find that it, too, is over the top.

LAND MANAGER

Vaughan Woods & Historic Homestead
Corner of Middle Street and Litchfield Road
Hallowell, ME 04347
(207) 622-9831
Info and trail map: vaughanhomestead.org

BREWERY/RESTAURANT

The Liberal Cup Public House & Brewery
115 Water Street
Hallowell, ME 04347
(207) 623-2739
www.theliberalcup.com
Distance from trailhead: 0.8 miles

WELLS RESERVE

REVEL IN THE DIVERSE ECOLOGY OF A SPRAWLING HISTORIC COASTAL FARMSTEAD

WELLS, ME

▷⋯ STARTING POINT	⋯✗ DESTINATION
LAUDHOLM FARM	**WELLS RESERVE CIRCUIT**
🍺 BEER	HIKE TYPE
JALI	**EASY**
🐾 DOG FRIENDLY	SEASON
NO	**YEAR-ROUND**
$ FEES	⏱ DURATION
YES	**2 HOURS**
⌂ MAP REFERENCE	↦ LENGTH
WELLS RESERVE AT LAUDHOLM	**3.9 MILES (LOOP)**
👁 HIGHLIGHTS	〰 ELEVATION GAIN
ESTUARIES, MEADOWS, BEACH, WILDLIFE, HISTORIC FARMHOUSE	**50 FEET**

INDIA PALE ALE

DEEP GOLDEN/SLIGHTLY AMBER

MALTY
PINE
TOUCH OF HONEY

BALANCED MALT AND HOPS

BITTERNESS

SWEETNESS

US1
ME9

Little River
Estuary

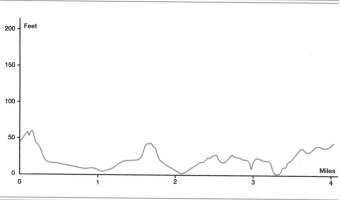

HIKE DESCRIPTION

Meander through the coastal ecosystems of a former farmstead that's now an important environmental research and education center. Then it's on to Wells Beach to "refuel and recharge" with a cold beer and tasty pub fare at Batson River Brewing.

The Wells National Estuarine Research Reserve encompasses 2,250 acres of diverse wildlife habitat—from grasslands, wetlands and woodlands to salt marshes, dunes and sandy beach—spanning the estuaries of the Webhannet River and the Little River along the Gulf of Maine. The Wells facility is one of 29 National Estuarine Research Reserves in the US that work to ensure healthy, productive and sustainable salt marsh estuaries through research and monitoring, education and training, stewardship and conservation, and preservation and protection.

Estuaries are formed where salt water from the ocean mixes with fresh water from inland rivers; they are incredible mixing grounds and some of the most dynamic and productive ecosystems on the planet. Estuaries like those at the Wells Reserve provide critical habitats for a variety of plant and animal life, help protect human communities from flooding, serve as buffers against coastal storms and filter pollutants out of fresh water before it reaches the ocean.

The extensive salt marshes from Kittery to Cape Elizabeth attracted European settlers to the area, as they could be transformed into pasture and hayfields. The Wells farmstead was first settled in 1641, and over the centuries has been owned by just four families. The name Laudholm (the word "laud" means to give praise, while the suffix "holm" means meadow on the shore) was given to the place around 1910, when it was the largest and most progressive saltwater farm in York

County. By the late 1970s, however, Laudholm Farm had fallen into a state of disrepair. Facing enormous development pressure, local citizens and key funding and conservation partners collaborated to acquire the property and adjacent lands, resulting in the establishment of the Wells Reserve in 1986.

Seven miles of trails crisscross the Wells Reserve, and our hike combines six different trails for a grand easy-walking tour through all of the major environments: from the Muskie, Pilger and Barrier Beach trails to the Laird-Norton, Farley and Saw Whet trails. You'll begin and end your walk at the Laudholm Farmhouse, which hosts the visitor center and a series of exhibits that describe the changes in the coastal landscape over the eons. A series of interpretive signs along the route offers insight into the ecology of this natural gem, and four observation platforms provide unobstructed views over the salt marshes. Laudholm Beach, at about the halfway point, is a wonderful spot to enjoy some sand and surf.

TURN-BY-TURN DIRECTIONS

1. From the fee and information kiosks, walk toward the large barn (restrooms), then bear right past the icehouse and water tower to the visitor center. The Muskie Trail begins just around the other side of the former farmhouse.

2. Follow the Muskie Trail across the road and through meadows and woods to the Pilger Trail at 0.9 miles. Here, a spur trail leads to an overlook platform on Webhannet Estuary. Continue the hike on the Pilger Trail.

3. On the Pilger Trail, pass the Laudholm Connector at 1.5 miles, then reach a dirt road at the junction of the Barrier Beach Trail and the Laird-Norton Trail at 1.8 miles. Turn right to follow the Barrier Beach Trail, which leads to Laudholm Beach at 2.1 miles.

4. Retrace your steps to the junction (2.3 miles) and turn right to continue on the Laird-Norton Trail.

5. At 2.5 miles, reach an overlook at the Little River Estuary; continue on the Laird-Norton Trail.

6. At 2.8 miles, reach a double four-way junction; with a gray gate on your right and the Cart Path to your left, proceed straight ahead a few yards to the next junction, then bear right to continue on the Farley Trail.

7. At 2.9 miles, a spur trail leads to an overlook on the Little River.

8. Ahead, pass the Farley Connector to reach an overlook on the Little River at 3.2 miles.

9. At a T-junction at 3.5 miles, turn left on the Laird-Norton Trail, and in another 0.1 miles, turn right on the Saw Whet Trail.

10. Pass the Forest Learning Center at 3.7 miles; then reach the entrance road and turn left along it to return to the parking lot.

FIND THE TRAILHEAD

From I-95, Exit 19 in Wells, drive east on ME Routes 9/109 for 1.6 miles to the junction with US Route 1. Turn left on US Route 1 and drive 1.5 miles to the blinking yellow traffic light at Laudholm Farm Road. Turn right on Laudholm Farm Road and proceed 0.4 miles; then turn left on Skinner Mill Road. In 0.1 miles, turn right into the Wells Reserve and drive 0.3 miles to the parking lot loop.

BATSON RIVER BREWING AND DISTILLING

Batson River Brewing and Distilling's craft beers and spirits capture the joy of sweet New England summers, salty ocean breezes and life in one of the most beautiful places on Earth. From its original brewpub in Kennebunk, opened in 2018, Batson River expanded to Portland, Biddeford and then Wells, which is home to its brewing operations. Sporting a fishing theme, the cozy, comfortable restaurant just steps from stunning Wells Beach is a relaxing spot to "refuel and recharge" with a cold beer and a scrumptious bite after a fun day in the Maine outdoors. Batson River's extensive menu of well-balanced brews features "different styles for different tastes" that pair nicely with their simple sandwiches and savory snacks. The easy drinking Cleaves Cove IPA is the flagship offering.

LAND MANAGER

Wells Reserve at Laudholm
342 Laudholm Farm Road
Wells, ME 04090
(207) 646-1555
Info and trail map: www.wellsreserve.org

BREWERY/RESTAURANT

Batson River Brewing and Distilling
73 Mile Road
Wells, ME 04090
(207) 360-7255
batsonriver.com/wells-maine/
Distance from trailhead: 3.9 miles

DEDICATION & ACKNOWLEDGEMENTS

Beer Hiking New England is dedicated to my wonderful wife and favorite trail companion, Fran Leyman, who loves hiking and beer almost (but not quite) as much as I do. It was Fran's gentle urging that I turn my passion for hikes and brews and my writing of the last few years into a book that kept me going over the course of this long and winding path to print. Thank you for being there always; I love you!

This book was born on a coast-to-coast walk across northern England two decades ago, when I tramped across hills, dales and moors by day, and at night would tuck into a village pub to enjoy a pint of good British ale. Hmmm, hiking and beer, I thought, what a concept. It wasn't until 2017, however, that the idea crystallized, and I began working in earnest on a book about hikes and brews in Maine. But that effort stalled a year later when a publishing deal fell through.

Enter Brandon Fralic and Rachel Wood, beer gurus, avid hikers and pioneering authors of *Beer Hiking Pacific Northwest*, a copy of which I happened upon quite by accident. I found Brandon on Facebook and immediately sent a message, which was met with a quick and enthusiastic response. We chatted about his book and my hoped-for book, and he provided contact info for his publisher, Helvetiq, in the unlikeliest of places, Switzerland.

Hadi Barkat, Helvetiq's CEO, was quick to reply to my inquiry and proposed expanding the scope to include not only Maine but hiking and beer across the six states of New England. Deal! And with that, I got back to work with renewed energy and focus. When an opportunity to thru-hike the 2,654-mile Pacific Crest Trail from Mexico to Canada the following summer was too good to pass up, Hadi graciously agreed to a 6-month pause in the book effort. Gearing up again post-hike, the project was further delayed by the complications of life during the COVID pandemic. But throughout the book process, Hadi believed in me and offered unwavering support. Thank you!

Sincere thanks are also due to Richard Harvell, Helvetiq's Head of USA Publishing, and Ashley Curtis, copy editor for Helvetiq. I truly appreciated how you both so deftly shepherded the book from a jumble of Word docs and images into a really beautiful finished product. You've been great to work with! I'm especially grateful to Daniel Malak for his many hours of work creating the maps, profiles and illustrations and for doing all the typesetting and corrections right up to the end.

Special thanks to my mom, Nora Kish, and my brother and sister-in-law, Kevin and Lynn Kish, all of whom live in Derry, New Hampshire, which proved to be an excellent (and cheap) base of operations for accomplishing a good chunk of the book's fieldwork. Thanks so much for the company, the beer and meals, and the heated pool.

My good friends, Amy Patenaude and Charlie Gunn of Henniker, New Hampshire, also provided great camaraderie on trail and off, as well as a comfy basecamp and plenty of good laughs. You rock!

Cheers and thanks to so many other amazing people who provided enthusiastic support and helpful information in the development of *Beer Hiking New England*, from friends along the trail and in the brew-pubs, land managers, trail managers, and tourism and hospitality pros to all the fabulous folks—the brewery owners, brewers, wait staff, kitchen staff, marketing and communication staff and all those behind the scenes—who make New England's craft beer industry so incredibly diverse and dynamic:

Maine: Dana Thurston, Robin Zinchuk, Gabe Perkins, Jessie Perkins and Jensen Bissell; Hope Rowan, Western Mountain Mapping; Kevin Sullivan, Maine Beer Geeks; Alex Mafucci, Atlantic Brewing; Tim Lo and Jared Lambert, Bangor Beer; Mary and Matt Weber, Monhegan Brewing; Gale White and McGinley Jones, Lubec Brewing; Jeff Chaisson, Ambition Brewing; Jim Yearwood, Northern Outdoors; Geoff Houghton, The Liberal Cup; Kailey Partin and Erin Cadigan, Rising Tide Brewing; Scott Fraser and James Kimball, Steam Mill Brewing; Tom Barthelmes and Ashley Charlton, Batson River Brewing; Sean Sullivan, Maine Brewers Guild; Stan Rintz, *Maine Brew & Bev Guide;* Heather Chandler, *Green & Healthy Maine.* **New Hampshire:** Peter Campbell, Sonja Carey, Stacie Illingworth, Leslie Turpin, Sharon Lavigne and Ellen Chandler; Maryalice Fischer, Friends of Northwood Meadows; Christina Pacuk, New Hampshire Dept. of Natural & Cultural Resources; Marti Mayne, Mt. Washington Valley Chamber of Commerce; Crispin Battles, Mt. Washington Auto Road; Dea Brickner-Wood, Great Bay Resource Protection Partnership; Tom Brightman and Jennie Berry, Town of Durham; Larry Garland, Appalachian Mountain Club; Marty Basch; the staff at the Derry Public Library; Ash Fischbein and Mike Frothingham, Hobbs Brewing; Ian Dowling, Marlaina Renton, Kyle Hatch and Phillip Renton, Rek'-Lis Brewing; Ian Ferguson and Cody Floyd, Ledge Brewing; Jon Shackett, Shackett's Brewing; Erin Marley, Woodstock Inn Brewery; Tom Mills and Rik Marley, The Flying Goose; Jeff Fenerty, Sarah Fenerty and Jeremy Fenerty, Northwoods Brewing;

Pete Beauregard, Stoneface Brewing; Debra Rivest, Steve O'Brien and Mike Barringer, Elm City Brewing. **Vermont:** Leah Mital, Ben Russell, Jeff York and Jim Ray; Mel Madison, Madison Brewing; Allan MacDonald, Next Trick Brewing; Tim Brady, Whetstone Station; Chris Kesler, Dan Sartwell and Karen Bisbee, Black Flannel Brewing; Emma Shea, Zero Gravity Craft Brewery; Steve Parkes, Drop-In Brewing; Dan Fulham, Long Trail Brewing; Renee and Matt Nadeau and Dylan Nadeau, Rock Art Brewery; Cullan Calvert, Nate Johnson and Kirstyn Quinn, Prohibition Pig; Jason Petrelli and Sara Jasinski, Beer Naked Brewery. **Massachusetts:** John Burk and Glenn and Helen Hersom; Mac Gallant, Hog Island Beer; Pete Henry, True West Brewery; Chris Webb, Newburyport Brewing; Jackie and Scott Cullen, River Styx Brewing; Chris McCarthy and Steve Bilodeau, Northampton Brewery; Christine Bump and Bill Heaton, Big Elm Brewing; Orion Howard, Bright Ideas Brewing; Sam Dibble, New City Brewing; Drew Brosseau and Allison DiMaggio, Mayflower Brewing; Gary Happ and Andrew Mankin, Barrington Brewery; Katie Stinchon, Massachusetts Brewers Guild. **Connecticut:** Linda Wilkinson, Vicki Morten and Judy Rugar; Spencer Meyer, Sandra Williams and Bill Bloss, Guilford Land Conservation Trust; Dave Boone, AMC Connecticut Chapter; Jim Mahoney and Cat Sullivan, Town of Berlin, CT; George Brierley, Berlin Land Trust; Clare Cain, Connecticut Forest & Parks Association; Aaren Simoncini, Beer'd Brewing; Stephannie Grant, Great Falls Brewing; Ralph Fiegel, Taylor Brooke Brewery; Bryan Hickey, Hopmeadow Brewing; Josh Norris, Witchdoctor Brewing; Frank Lockwood, Reverie Brewing; Justin Gargano and Kelley Gargano, Thimble Island Brewing; Heather Wilson, Hop Culture Farms; Dave Littlefield, Housatonic River Brewing. **Rhode Island:** Chris Mishoe, Bravo Brewing; Jeremy Ruff, Linesider Brewing; Bill Christy, Coddington Brewing; Gary Richardson, Rhode Island Brewers Guild.

If I've forgotten anybody along the way, I'm sorry; thank you for your assistance just the same.

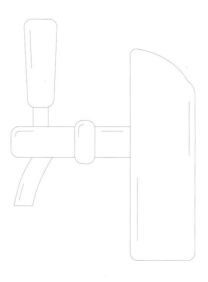

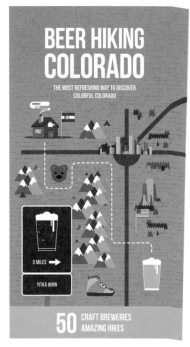

Coming soon:

BEER HIKING NEW YORK

BEER HIKING CANADIAN ROCKIES